T0407835

Exploring Hope

DIVERSE PERSPECTIVES ON CREATING A FAIRER SOCIETY

A fair society is one that is just, inclusive and embracing of all without any barriers to participation based on sex, sexual orientation, religion or belief, ethnicity, age, class, ability or any other social difference. One where there is access to healthcare and education, technology, justice, strong institutions, peace and security, social protection, decent work and housing. But how can research truly contribute to creating global equity and diversity without showcasing diverse voices that are underrepresented in academia or paying specific attention to the Global South?

Including books addressing key challenges and issues within the social sciences which are essential to creating a fairer society for all with specific reference to the Global South, *Diverse Perspectives on Creating a Fairer Society* amplifies underrepresented voices showcasing Black, Asian and minority ethnic voices, authorship from the Global South and academics who work to amplify diverse voices.

With the primary aim of showcasing authorship and voices from beyond the Global North, the series welcomes submissions from established and junior authors on cutting-edge and high-level research on key topics that feature in global news and public debate, specifically from and about the Global South in national and international contexts. Harnessing research across a range of diversities of people and places to generate previously unheard insights, the series offers a truly global perspective on the current societal debates of the 21st century bringing contemporary debate in the social sciences from diverse voices to light.

Previous Titles

- *Disaster, Displacement and Resilient Livelihoods: Perspectives from South Asia* edited by M. Rezaul Islam
- *Pandemic, Politics, and a Fairer Society in Southeast Asia: A Malaysian Perspective* edited by Syaza Shukri
- *Empowering Female Climate Change Activists in the Global South: The Path Toward Environmental Social Justice* by Peggy Ann Spitzer
- *Gendered Perspectives of Restorative Justice, Violence and Resilience: An International Framework* edited by Bev Orton
- *Social Sector Development and Inclusive Growth in India* by Ishu Chadda
- *The Socially Constructed and Reproduced Youth Delinquency in Southeast Asia: Advancing Positive Youth Involvement in Sustainable Futures* by Jason Hung
- *Youth Development in South Africa: Harnessing the Demographic Dividend* edited by Botshabelo Maja and Busani Ngcaweni
- *Debt Crisis and Popular Social Protest in Sri Lanka: Citizenship, Development and Democracy Within Global North-South Dynamics* by S. Janaka Biyanwila
- *Building Strong Communities: Ethical Approaches to Inclusive Development* by Ifzal Ahmad and M. Rezaul Islam

- *Family Planning and Sustainable Development in Bangladesh: Empowering Marginalized Communities in Asian Contexts* by M. Rezaul Islam
- *Critical Reflections on the Internationalisation of Higher Education in the Global South* edited by Emnet Tadesse Woldegiorgis and Cheryl Qiumei Yu

Forthcoming Titles

- *'Natural' Disasters and Everyday Lives: Floods, Climate Justice and Marginalisation in India* by Suddhabrata Deb Roy
- *Social Constructions of Migration in Nigeria and Zimbabwe: Discourse, Rhetoric, and Identity* by Kunle Oparinde and Rodwell Makombe
- *Rural Social Infrastructure Development in India: An Inclusive Approach* by M. Mahadeva
- *Neoliberal Subjectivity at Work: Conduct, Contradictions, Commitments and Contestations* by Muneeb Ul Lateef Banday
- *The Emerald Handbook of Family and Social Change in the Global South: A Gendered Perspective* by Aylin Akpınar and Nawal H. Ammar
- *An Introduction to Platform Economy in India: Exploring Relationality and Embeddedness* by Shriram Venkatraman, Jillet Sarah Sam, and Rajorshi Ra
- *Unearthing the Institutionalised Social Exclusion of Black Youth in Contemporary South Africa: The Burden of Being Born Free* by Khosi Kubeka

Diverse Perspectives on Creating a Fairer Society

Exploring Hope: Case Studies of Innovation, Change and Development in the Global South

EDITED BY

MARCELO SILI (EDITOR-IN-CHIEF)
National Scientific and Technical Research Council (CONICET) - Universidad Nacional del Sur, Argentina

ANDRÉS KOZEL
National Scientific and Technical Research Council (CONICET) – Universidad Nacional de San Martín, Argentina

SAMIRA MIZBAR
National Assessment Body of the Higher Council of Education, Training and Scientific Research, Morocco

AVIRAM SHARMA
University of Vigo, Spain

AND

ANA CASADO
National Scientific and Technical Research Council (CONICET) – Universidad Provincial del Sudoeste, Argentina

United Kingdom – North America – Japan – India – Malaysia – China

Emerald Publishing Limited
Emerald Publishing, Floor 5, Northspring, 21-23 Wellington Street, Leeds LS1 4DL.

First edition 2024

British Library Cataloguing in Publication Data
A catalogue record for this book is available from the British Library

ISBN: 978-1-83549-737-1 (Print)
ISBN: 978-1-83549-736-4 (Online)
ISBN: 978-1-83549-738-8 (Epub)

Printed and bound by CPI Group (UK) Ltd, Croydon, CR0 4YY

Contents

Part 4: Ensuring Environmental Sustainability

Part 5: Inclusive and Caring Worlds

List of Editors

Marcelo Sili [Editor] — *National Scientific and Technical Research Council (CONICET) - Universidad Nacional del Sur, Argentina*

Andrés Kozel [Co-editor] — *National Scientific and Technical Research Council (CONICET) - Universidad Nacional de San Martín, Argentina*

Samira Mizbar [Co-editor] — *National Assessment Body of the Higher Council of Education, Training and Scientific Research, Morocco*

Aviram Sharma [Co-editor] — *University of Vigo, Spain*

Ana Casado [Co-editor] — *National Scientific and Technical Research Council (CONICET) - Universidad Provincial del Sudoeste, Argentina*

Gustavo Valente [Producer of maps and photographs] — *Centro ADETER, Departamento de Geografía y Turismo, Universidad Nacional del Sur, Argentina*

Antonella Mauri [Producer of maps and photographs] — *Centro ADETER, Departamento de Geografía y Turismo, Universidad Nacional del Sur, Argentina*

List of Contributors

Fazlullah Akhtar	*Center for Development Research (ZEF), Bonn, Germany*
Murad Ali	*University of Malakand, Pakistan*
María José Aparicio Meza	*Universidad Nacional de Asunción, Paraguay*
Deyani Alejandra Ávila Martínez	*National Autonomous University of Mexico (UNAM), Mexico*
Usman Khalid Awan	*Center for Development Research (ZEF), Bonn, Germany*
Abdul Haseeb Azizi	*Center for Development Research (ZEF), Bonn, Germany*
Mairon G. Bastos Lima	*Stockholm Environment Institute, Sweden*
Christian Borgemeister	*Center for Development Research (ZEF), Bonn, Germany*
Fernando Calderón Gutiérrez	*Universidad Nacional de San Martín, Argentina*
Anwesha Chakraborty	*University of Bologna, Italy*
Rosa Cuesta	*Instituto Geográfico Militar, Ecuador*
Ahmad Dermawan	*School of Economics and Business, Norwegian University of Life Sciences, Ås, Norway*
Idrissa Yaya Diandy	*Université Cheikh Anta Diop de Dakar, Senegal*
Sangay Dorji	*Paro College of Education, Royal University of Bhutan, Bhutan*
Driss El Yazami	*Conseil National des Droits de l'Homme, Morocco*

María Luisa Eschenhagen	*Universidad Nacional de Colombia, Colombia*
Federico Escribal	*Universidad Nacional de las Artes, Argentina*
José Andrés Fuentes	*Consejo Directivo del Grupo Cooperativo Yomol A'tel, México*
Beatriz Garcés Beltrán	*Engineer and philosopher, Medellín, Colombia*
Juan José García Pérez	*Fundación para el desarrollo colectivo y autónomo del hábitat Cíclica (Fundación CÍCLICA) Chile*
Camila Gonçalves De Mario	*Universidade Candido Mendes (UCAM), Brazil*
Pablo Grilli	*Universidad Nacional Arturo Jauretche, Argentina*
Otto Hospes	*Wageningen University, Netherlands*
Amado Insfrán Ortíz	*Universidad Nacional de Asunción, Paraguay*
Sandra Iturrieta Olivares	*Pontificia Universidad Catolica de Valparaiso, Chile*
J. Enkhsaikhan	*Blue Banner NGO, Mongolia*
Elizabeth Jiménez	*CIDES-UMSA, Universidad Mayor de San Andrés, Bolivia*
Li Juan	*Shanghai International Studies University, China*
Kavitha Kuruganti	*Alliance for Sustainable and Holistic Agriculture, India*
Alejandra Larrazábal	*Universidad Nacional Autónoma de México (CIGA-UNAM), Mexico*
Pema Latsho	*Paro College of Education, Royal University of Bhutan, Bhutan*
Diana Tamara Martínez Ruiz	*National Autonomous University of Mexico (UNAM), Mexico*

Javier Enrique Medina Vásquez	*Universidad del Valle, Cali, Colombia*
Yadira Méndez Lemus	*Universidad Nacional Autónoma de México (CIGA-UNAM), Mexico*
Asaah Sumaila Mohammed	*CK Tedam University of Technology and Applied Science, Ghana*
Édgar Adrián Mora	*Universidad Iberoamericana e Instituto de Educación Media Superior de la Ciudad de México, México*
Ossere Nganongo	*Université Marien NGOUABI, Republic of Congo*
Paula Lucía Olaizola	*Instituto Nacional de Tecnología Agropecuaria, Argentina*
Claudia Ospina Aldana	*Rimisp – Centro Latinoamericano para el Desarrollo Rural, Colombia*
Poonam Pandey	*University of Vigo, Spain*
Fabricio Pereira da Silva	*Universidade Federal do Estado do Rio de Janeiro (UNIRIO), Brazil*
Alejandro Rivero Villar	*Centro de Investigación y Posgrado en Humanidades, Ciencias e Ingeniería – Instituto de Estudios Superiores de la Ciudad de México "Rosario Castellanos", Mexico*
Norma Angélica Rodríguez Valladares	*Centro de Estudios en Geografía Humana de El Colegio de Michoacán A.C., Mexico*
Cinthia Fabiola Ruiz López	*Universidad Nacional Autónoma de México (CIGA-UNAM), Mexico*
Nelida Sotelo	*Centro de Estudios sobre la Acción y el Desarrollo Territorial (ADETER), Departamento de Geografía y Turismo, UNS, Argentina*
Carmiña Soto	*Universidad Nacional de Asunción, Paraguay*
Crain Soudien	*Nelson Mandela University, Gqeberha (Port Elizabeth), South Africa*

Bernhard Tischbein — *Center for Development Research (ZEF), Bonn, Germany*

Rodrigo Tizón — *Instituto Nacional de Tecnología Agropecuaria (INTA), Argentina*

Milena Umaña Maldonado — *Rimisp – Centro Latinoamericano para el Desarrollo Rural, Colombia*

Antonio Vieyra — *Universidad Nacional Autónoma de México (CIGA-UNAM), Mexico*

Martha Villagómez — *Instituto Geográfico Militar, Ecuador*

Seetha I. Wickremasinghe — *National Science Foundation, Sri Lanka*

Zhongshi Yuan — *Shanghai International Studies University, China*

Jingting Zhang — *Shanghai International Studies University, China*

Foreword

Rahma Bourquia
Sociologist and Anthropologist, Member of the Academy of the Kingdom of Morocco

This book brings together articles by authors from countries on three continents: Africa, Latin America and Asia, presenting experiences of projects and initiatives reflecting the dynamics of development. What emerges from these articles is that many countries that in the past had to live through the colonial experience have, in the post-colonial period, undertaken reconstruction by establishing institutions and putting in place policies to overcome deficits in human development in the fields of education, health and employment, while at the same time deploying technological infrastructures and strengthening both agriculture and environmental conservation. In terms of political institutions, initiatives are being undertaken in several countries to strengthen the democratisation process, and by putting in place mechanisms for social inclusion. There have also been initiatives and significant progress in improving the conditions of women and their integration into the economic fabric, with measures to strengthen their capacities. Other articles deal with immigration policies that make the mobility of populations a phenomenon that promotes human intermingling and preserves links between peoples. Progress has been made, and much remains to be done in the countries of the South, where successful experiments are emerging.

In some countries of the South, young people are trying to assert themselves and express their ideas, driven by a desire to play a part in building their countries. New forms of political expression are emerging to break free from the shackles of the past and make their voices heard, both in their own countries and on the world stage. In most of these countries, civil societies are serving as vectors of innovation in the fields of education, health, democratisation and the fight against corruption. Countries that have experienced social, political and ethnic upheaval have been able to find mechanisms for conflict resolution and reconciliation in favour of appeasement and reconstruction and serve as a model of reference.

At present, all countries are going through a period marked by the end of a pandemic that has revealed the vulnerability of those who were unable to protect themselves against the scourge. The post-pandemic period has also disrupted economies and created inflation, which is not happening without reinforcing inequalities between populations, and testing the resilience of societies to overcome its effects. Today, the Russia–Ukraine war raises the spectre of an upheaval in the global balance of power. Despite all the constraints that accompany this global upheaval, the promising beginnings of a new era are on the horizon. Against this backdrop, the Global South is attempting to chart a new path of hope through the experiences of a development process at work, so that it becomes a plural voice that is heard throughout the world.

In the context of the significant changes that the world is going through, the dynamics of the countries of the Global South, despite structural and cyclical constraints, have become a reality. The chapters in this book reflect the idea of a South that speaks for itself and demonstrates the dynamics of concrete experiences that hold out the promise of hope. By recounting initiatives and projects from countries in Africa, Latin America and Asia, the authors collectively draw up a map of success stories and tell of a hope for the present that presages a promise for the future.

Acknowledgements

The search for new and innovative ways to improve the quality of life and sustainability of the countries of the Global South is not a solitary task. Hundreds of thousands of people around the world are building new ideas and initiatives every day to change reality with hope. Building the future is a collective task.

Through this work, we have gathered many people who intend to raise their voices and show concrete examples that allow us to affirm the hope for a better future.

We would like to thank all of them for their hard work in the preparation of each of the chapters, which are definitely messages of hope.

Special thanks to the editors of Emerald for believing in this call for ***Exploring Hope*** in all the countries of the Global South. They have supported this work with total freedom and breadth of vision, thus contributing to spreading a new message about the reality of the countries of this part of the world.

A special thanks to Rahma Bourquia, who inspired this work and accompanied us with immense wisdom and human quality since its beginning.

To Fernando Calderón Gutiérrez, who has given us his wise words at the conclusion of this work, reinforcing the idea and the call to build a more humane future for all of us who live in the Global South.

Finally, particular thanks to Andrés Kozel, for his advice and support in the construction of new ideas and proposals for the future of the countries of the Global South.

General Introduction: Building Hope, Perspectives and Experiences from the Global South

Marcelo Sili

CONICET, Universidad Nacional del Sur, Argentina

The idea and concept of the global south are controversial and polysemic. It is used to group together all those countries and territories that have less beneficial development conditions, with significant levels of poverty, inequality and marginalisation, often linked to their heavy colonial history and economic and cultural dependence. The concept of the global south has been referenced to the countries formerly known as the third world. In recent decades, however, this concept has been extended and applied not only to the previously mentioned third-world countries, but also to cities and regions. Thus, it is argued that there are not only countries in the global south, but also territories that can be called 'souths' in northern countries, referring to poor and marginalised areas in richer countries, as well as 'northern' or rich areas in the countries of the global south.

The common element of these territories, countries or regions, is the presence of a heavy legacy of colonisation and imperial hegemonies, which defined conditioned but very heterogeneous development trajectories, resulting in very different situations today. There are countries and regions where very traditional production systems persist, based on dense family farming, with communities trying to sustain themselves in very discouraging contexts, marked by a lack of infrastructure and employment and by high levels of poverty and violence. The existence of difficult determinations, conditioning factors and realities in the global south cannot be ignored: famine, violence and corrupt leaders, massive migration, environmental deterioration, among many other things. There is clearly a profuse bibliography on these problems around the world, both in developed countries and in the countries of the global south, as well as hundreds of institutions and research networks that point out and diagnose all these problems.

However, in spite of the strong conditionalities derived from the forms of insertion of countries in global contexts, four key elements have been observed in recent decades that can generate new conditions for the reconfiguration of social,

Exploring Hope: Case Studies of Innovation, Change and Development in the Global South, 1–6

Published under exclusive licence by Emerald Publishing Limited
doi:10.1108/978-1-83549-736-420241001

political and economic relations. These are, firstly, the profound technological change in terms of communications, mobility and production systems; secondly, the social and cultural change around the relationship between society and nature; thirdly, the change in the global conditions of accumulation, which entails profound novelties in terms of geopolitics and the game of actors. Fourthly, the demand coming from developing societies for an accelerated process of development in terms of democracy and justice led by actors of civil society, youth and media. These four elements open up possibilities for the generation of new initiatives, eventually capable of reconfiguring the dominant socio-technical model.

For example, at the level of political and social development, new initiatives are emerging in the political arena in some countries of the global south that are engaging in the democratic process. We find also other countries that have established ways for reconciliation after periods of violence. Many other developing countries have undertaken reforms of education or adopted a gender policy to improve the status of women or policies to reduce poverty. The issue of the role of the state in development is raised, especially since the pandemic period has created a concern about the role of the state and its reform. New initiatives can be observed also in terms of production (small industries, agroecology, bioeconomy with high added value, renewable energies, etc.), as well as in other dimensions: tourism and enjoyment of spaces; rescue and revaluation of sociocultural heritage (recovery of sites, recovery of gastronomic heritage, etc.); protection of natural resources, landscape and habitat (revaluation of landscapes, bioconstruction); migration and installation of young people in rural areas or small cities, among others.

These developments feedback on each other, generating retroactive loops, system effects, causal chains, etc., in many cases creating virtuous processes of varying size and complexity. These initiatives are triggered by profound technological change, by the search for democracy and peace and also by a growing concern and interest in the protection and care of the environment.

There is no doubt that development is a holistic model dealing with the integration of developing countries into the global economy, considering the role of the state in each country in leading development and setting policies, in providing innovative solutions to the economic constraints, in establishing the democratic process, in establishing a system of governance and accountability, and in developing culture and capacity building among the population.

Thus, there seems to be reason to believe that the undeniable panorama of constraints and difficulties may finally begin to be reversed and overcome, giving way to more hopeful dynamics and realities.

The main idea of this book is to identify in developing countries of the global south specific innovative and successful projects and processes that are having a structural impact in changing the model of development, and that make it possible to imagine new development paths in the Global South. Thus, this book seeks to qualify, question and even refute the monolithic ideas and images of the impossibility of building opportunities for improving the quality of life and overcoming the different constraints of development in the Global South. It is a book based on the premise as it is stated in the book *New Paths of Development: Perspectives from the Global South*

> The first premise is that it is necessary to regain confidence in the future. This means to overcome any determinism that mainstreams the defining features of the current scenario or the undesirable consequences it potentially contains. It is essential to believe in the viability of other future world-systems. Therefore, overcoming fatalism and restoring confidence in the future is a fundamental stance, as trust is the basic raw material for building visions and alternative pathways for a more equitable future. (Bourqia & Sili, 2021, p. 13)

In this sense, the book can be considered and understood as a kaleidoscope of opportunities and potentialities in the global south, which opens the doors to think about the future with more hope.

Hope Is the Keyword in This Book

Indeed, one of the most notorious features that characterise the countries of the global south is the double meaning of the idea of the future. On the one hand, the future is viewed and perceived critically, with a certain disillusionment, as it is a view constructed from the inertia of a present that does not offer peace, justice, wealth and happiness; it is a view constructed from poverty, marginality, war and chaos. If the countries of the global south stick to and persist in this outlook, it is logical to remain in a vicious circle of disillusionment and lack of future projects, because the future has no meaning. However, in the pain of everyday life, hunger, war and marginalisation, new ideas about the future are also being built, about possible futures, which are always in the process of being realised and which are based on the idea of hope.

Hope constitutes, by definition, the search for alleviation of everyday problems; it is, as Bloch says (Bloch, 2004), a consciousness that seeks in the future what has not yet been given, an anticipatory consciousness of a possible world, of a better world. This hope is based on the human impulse towards Happiness, which is why it clearly constitutes the motor of history, since it does not remain a simple utopia, but is an action that builds new futures.

Hope constitutes a movement towards the good, not simply a desire (Eagleton), therefore it does not arise on its own, it needs a process of conscious, arduous, systematic construction, anchored in everyday reality. An inactive society does not build hope but remains submerged in the conditioning facts of history and in dependence on other societies or countries. Hope is built with patience, not like wishes that are sporadic, fleeting and random, this construction of hope requires not only enthusiasm, but also reason anchored in real and significant facts, with experiences, with people's work, because hope is also a pedagogical process of learning how people build the world and their future (Eagleton, 2016). People, societies and countries themselves construct hope at the same time as they construct their daily actions and projects in search of a better future. Therefore, hope is not an empty element of reality, but is nourished by reality itself, which, although hard and often suffering, is a conscious reality and, therefore, thought and understood in order to be overcome. Thus, hope is not a magical and naïve force; on the contrary, there is only hope when there are also possibilities for the future, but also possibilities for failure and darkness.

Hope is also to be understood as the vital energy that builds, despite all restrictions and limitations, new goals and new meanings of the future, a future expressed in potential, for which it is important to strive, because it creates meaning in the empty course of time (Bloch, 2004). Hope, understood as the vital energy of a society, contributes to effective action, since hoping for that desired future implies striving to make it a reality.

This book is based on the idea that innovation processes and people's projects are an input for the construction of a better future. We think of the actions, or innovative projects that emerge in the countries of the global south, not only as innovative processes in themselves, but also as instruments illuminated by hope for building a different future.

Five interrelated questions emerge to identify innovative policies or actions and new realities and processes that have a structural impact on society:

1. What type of initiatives can be observed, and what are their trajectories? We are interested in understanding the socio-cultural and economic motivations that encourage these new practices, as well as their trajectories, in order to understand their contextual conditions and their opportunities for replication.
2. What are the factors that make or limit the development of these initiatives? Understanding this will make it possible to systematise causes and effects and also to define more clearly the policy options for sustaining the new dynamics.
3. Who are the key actors in these processes of change and what forms of organisation have they promoted? (governance). We are interested in understanding the forms of organisation of collective action and private action, because this is relevant for thinking about new forms of governance and the promotion of national development.
4. Do these innovations really contribute to the structuring and organisation of new sustainable development dynamics?
5. Do these initiatives, which currently appear as 'niche' activities, have the capacity to transform themselves into a stable system of action and thus influence and modify the dominant socio-technical model, structuring a new development logic and dynamics? This question is crucial, as it invites us to analyse whether these initiatives can overcome the instance of 'special cases', to become structuring initiatives of another development model.

The backbone hypothesis of the book is that in the Global South there are emerging initiatives sustained on the basis of new contextual conditions, expectations and visions of development, such as the growing concern for the environment and habitat, new forms of relationship with nature, new consumption patterns, new demands for rights and democracy, and the search for new and greater opportunities for economic development and employment. These innovative processes are integrated into the current socio-technical regime and modified over time; this dynamic would make it possible to reconfigure the current socio-technical regime and from there modify and build new development itineraries and trajectories, capable of offering new opportunities to the population.

Clearly, the structural problems of the Global South are not denied, but the book defines itself precisely as the 'book of current and future opportunities' or as the 'book of ongoing experiences that should be enhanced'. This contrast is legitimate and important and defines and distinguishes this work. Seen in this way, this book has a clear political intentionality, aimed at generating and focusing a new message on the opportunities for building a better future. It is a work that extends several of the lines opened by the book *New Paths of Development*, published in 2021.

In order to open the debate and to reflect on the opportunities for development in the countries of the Global South, this book presents a number of significant cases of innovation (36 cases), which suggest new ways of solving structural problems. In brief, each case will be a 'lesson to be considered', an example of opportunities for development alternatives. These are successful experiences that have left their traces have had an impact on the development of their societies and have opened the doors to new paths of development. Each of these 36 cases or experiences is presented by different authors from Latin America, Africa and Asia, as well as by colleagues from other continents related to the development problems of their countries and regions of origin.

These innovative experiences or cases have been regrouped and organised into five main thematic parts, as follows:

1. **In Search for Peace and Democracy-Building.** This part emphasises experiences that have made it possible to overcome violence in many countries as a result of guerrilla warfare, inter-ethnic wars, border conflicts, conflicts over the monopolisation of resources, or reconciliation and transitional justice after dictatorship or apartheid etc. But also, through this part, we can observe cases of strengthening identities and revaluing cultural heritage in a broad sense. The aim is to show through these cases how the countries of the Global South manage to build their own culture, revaluing their roots and their cultures, which are ultimately what allows them to sustain themselves in the dynamics of globalisation. In this thematic part, 6 cases or innovative experiences are presented.
2. **Organising Territories and Infrastructures to Improve Life.** The objective in this part is to identify innovative experiences in territorial planning and organisation and in the creation and management of infrastructures (roads, water, energy), improvements in collective facilities (community centres, schools, hospitals) and housing, to generate better living conditions, improve the quality of life and reduce territorial imbalances and conflicts. We observe how societies are constructing decentralisation and innovative forms of territorial management of the countryside, of cities, which can point to new itineraries of territorial planning, management and development. In this thematic part, 7 cases or innovative experiences are presented.
3. **Revitalising the Economy with a Sustainable Approach.** Emphasis is placed on showing experiences of overcoming the traditional productive matrix and the construction of other productive itineraries capable of generating employment in a dignified and sustainable manner. Innovative processes are presented that can mark alternative paths of development, but not only product innovations,

but above all innovations in the ways of producing, linking societies, solving problems, and illuminating new paths and ways of doing things. We also explore the new opportunities generated in each of the countries, beyond the approach of adaptation and competitiveness that marks the dynamics of capitalist globalisation, and which has allowed many countries to compete in the world market. In this thematic part, 8 cases or innovative experiences are presented.

4. **Ensuring Environmental Sustainability.** In this part, the aim is to identify experiences that point the way to environmental sustainability, both in urban and rural areas. These may be experiences linked to the protection of natural ecosystems (forests, forests, grasslands, and maritime coasts), as well as to the reduction of environmental risks and conflicts and the deterioration of the environment due to human intervention (solid waste, pollution in general, reduction of species, among others). In this thematic part, 6 cases or innovative experiences are presented.
5. **Inclusive and Caring Worlds.** In this part, we want to present cases of socially innovative processes or policies that were applied with success and had a great impact in education, building capacities, health, poverty, gender, youth, etc. This part emphasises experiences that have made it possible to overcome violence in many countries as a result of guerrilla warfare, inter-ethnic wars, border conflicts, conflicts over the monopolisation of resources, or reconciliation and transitional justice after dictatorship or apartheid, etc. But also, through this part, we can observe cases of strengthening identities and revaluing cultural heritage in a broad sense. In this thematic part, 9 cases or innovative experiences are presented.

Many of the initiatives analysed can be considered niche actions and special cases, but in other cases, many of these have given rise to more structured and sustainable public policies over time. In sum, this book will offer a kaleidoscopic panorama of some 36 cases linked to hopeful experiences of development alternatives in the Global South, enriched with cartography, infographics and photographs.

The book is organised as follows: in addition to this general introduction, five main thematic parts are presented, within each of which there is a brief introduction that explains the different cases of this part from a cross-cutting and comparative perspective. Then, within each of these parts, the different chapters or case studies are presented. Finally, a general conclusion of the whole book is presented, in terms of a general reflection on the future and Hope in the countries of the Global South.

References

Bloch, E. (2004). *El principio de Esperanza*. Trotta.
Bourquia, R., & Sili, M. (Eds.). (2021). *New paths of development*. Springer.
Eagleton, T. (2016). *Esperanza sin optimismo*. Taurus.

Part 1

In Search for Peace and Democracy-Building

Introduction

Javier Enrique Medina Vásquez

Universidad del Valle, Cali, Colombia

The foresight required by the contemporary world must provide comprehensive answers to the acute questions arising from this relevant historical moment, especially from the Global South. We are witnessing a turning point in the contemporary world, as a result of the Russia-Ukraine conflict crisis, the accumulation of crises derived from the COVID-19 pandemic, high inflation, among others. In Latin America, there is also the lost decade of growth in the region between 2010 and 2019, the legacy of historical inequalities, and so on. The techno-economic forces driven by globalisation alone do not explain all the structural change underway. All this is leading to a breakdown of the planetary order that has been in place since the 1990s, with unsuspected repercussions.

A very important debate to explain this situation is whether we are living through small adjustments within an 'uncontroversial' development model, or whether a change of the model is required. In the 1980s, some authors characterised the former position, warning about the increasing difficulty of organisations to manage volatile, uncertain, complex and ambiguous (VUCA) environments. Later, towards the middle of the last decade, other authors called them turbulent, unpredictable, too novel or opaque environments (TUNA). Now, in the midst of the pandemic, other authors call this type of environment (BANI), i.e. fragile, anxiety-inducing, non-linear and frankly incomprehensible.

Many authors line up behind the hypothesis that we are in a time of change, focusing on the symptoms, but not on the causes that give rise to this situation. On the other hand, other authors hold the opposite hypothesis. The world is immersed in an epochal change. This is not about small changes within an order of things that should remain the same, but about a moment of transitions and transformations of humanity that configure a change of development model, in a multidimensional sense. However, the position to be adopted in the face of this heated intellectual debate is that, whether it is an era of change or a change of era, it is occurring more rapidly and in a more oscillating manner than one might have thought. Regardless of the position taken, i.e. the change-era view, or the epochal change hypothesis, the key idea is that global interconnectedness requires new frames of reference for its understanding and management.

Exploring Hope: Case Studies of Innovation, Change and Development in the Global South, 9–12

doi:10.1108/978-1-83549-736-420241002

This shift also represents an ethical imperative of this decisive moment in history. This fact invites us to reflect and not follow the inertia of thinking and doing the same things that led to this state of affairs (Medina Vásquez, 2020).

Human and Social Foresight, proposed by the Italian professor Eleonora Barbieri Masini, is a rich resource for thinking about and discovering the seeds of change in the contemporary world. This is understood as a 'research perspective on the possible futures of humanity, which allows for the development of elements of social prevention and the construction of visions and future projects' (Alonso Concheiro & Medina Vásquez, 2013).

Professor Masini has been one of the pioneers of future studies since the 1960s, and her theoretical legacy is especially useful for the construction and negotiation of shared visions of the future, in conditions of conflict and social fragmentation. Her texts invite us to focus on discovering and cultivating the visions, values and capacities that can renew contemporary society (Masini, 2000). However, Masini (2014) always argued that the exhaustion of Western visions of the future was very difficult to remedy from Europe or North America.

Precisely, the texts that make up this first part of the present book contribute with a profound reflection on the seeds or possibilities of change for humanity, with a view to improving and transforming the repertoire of mental models and collective behaviours in order to imagine and build a better world. The main added value of the chapters that make up the first part of this book is that it shows how the current crisis of the development model framed by democracy and the market economy can be confronted by an active civil society, capable of building shared visions of the future and accelerating a transformative recovery from Africa, Asia and Latin America. This is how innovative visions, values and capacities are presented that demonstrate the power of peace processes and dialogues, the development of inclusive policies and new forms of political participation of young people, the democratisation of political opportunities for indigenous peoples, the management of migrants' problems and the curbing of electoral corruption.

The renewal of these visions begins in Colombia, with the experience of a peace agreement focused on transforming living conditions in rural territories, which are the poorest and have the least equity and opportunities for their inhabitants, in a situation of acute armed conflict, institutional weakness and the presence of illicit groups and illegal economies. The second experience takes place in Mongolia and denotes an immense effort on the part of a state located between Russia and China, which has struggled for several decades to be recognised as an arms-free country, being of special relevance in the process of establishing global policies from the periphery.

The third case comes from Chile and shows how youth develop sophisticated cultural and communicational tools to forge opportunities and counteract the social inequality of the inhabitants. This is how a process was designed and implemented that culminated in a campaign whose slogan was 'for hope and social justice', which won the 2021 elections with Gabriel Boric, a charismatic youth leader who comes from below and shares the popular mentality. The fourth case comes from Brazil and highlights a set of institutional innovations and social policies implemented during the first decade and a half of the 21st century. This model produced a strong cycle of social inclusion, poverty reduction, improved quality of life and the promotion of sustainable development, with tangible results in access to universal health care, the expansion of the national public education system, social security and the transfer of income to families.

The fifth experience is that of African migrants, either as foreigners seeking asylum or as refugees as a result of political or social conflict. These groups often find themselves in situations of illegality, clashes with law enforcement and diverse and complex economic dynamics. Finally, the last case presents two South Asian civil society efforts to build strong democracies in India and Bangladesh. Here civil society's struggle to control corruption is highlighted, with organisations independent of the public and private sector contributing to the creation of active citizenship at the grassroots level.

These clear and sharp examples of peace-seeking and democracy-building are particularly noteworthy in view of the dismal results of pandemic management in the global south. This situation confirmed the persistence of poor quality in strategic decision-making, in the various pandemic cycles, in the vaccination process and in recovery management. Lack of government vision and public policy biases demonstrated the vulnerability of the population and the high risks and costs of accumulating complex problems. Governments grappled with the consequences of their lack of empathy and understanding of the new contexts. They have taken unprecedented paths, where the main issue was not a lack of knowledge, but paradigmatic blindness and a lack of political and social sensitivity. The lack of common sense and the lack of a shared vision of the future ended up aggravating the problems.

Today, more than ever, in a situation of progressive accumulation of crises, it is necessary to think about the future with foresight and institutional resilience, with the capacity to resist the crisis, with recovery and adaptation to the new situation. The Global South must counteract the effects of global shocks, systemic phenomena of interconnectedness and cascading effects. It is imperative to close development gaps, especially in the areas of productivity, gender, health and biosafety, and social, green and digital development. New public policy approaches require holistic, cross-cutting, multidimensional, and intertemporal solutions. Also, they must listen to the different voices of civil society (Medina Vásquez, 2023).

In the current decade, an unprecedented collective learning effort must be made to generate a triple dynamic of economic growth, institutional development and sustainable human development. Public policies must be adjusted with long-term horizons and short-term actions, with people in mind, in order to preserve and strengthen democratic governance (Bitar et al., 2021).

The seeds of change identified by civil society in this text demonstrate the capacity of the Global South to build hope, innovation and change. They are contributions that generate hope and inspire new generations to socially construct the future, that is, to design visions of the future, forge values for the common good, and implement life projects that enrich the quality of life of the inhabitants, especially those of the least favoured.

We are facing a great epochal change and these seeds show that it is possible to leave the status quo behind and turn the situation around. It is time to share these experiences and believe in the potential of the Global South to build its future. It is now or never!

References

Alonso Concheiro, A., & Medina Vásquez, J. (2013). *Eleonora Barbieri Masini. Alma de los estudios de los futuros*. Fundación Javier Barros Sierra.

Bitar, S., Máttar, J., & Medina, J. (2021). *El Gran Giro de América Latina*. Programa Editorial, Universidad del Valle.

Masini, E. (2000). *Penser le futur*. Dunod.

Masini, E. (2014). Repensar los estudios del futuro. In L. Leal, M. Escobar, H. Mosquera, J. Medina Vásquez, & A. Mosquera (Eds.), *Construyendo la calidad en los ejercicios de Prospectiva y Vigilancia Tecnológica*. Programa Editorial Universidad del Valle.

Medina Vásquez, J. (2020). *Abriendo caminos en la Prospectiva de América Latina y el Caribe*. Programa Editorial Universidad del Valle.

Medina Vásquez, J. (2023). *Prospectiva para un mundo interdependiente*. Academia Colombiana de Ciencias Económicas.

Chapter 1

Peace Can Be Built from the Territories: Experiences of Networking in South-Western Colombia

Milena Umaña Maldonado and Claudia Ospina Aldana

Rimisp – Centro Latinoamericano para el Desarrollo Rural, Colombia

Colombia lived through an armed conflict with the FARC[*] *guerrilla* for more than half a century. After several years of negotiations, the Peace Agreement was finally signed in November 2016, with the main objective of putting an end to the conflict and guaranteeing its non-repetition. A crucial point to achieve this purpose is to achieve the transformation of living conditions in rural territories, taking into account that poverty in these areas is much higher than in urban areas, which is one of the reasons why the conflict has lasted for so long. For this reason, Point 1 of this Agreement, the Integral Rural Reform (RRI), includes actions to close urban–rural gaps, seeking greater equity and opportunities for rural inhabitants and territories. One of the main mechanisms for implementing the RRI is the Territorially Focused Development Programmes (PDET), which were targeted at 170 municipalities divided into 16 sub-regions (Fig. 1.1). Although the process of structural transformation of the countryside should cover all of the country's rural areas, these municipalities were prioritised taking into account poverty levels, the level of armed conflict, institutional weaknesses and the presence of illicit crops and other illegal economies (Point 1.2.2 of the Agreement).

Although there are still around 10 years of implementation of the Peace Agreement and many more will surely be needed to achieve a stable and lasting peace, 6 years after its signing, the balance of its implementation is not very positive, especially from the point of view of the communities, who have felt that once again they have not been fulfilled what was promised in the participatory processes (which in this case gave rise to the Action Plans for Regional Transformation – PATR) and with the full implementation of the Agreement. This panorama

[*]The Revolutionary Armed Forces of Colombia (FARC guerilla, after the initials in Spanish)

Exploring Hope: Case Studies of Innovation, Change and Development in the Global South, 13–17

doi:10.1108/978-1-83549-736-420241003

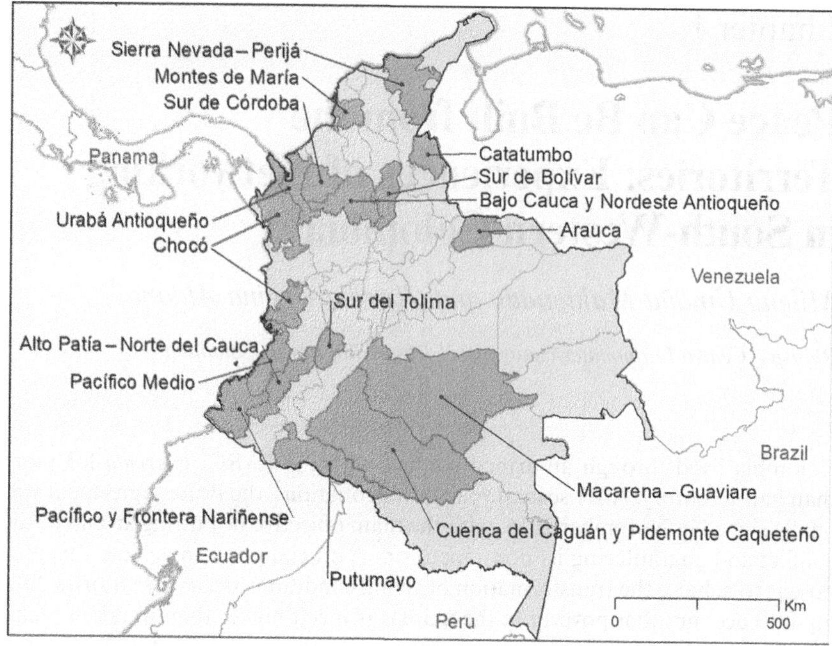

Fig. 1.1. Sub-regions Prioritised for the Implementation of the Integrated Rural Reform (PDET Sub-regions). *Source*: Own Elaboration Based on Information from the Agencia de Renovación del Territorio (ART).

has a chance to change with the current 2022–2026 government, which has so far committed itself to this implementation, unlike the 2018–2022 government, whose political party opposed the signing of the Agreement and ensured that its implementation would begin at a very slow pace.

However, it should be noted that, despite the obvious disappointment, civil society organisations and delegates from the PDETs' driving groups have not stopped working for peace building from their territories. As part of these processes, we would like to highlight two experiences that we have had the opportunity to accompany in our work with Rimisp – Latin American Centre for Rural Development. Thanks to funding from the European Union, in 2018 Rimisp, the Institute of Intercultural Studies of the Javeriana University in Cali (IEI) and the Avina Foundation implemented the project 'Support for the Participation and Peace Building Process in Northern Cauca and Alto Patía' (Capacities for Advocacy project) in the 24 municipalities of the departments of Valle del Cauca, Cauca and Nariño that are part of this PDET sub-region (Fig. 1.2).

This project promoted different processes for the construction of peace in civil society. It supported the articulation of a network of civil society organisations that were committed to public policy advocacy and peace building in their municipalities, forming the Tedapaz Platform (Territory of Life and Peace). This network was made up of 141 civil society, indigenous, peasant, environmental,

Fig. 1.2. Northern Cauca and Alto Patía. *Source*: ID 144907142 © Harold Song | Dreamstime.com.

youth, community, women's, productive, victims' and Afro-Colombian community organisations, among others. As part of the strengthening of the network's organisations, 87 people participated in a diploma course to strengthen their capacities for intercultural dialogue and community and territorial advocacy.

Capacity building for advocacy was complemented by the production of relevant information to build an informed multilevel dialogue. In this way, a measurement of 'everyday indicators' designed in a participatory manner was carried out. These indicators seek to account for day-to-day changes in peace building and well-being issues and to measure them closer to the communities.

With these and other tools from the political and community work of civil society organisations, this network supports the participatory monitoring of the implementation of the PDETs through the social and virtual platform Tedapaz, its Administrative Committee and the Citizen Oversight Committee (Veeduria Regional). The objective of this committee, formed within the framework of the project, is to exercise vigilance over the public management of the PATR of the PDET of Alto Patía and Norte del Cauca. At present, they have already submitted monitoring reports on this PDET to feed the reports of the Comptroller General's Office to the Congress of the Republic.

Based on the lessons learned from this process, the need was identified to contrast the dynamics of Alto Patía – Norte del Cauca with other PDET sub-regions in south-western Colombia, in order to have a broader overview of the advances and setbacks in the implementation of the Agreement and to strengthen regional work. For this reason, it was proposed to strengthen a territorial observatory that would be at the service of platforms such as Tedapaz and that would have the particularity of being made up of civil society organisations, that would be nourished by the interculturality of the western mountain range and the Pacific coast, and that would strengthen women's leadership.

In this way, the Cordilleras Pazcíficas Observatory was consolidated between 2021 and 2022, a territorial observatory currently made up of 43 organisations, which is aimed at measuring and making visible the territorial transformation of the southwest of Colombia (Alto Patía – Northern Cauca, Pacífico and Nariñense Border and Middle Pacífico Sub-regions), in order to monitor public policies and contribute to peace building.

One of the first questions that the observatory had to answer was the specific dimensions to be monitored. To this end, a participatory process was developed in which it was decided to monitor changes in those dimensions associated with the inhabitants' living well. This process opened up spaces for discussion and reflection, which were highly appreciated by the social organisations, even in complex scenarios of intensification of the armed conflict, the COVID-19 pandemic and the National Strike (Fig. 1.3).

Accordingly, for the Cordilleras Pazcíficas Observatory, Living Well for the southwest of Colombia refers to

> Enjoying all the rights to be able to live in the territory in harmony with nature, based on ancestral knowledge, tranquillity and emotional balance. It implies that women can enjoy the same rights as men, that citizens have the guarantees to participate in politics and to monitor public affairs, and that they are in a safe and peaceful territory where social problems are properly managed collectively.

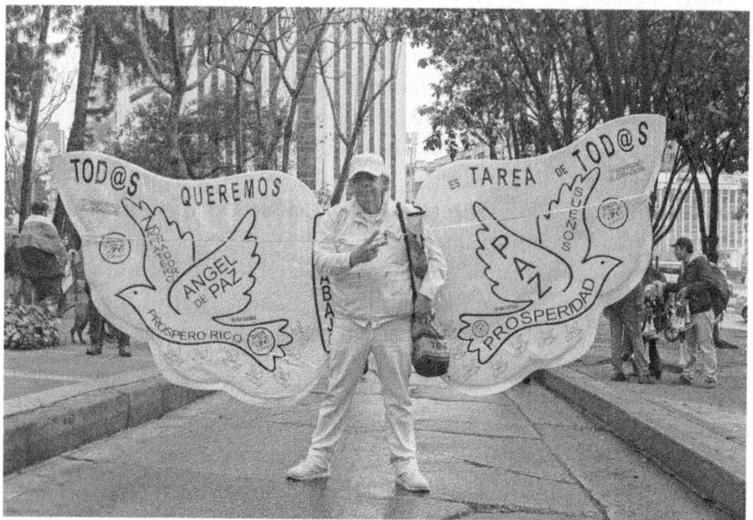

Fig. 1.3. 18 March 2019 – March for the Defence of the JEP, Special Jurisdiction for Peace Bogota Colombia. *Source:* DNI 142421474 © Gabriel Leonardo Guerrero Bermúdez | Dreamstime.com.

Fig. 1.4. Exercise 'Weaving the Network' Carried Out by the Participants of the Observatory. *Source:* Cordilleras Pazcíficas Observatory Photographic Archive.

For this reason, the observatory monitors the dimensions of a dignified and just life, the environment, emotional balance, gender equality, citizen participation, territorial security and the management of social problems (Fig. 1.4).

The strengthening of the Cordilleras Pazcíficas Observatory was carried out thanks to funding from the Territories of Opportunity Programme and was executed by Rimisp together with the IEI with the aim of laying the foundations for consolidating a sustainable observatory over time. This process was carried out, first, by strengthening the capacities of the social organisations that make up the Observatory in the analysis and monitoring of planning processes and the execution of public policies for territorial development; second, by mobilising concrete actions to influence public policy instruments and tools in order to contribute to processes of territorial transformation; and third, by generating greater knowledge and understanding of the realities of these territories through innovative measurements (such as the everyday indicators of living well), the visibility of peace-building initiatives and the promotion of dialogue with public institutions.

Conclusions

These two experiences made it possible to demonstrate to various actors the strength of civil society organisations in the southwest of the country, which on a daily basis develop various initiatives that are committed to peace building in their territories and to living well, including the creation of networks, platforms and monitoring of the implementation of the Peace Agreement. This explains the leading role that the citizens of the southwest of the country demand in the formulation and execution of territorial development projects, so that their recognition and inclusion can be taken into account by public policy and the effective transformation of their territories towards territories of peace.

Chapter 2

Non-Proliferation in Asia: Time to Un-tap the Potential of NWFZs

J. Enkhsaikhan

Blue Banner NGO, Mongolia

Introduction

International relations are witnessing an intensification of great power rivalry and tension, a renewed and qualitatively new level of nuclear arms race that involves hypersonic and dual-use delivery vehicles, offensive cyber capabilities, artificial intelligence, etc. Nuclear-weapon states (NWS or the P5)[1] and nuclear-armed states[2] are increasing their weapons spending to modernise, upgrade or expand their arsenals and are placing greater emphasis on increasing the role of such weapons in their security policies. This is accompanied by thinly veiled or even direct threats of the use of nuclear weapons as instruments for military or political coercion, blackmail and intimidation. As such they demonstrate the fallacy of nuclear deterrence doctrines that go against the spirit and goal of a nuclear-weapon-free world (NWFW) that we are all trying to establish.

The unsuccessful conclusion in August 2022 of the 10th Review Conference of States Parties to the Treaty on the Non-proliferation of Nuclear Weapons (in short NPT Revcon) has shown that despite many constructive proposals by the non-nuclear-weapon states (NNWS) and non-state actors, the P5 are not prepared not only to honour the commitment taken by them by Article VI of the

[1]Nuclear weapons states (NWS) are the United States, Russia, China, UK and France that are recognised as such by the Treaty on the Non-proliferation of Nuclear Weapons (NPT) and the states parties to it. Thy are also known as the P5.

[2]These are states that besides the NWSs de facto possess nuclear weapons: India, Pakistan, Israel and North Korea.

Exploring Hope: Case Studies of Innovation, Change and Development in the Global South, 19–23

Published under exclusive licence by Emerald Publishing Limited
doi:10.1108/978-1-83549-736-420241004

NPT[3] more than half a century ago, i.e. abolishing nuclear weapons, but even to commit not to use nuclear weapons first.[4] The failure of the Revcon as well as the exchanges of nuclear-weapon threats being made in different forms throughout the war in Ukraine have weakened further the NPT regime. If serious conclusions are not drawn, some NNWSs may go nuclear for their own protection or join the nuclear alliance of NATO as has already been the case with neutral Finland and Sweden giving thus credence to the nuclear deterrence doctrine.

In the Indo-Pacific region, the increase of US–China rivalry, reviving of the Quadrilateral security dialogue and establishing of AUKUS, a provocative trilateral security pact between the UK, the US and Australia (which is a state party to the South Asian nuclear-weapon zone) to help the latter to acquire nuclear-powered submarines, India's accidental firing of a supersonic missile into Pakistan, recurring incidents at the border of China and India are the signs of possible troubles ahead. The deepening crisis on and around the Korean Peninsula is raising deep concerns of the states of the region that if not seriously addressed can lead to the nuclear arms race in Northeast Asia involving the US, Russia, China, the two Koreas, Japan and even some other members of the NATO alliance. Members of the Pacific Islands Forum (PIF) express concern with the possible risks of the nuclear arms race involving the vast Pacific region.[5] Thus the Melanesian Spearhead Group is discussing the issue of declaring their sub-region or the entire Blue Pacific a zone of peace and cooperation.

NPT Commitments

Though the state parties to the NPT have committed to preventing the proliferation of nuclear weapons and abolishing them, efforts of NNWS to influence the policies of the P5 and their allies represent a hefty challenge, to say the least. Besides strengthening the Treaty on the Prohibition of Nuclear Weapons (TPNW), NNWS need to continue to put pressure on NWS that have not done so to become party to the Comprehensive Nuclear-Test-Ban Treaty (CTBT) without further delay, prohibit fissile materials production for nuclear weapons purposes and demand concrete results on other issues that have for years and even decades been on the multilateral negotiating table. However, all these activities are not enough today. NNWS and non-state actors need to be even more actively involved in addressing all issues of vital importance to the international

---

[3]Article VI of the NPT reads as follows: 'Each of the Parties to the Treaty undertakes to pursue negotiations in good faith on effective measures relating to cessation of the nuclear arms race at an early date and to nuclear disarmament, and on a treaty on general and complete disarmament under strict and effective international control'.

[4]https://news.un.org/en/story/2022/08/1125572

[5]Pacific Island states' exclusive economic zones (EEZs) cumulatively cover over 10 mln square miles of space with rich living and non-living resources, including energy resources. Many of these states are also located on or near important international shipping lanes.

community as a whole. NNWS need to go beyond the above measures by making use of their inherent sovereign right to restrict P5 activities in areas of their sovereign competence by expanding and making fuller use of the nuclear-weapon-free zone (NWFZ) concept.

Role of NWFZ

Nuclear-weapon-free zones (NWFZs) are recognised as strategically important and practically useful regional measures of NNWS in curbing nuclear weapon proliferation. The five NWFZs established in inhabited areas so far are Latin America and the Caribbean, the South Pacific, Southeast Asia, the entire African continent and Central Asia. They include more than 115 states, the territories of which cover about 84 million km^2 of the world's landmass, representing 39% of its population and making up almost 60% of United Nations membership. The total absence of nuclear weapons in the states parties to NWFZs and expected legally based commitments of the P5 to respect their status and refrain from using or threatening to use nuclear weapons against them make up the very basis of such zones. Establishing of the second-generation zones, i.e. in regions of conflict or of direct geopolitical interest of great powers, is currently under consideration in the Middle East,[6] while informal discussions for such zones are underway in Northeast Asia and the Arctic. When established, these zones would reduce further the geographical scope of nuclear-weapon-related activities of the P5 or other nuclear-armed states.

However, to enjoy the full benefits of NWFZs, its weakness, i.e. its narrow, restricted approach to zones ought to be changed. So far the concept follows the NPT approach[7] that believes that such zones need to be established 'on the basis of arrangements freely arrived at among the States of the region concerned',[8] known as traditional zones. At the time when the NWFZ was initially being defined, to start the ball rolling the two superpowers and their allies were focusing on involving large numbers of states, i.e. involving groups of states in various regions. That might have been logical and understandable at the time. However, the situation has changed in the past half-century. In order to ensure that no blind spots emerge in the NWFW, the rights, interests and roles of two dozen if not more individual states ought to be recognised. Moreover, in order to prevent the expansion of the number of nuclear umbrella states, the P5 should commit not to expand further their umbrellas and, as a confidence-building measure, provide NNWSs not parties to NWFZs with a political assurance in the form of a joint P5 declaration that they would not use the territories of such states in their nuclear-weapon-related policies and activities.

---

[6]Known as a Weapons of Mass Destruction Free Zone in the Middle East.

[7]Article VII of the NPT reads as follows: 'Nothing in this Treaty affects the right of any group of States to conclude regional treaties in order to assure the total absence of nuclear weapons in their respective territories'.

[8]UNGA resolution 3472 (XXX) B of 11 December 1975.

Mongolia's Experience

Mongolia is a small state situated between Russia and China. During the Cold War, it was an ally of the Soviet Union and hosted the latter's military bases where dual-use weapons were based. At that time politically and militarily Mongolia was caught between two cold wars: East-West and Sino-Soviet. During the height of Sino-Soviet military confrontation in 1969, there was the danger of a larger conflict that might involve the use of nuclear weapons not only by its two neighbours but also by the US. In such a case, Mongolia could have been turned into an 'irradiated grass'.

At the end of the Cold War when Russia was completing the withdrawal of its bases, Mongolia declared its territory an NWFZ and pledged to have that status internationally guaranteed. However, since it bordered on two nuclear weapon states only, the narrow concept of NWFZ could not be applied in its case. Its long talks and discussions with the P5 have revealed that they were reluctant to accept its single-state NWFZ policy seeing it as setting an unwelcome for them precedent which could also undermine the establishment of traditional (group state) zones.[9] The talks have shown that unless politically pressured, the P5 would be reluctant to agree to the concept and practice of single-state zones. Of the five NWFZs mentioned above, three were established after Mongolia had announced its single-state zone initiative. The three NWFZ cases under consideration or discussion mentioned above also demonstrate that establishment of single-state zones is not at all undermining the establishment of traditional zones. After many meetings and talks, in 2012 the P5 signed a joint declaration whereby they pledged to respect Mongolia's nuclear-weapon-free status and not to contribute to any act that would violate it. Mongolia sees it as a sign of the P5 in gradually accepting the concept of single-state zones as an important part of the NWFW that would foreclose the appearance of any Achilles' heels in the NWFZ or the NPT regimes.

Recognising single-state zones would complement the traditional zones and strengthen the NWFZ regime. Cumulatively these individual states in number of states involved and territories covered far exceed those of the Central Asia and Southeast Asian NWFZs. From the purely legal point of view disregarding of the rights of individual states and their interests grossly violates the principle of sovereign equality of states as enshrined in the Charter of the United Nations that form the very basis of contemporary international law. International law should serve the interests of all states and not particular groups. If needed, the international community can seek the Advisory opinion of the International Court of Justice on the issue of sovereign equality of states regarding acquiring nuclear security assurances. Artificial division among NNWSs would only weaken their concerted action.

---

[9] https://www.globalasia.org/v15no4/feature/lessons-from-mongolia-reinvigorating-the-approach-to-nuclear–weapon-free-zones_jargalsaikhan-enkhsaikhan, https://www.brookings.edu/wp-content/uploads/2016/06/08-nuclear-weapon-free-mongolia-tuya.pdf

Realpolitik logic shows that individual states that are not protected by international law might be perceived by the P5 as low-hanging fruits that could easily be used for their narrow geopolitical purposes. Therefore, only by broadening the definition of NWFZs and recognising the rights of individual states to establish single-state zones (i.e. mini-zones) will it be possible to expand horizontally NWFZs to all corners of the world without exception. Doing that would restrict the possible frivolous actions of the P5 in vast areas of the world. This would also open the way for individual neutral states to acquire security assurances from the P5 and at the same time add their voices in support of the common goal of establishing a NWFW. On the other hand, as already mentioned, ignoring the role of individual states would create grey areas, international legal loopholes and Achilles' heels that would weaken not only the entire NWFZ regime but also the future of the NWFW.

What Next

In the case of the Indo-Pacific region, especially the West Pacific,[10] un-tapping of the full potential of NWFZs could reduce by millions of square miles the areas of possible unfettered activities of NWS at a time of great power rivalry. This is important since international practice shows that the risks of conflicts and frictions of the P5 in the form of proxy conflicts and wars would be greater on territories of NNWS or of those of their allies as per logic *lupus non mordet lupum* (i.e. wolf does not bite a wolf).

An inclusive approach to NWFZs would be an important form of NNWS prevention or proliferation of deterrence policies, including in Europe, and would serve as a practical stepping stone to the NWFW. Such policy needs to come especially from the NNWSs of the Indo-Pacific region where not only de jure and de facto nuclear weapon states but also nuclear-capable states and many small vulnerable states are located, a region where the absence of an NWFZ in Northeast Asia and the possible nuclear domino effect could lead to the proliferation of nuclear weapon states in the region and well beyond it. Hence, the United Nations General Assembly needs to undertake ASAP the second comprehensive study of NWFZs in all their aspects bearing in mind that the first such study had been undertaken as far back as in 1975. The rich experience gained since then would be useful not only in establishing further traditional zones but also in recognising and including single-state zones in the NWFZ regime.

[10]https://carnegieendowment.org/2022/03/23/what-island-nations-have-to-say-on-indo-pacific-geopolitics-pub-86700

Chapter 3

Youth and New Forms of Politics in Chile

Sandra Iturrieta Olivares

Pontificia Universidad Catolica de Valparaiso, Chile

As a tri-continental country located in the southwest of South America between mountains, seas, desert and snow, Chile is entering the third decade of the century under strong social pressures derived from citizens' expectations to achieve greater levels of equity, social justice, political transparency, multiculturalism and a balance between environmental preservation and economic production. Advances in modernisation, access to more consumption, more education, and techno-sociability have led citizens to notice increasing social inequalities and greater deterioration of their natural environment (Letelier, 2020). Everyday lives are alerted in different ways to the fact that Chile is one of the countries with the greatest social inequality in the world (OECD, 2020). There is a growing public clamour for the state to assume a more central role in the economy and society (Calderón & Castells, 2019). The happiness of the Chilean population is undermined by the rigours of the daily grind of inserting and maintaining oneself in a society labelled as successful, and by the decline of national pride sustained by the probity of its institutions, now called into question. Citizen subjectivities are strongly affected, by the delegitimisation of institutionality and of the political orientations that guide its development taking shape (Calderón & Castells, 2019; Letelier, 2020). Political apathy and hopelessness about the future are taking over the national scene. 'A kind of frustration of expectations positioned itself at the political centre of the different Latin American countries' (Calderón & Castells, 2019, p. 51). Chile was no exception.

However, as a result of the progress made in the country, young people have greater opportunities to 'observe social inequality from a better cultural position and react to it with more sophisticated tools' (Letelier, 2020, p. 53). They have grown up in a democracy and feel that they have inherited the responsibility to generate better opportunities for every inhabitant of the territory. They have been protagonists of the Penguin Revolution of 2006 and the Student Movement of 2011, managing to lay the foundations for free higher education in the country.

Exploring Hope: Case Studies of Innovation, Change and Development in the Global South, 25–29

doi:10.1108/978-1-83549-736-420241005

Based on these achievements, they support the idea that another Chile is possible, and in 2019 they initiated the first steps of what will be the largest social revolt in the history of democratic Chile, *October 2019*, which, like a leap of hope (Iturrieta, 2020), will remain in the memory of every inhabitant of this territory eager for transformation (Fig. 3.1).

The adult citizenry and part of the youth watch with disbelieving and hopeful, nostalgic and fearful eyes, as this group of young people, without trembling, argue for dignity and inclusion. Gradually, self-convened voices are being added through social networks. Airs of hope fill the voids left by years of sour taste of inequality. Hope is intertwined with the fear and nostalgia of the adult generations that lived through the democratic rupture of 1973 in the country. Those disenchanted youth of yesterday are beginning to identify with the powerful message of today's youth. Nostalgia and hope build bridges that seemed broken or nonexistent until then, symbolised, for example, in the complicity between *Tevito*, the chinchinero dog, official mascot of Chilean public television between 1969 and 1973, and the dog of the protests who, replicated in thousands of dogs throughout the country, proudly participated in the social mobilisations of 2019 wearing a red scarf. The image of the iconic mascots together, twinning the nostalgia of the past with the hopes of the present, to project an idealised future. The youth of yesteryear and the youth of today, united by the same ideal of social justice, assume a central role in the National Plebiscite in October 2020 in which the citizens, with the largest vote in the history of Chile (7,562,173 votes), approved the drafting of a new Constitution to govern the destiny of the country (SERVEL, 2020). *Hasta que la dignidad se haga costumbre* (Until dignity becomes customary) was the slogan that brought voters together on that epic day.

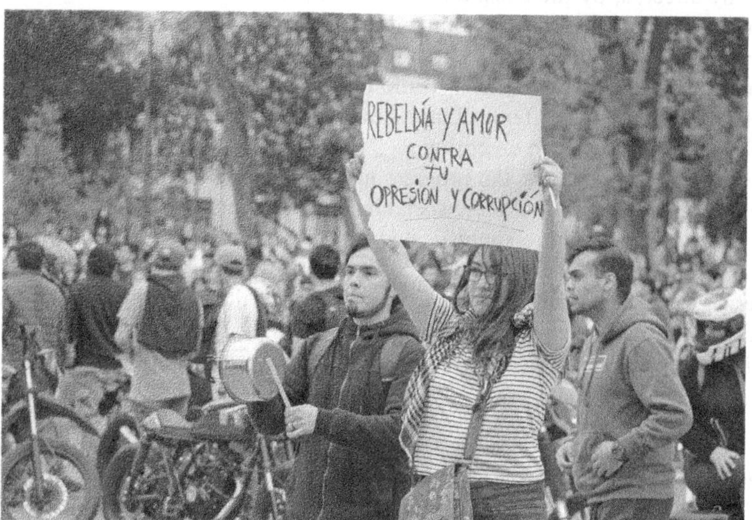

Fig. 3.1. National Protest Day in Chile, October 2019. *Source:* ID 161991821 © Marcelo Vildósola Garrigo | Dreamstime.com.

In 2021, one of the youngest presidents in the world, and one of the leaders of the Chilean student mobilisations, is elected. The chords of the campaign jingle (Gabriel Boric Font, 2021) filter through the cracks of everyday life: *Un Chile para vivir mejor* fleeds the country with renewed hopes. *Haciendo crecer Chile como nadie más lo ha hecho*; *Ya marchamos mucho tiempo, no perdimos la fe*; *El momento es ahora para cambiar la historia*; *Chile necesita juventud*; *Lo haremos juntos y esa será la virtud*; *Que en el nuevo Chile paso a paso, nadie quede atrás*, is the hopeful promise for those who live day by day the disappointments of frustrated expectations. *¡Generación dorada que va a todas!*, is the historical account with which the catchy melody alludes to the power of youth to bring about social transformations. Hope brings together self-convened voices, which, without political banners, take over the technological platforms. The country is polarised between the continuity and radicalisation of the current model, and the youthful hopes of transformation (Fig. 3.2). The tense contest is being waged on social networks and through the mass media, which are struggling to position their truth. Aware of the digital divide, the vigorous golden generation is setting itself the challenge of walking through Chile: 'Vamos a llevar la esperanza de vivir mejor a lugares donde aún no hemos llegado' (Página 19, 2021, p. 19). In the meantime, the *Bus de la Esperanza*, loaded with convictions, travels the territories from north to south, seeking to 'survey the problems and get to know the opinions of the citizens regarding the social, economic and political development of the regions' (Nostalgica, 2021).

Expectations of change transcend national borders to nestle in the nostalgia, yearnings and hopes of fraternal peoples. León Gieco, one of Argentina's most prominent singer-songwriters, authorises the use of his composition *Los Salieris de Charly* as part of the Chilean presidential campaign. The song, originally

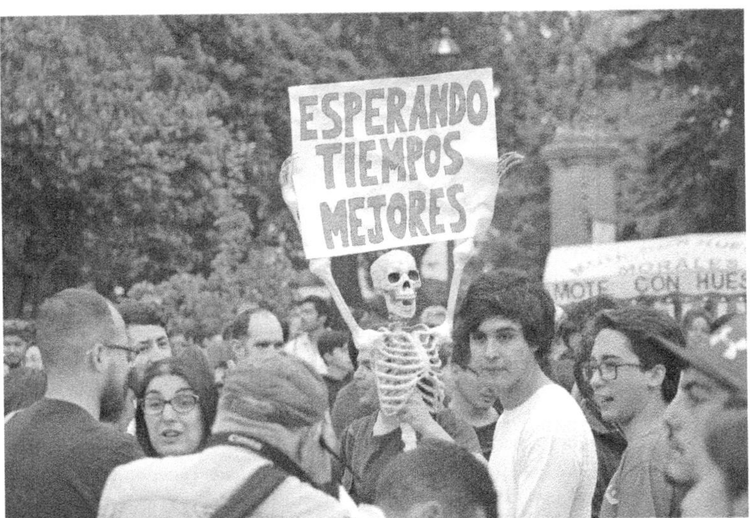

Fig. 3.2. Massive Protests in the Cities of Chile. *Source:* DNI 142421474 © Gabriel Leonardo Guerrero Bermúdez | Dreamstime.com.

published in 1992, is filled with magic the links between the youth of the 1980s and 1990s and the new generation, heir to their democratic impetus. The reflection of past, present and future yearnings and hopes amalgamates wills and illusions. The reference to the desire to have a young president, lover of life, lacking experience (to steal and lie) is part of the lyrics with which this rap-rock brings together souls yearning for a life in harmony with Nature and Human Rights. It is also a reflection of the citizen's aspiration to return to a life in a probative environment.

The visual arts concur with everyday images that, in perfect harmony with the chords and lyrics of the song, contribute to the identification with a charismatic youthful leader, who comes from the people, has lived their vicissitudes, participates in their longings and is capable of humbly recognising mistakes.

The noise of the cities and the rural quietness intermingle with art to develop the local version of the trans-Andean theme: dignity is demanded from the streets, it is declared that fear will not defeat hope and an invitation is made to elect a young president (Single 2; Illapu, 2021), they call for the election of a young president. Renowned Latin American academic voices, united under the slogan *por la esperanza y la justicia social* audiovisual capsules are being produced urging university youth to join the campaign and turn out to vote. A halo of uncertainty, with the scent of tense calm, covers the hours of the day when 55.6% of the population goes to the polling stations. On a peaceful, transparent day, and with the highest turnout ever recorded for a presidential election in Chile, citizens entrusted their destinies to the golden generation, with 55.87% of the vote (SERVEL, 2021). At 36 years of age, amidst cheers and celebrations fragrant with hope, the youngest president in Chile's history took office, and in his first speech, he declared: 'Let us walk together on the road of hope and let us all build the change towards a country that is dignified and just. Dignity, what a beautiful word' (Prensa Presidencia, 2022).

References

Calderón, F., & Castells, M. (2019). *La nueva América Latina*. FCE, Fondo de Cultura Económica.

Gabriel Boric Font. (2021, November 16). *Jingle – Nuevo Chile* [Video]. YouTube. https://www.youtube.com/watch?v=PVYDOGU2SxQ)

Illapu. (2021, December 14). *Con el miedo no nos van a vencer* [Video]. Facebook. https://m.facebook.com/watch/?v=210730467804312&_rdr

Iturrieta, S. (2020). Un salto a la esperanza en tiempos convulsionados: Hacia la inteligencia pronóstica. *ConCienciaSocial*, *4*(8), 48–66. https://revistas.unc.edu.ar/index.php/ConCienciaSocial/article/download/32874/33493

Letelier, R. (2020). Chile: La necesidad de cambio constitucional. In V. Petinnà & R. Rojas (Eds.), *América Latina: Del estallido social a la imposición económica y sanitaria post COVID-19* (1st ed., pp. 51–62). Editorial Planeta Perú.

Nostalgica. (2021, December 8). *"Bus de la Esperanza" del comando de Boric recorrió Atacama*. https://www.nostalgica.cl/bus-de-la-esperanza-del-comando-de-boric-llego-a-atacama/)

OECD. (2020). *How's life? 2020: Measuring well-being*. OECD Publishing. https://doi.org/10.1787/9870c393-en

Página 19. (2021, December 2). *Un Millón de Puertas por Boric: Vamos a Llevar la Esperanza de Vivir Mejor a Lugares Donde aún no Hemos Llegado*. https://pagina19.cl/politica/un-millon-de-puertas-por-boric-vamos-a-llevar-la-esperanza-de-vivir-mejor-a-lugares-donde-aun-no-hemos-llegado/

Prensa Presidencia. (2022, March 11). *Primer discurso en el Palacio de La Moneda del Presidente Gabriel Boric Font*. Gobierno de Chile. https://prensa.presidencia.cl/discurso.aspx?id=188237

SERVEL. (2020, October 26). *Plebiscito Nacional 2020 fue la mayor votación de la historia de Chile*. Servicio Electoral de Chile. https://servel.cl/plebiscito-nacional-2020-fue-la-mayor-votacion-de-la-historia-de-chile/

SERVEL. (2021). *Resultados Plebiscito Constitucional*. Servicio Electoral de Chile. https://www.servelelecciones.cl/

Chapter 4

Public Policies for Social Inclusion in Contemporary Brazil

Camila Gonçalves De Mario[a] *and Fabricio Pereira da Silva*[b]

[a]*Instituto Universitário de Pesquisas do Rio de Janeiro – Universidade Candido Mendes (IUPERJ – UCAM), Rio de Janeiro, Brazil*
[b]*Universidade Federal do Estado do Rio de Janeiro (UNIRIO), Rio de Janeiro, Brazil*

During the first decade and a half of the 21st century, Brazil experienced a strong cycle of social inclusion, with a reduction in poverty and social inequalities. This cycle was driven by a combination of public policies aimed at improving the quality of life and promoting sustainable development. Some actions and experiences played a key role in this process, among them the democratisation of access to universal health care, the expansion of the national public education system, the expansion of access to social security, and the creation of income transfer programs such as the Continuous Cash Benefit (*Benefício de Prestação Continuada*, BPC) and the Bolsa Família Program (*Programa Bolsa Família*, PBF), whose experience is considered a model. In this period, we have seen a significant increase in family income, in the average time of schooling of the Brazilian population, and a significant decrease in the poverty and extreme poverty indexes. Important indicators of this change can also be seen in health, through the reduction in infant, neonatal and maternal mortality.

The Bolsa Família Program (Fig. 4.1) was implemented in 2003 by Luiz Inácio Lula da Silva's government and lasted for 18 years. It was the most important experience in income transfer policy in Brazil, and an international reference for the promotion of social inclusion. Aimed at families living in poverty and extreme poverty, the PBF unified pre-existing federal cash transfer programs. It started serving about 4.1 million families in 2004, until reaching about

Exploring Hope: Case Studies of Innovation, Change and Development in the Global South, 31–34

Published under exclusive licence by Emerald Publishing Limited
doi:10.1108/978-1-83549-736-420241006

Fig. 4.1. Rio de Janeiro, Brazil – September 5, 2020: Logo Bolsa Família. Financial Aid Given by the Brazilian Federal Government. *Source:* DNI 195459627 © Agfotografia74 | Dreamstime.com.

14.7 million families in 2021. The program has helped lift 3.4 million people out of extreme poverty, while another 3.2 million have moved above the poverty line.[1]

In addition to the increase in family income, the PBF had an important impact on people's quality of life. A 16% reduction in infant mortality (children between 1 and 4 years old) was observed among beneficiary families. The effect was even more significant when considering families with black mothers: in these families, the reduction was 28% (Ramos et al., 2021). Another relevant fact was the increase in school attendance by children and adolescents. One study, which analysed data from 2005 to 2009, showed that this impact was more significant among girls, whose school attendance and progression between grades increased by 8 and 10 percentage points, respectively. The income guarantee, linked to school attendance, has freed from housework an important portion of the daughters of the families benefiting from the program (de Brawn et al., 2015).

As effects directly linked to access to income, the PBF was important in promoting the food and nutritional security of families. About 87% of beneficiary families spent the amount received on food purchases, which enabled not only an increase in the amount of food to which families had access, but also ensured a greater variety of foods, essential for nutritional security. Additionally, it boosted the consumption of the poorest families, generating a multiplier effect on the Brazilian Gross Domestic Product (GDP), as it is estimated that every 1 real spent on Bolsa Família generated an impact of 1.78 reais on GDP (Campello & Neri, 2013).

As important as redistribution and access to income are, these results are due to a combination of policies and strategies that were promoters of social inclusion.

[1]For the reader to have a reference, the base value for defining the poverty line in Brazil, established in February 2022, is a per capita monthly income of up to R$105.00 – equivalent to $22.00 – for extreme poverty, and of R$105.01 to R$210.00 – from $22.01 to $44.20 – for poverty. The reference values were calculated according to the quotation of the Dollar in the Brazilian market on 25 March 2022.

The PBF carried out cash transfers through two important conditionalities: school attendance, with compulsory attendance of 85% of classes for young people between 6 and 15 years old, and compulsory attendance of 75% for young people between 16 and 17 years old; and the regular monitoring of pregnant women and children under 7 years old by the Unified Health System (*Sistema Único de Saúde*, SUS), focusing on vaccination and nutritional surveillance for children and with assistance from prenatal to puerperium in the case of pregnant women.

The program was implemented from a shared management that directly involved three areas of the federal government through their respective Ministries: social assistance, education and health. While the Ministry of Social Development, responsible for coordinating the Unified Social Assistance System (Sistema Único de Assistência Social, SUAS), oversaw registering and monitoring the families that were beneficiaries of the program, the Ministries of Health and Education were directly in charge of controlling the conditionalities.

The objective of the program transcended the guarantee of access to income; its focus was to guarantee access to the basic social rights of health, food, education and social assistance. Among the program's constitutive elements were the overcoming of poverty and its intergenerational cycle, the protection of the family, the construction of public management configured in networks, and the assumption of health as a universal right and education as a subjective and inalienable universal right.

It is important to emphasise that the implementation and management of the PBF was only possible because there was state capacity and centralised management coordination at the federal level, combined with a local production of public policies with decentralised and territorial organisation and management (Fig. 4.2). Since the 1988 Constitution, health and education were recognised as universal rights of every Brazilian citizen and duty of the state. During the 1990s,

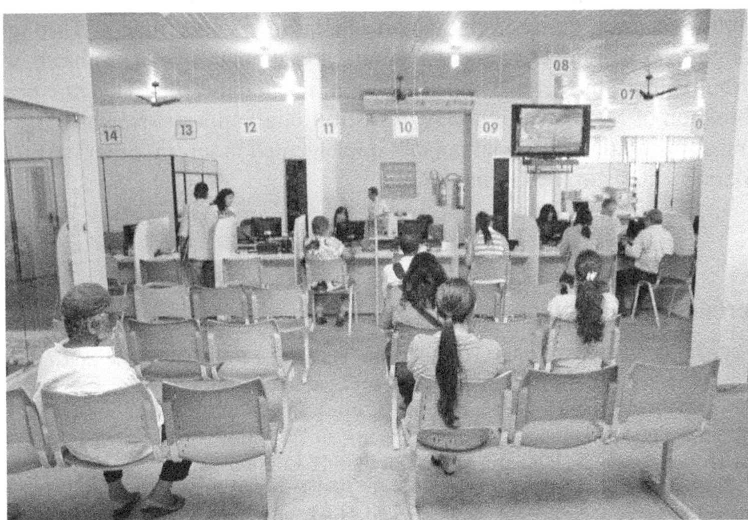

Fig. 4.2. Enrolment in the Bolsa Família Program. *Source:* DNI 223652171 © Joa Souza | Dreamstime.com.

a broad network of services and programs was built and present throughout the territory that was fundamental for the implementation of the PBF later.

The SUS has been working to promote health and reduce social inequalities and inequities in health since its inception in 1990. It is based on the approach of the social determinants of health, understanding the health-disease process as social. This means that people's health is impacted by social inequalities that transcend the supply of and access to health services. Among the social determinants of health, there is a consensus that access to income, work, education, food and nutritional security are fundamental to the health of individuals and of a society.

The results achieved in terms of reduction in infant mortality and malnutrition, as well as maternal and neonatal mortality, is an achievement of the recognition of the universal right to health, but also of intersectoral and collaborative management. Evidence of the need and effectiveness of this type of collaborative coordination in the management of public policies is in the reduction of child malnutrition from 13.5% in 1996 to 6.8% in 2006; a reduction that is attributed to at least four factors: increased maternal schooling, crescent purchasing power because of income transfer programs, expanded health care and improved sanitation conditions.

Universalising access to basic education was another important challenge for which the Brazilian educational system sought solutions. As in health, the existence of a public-school network and a wide offer of places is not enough in a context marked by poverty and social vulnerability, since the permanence of students in school is impacted by social and economic inequalities, leading to the early insertion of children and youth in the formal and informal labour market. In this respect, the PBF was strategic for the promotion and assurance of permanence in schools of children and youth at risk and social vulnerability.

Thus, the democratic period established since the 1988 Constitution favoured the search for ways to implement and expand social rights in the following years. The cycle of economic and political stability inaugurated by Fernando Henrique Cardoso's presidential terms culminated in the cycle of 'progressive' governments that followed, particularly Luiz Inácio Lula da Silva's government. Throughout this large process, innovative and democratic social policies were produced, which contributed to a considerable improvement in social indicators. This rare positive combination of factors left a legacy of institutional innovations, which has been serving as inspiration for social policies implemented in several other parts of the world, particularly in the Global South.

References

Campello, T., & Neri, M. C. (Orgs.) (2013). *Programa Bolsa Família: uma década de inclusão e cidadania*. IPEA Instituto de Pesquisa Econômica Aplicada.

de Brawn, A., Gilligan, D. O., Hoddinott, J. F., & Roy, S. (2015). The impact of Bolsa Família on schooling. *World Development*, *70*, 303–316.

Ramos, D., da Silva, N. B., Ichihara, M. Y., Fiaccone, R. L., Almeida, D., Sena, S., Rebouças, P., Pinto Júnior, E. P., Paixão, E. S., Ali, S., Rodrigues, L. C., & Barreto, M. L. (2021). Conditional cash transfer program and child mortality: A cross-sectional analysis nested within the 100 Million Brazilian Cohort. *PLoS Medicine*, *18*(9), e1003509.

Chapter 5

Human Mobility as a Resource and an Asset

Driss El Yazami

Conseil National des Droits de l'Homme, Morocco

There are only two ways to talk about the foreigner, the refugee, or the asylum seeker. Either within the tragic-security-based approach, which focuses on individuals and groups who try to cross borders illegally, often giving rise to images of clashes between migrants and law enforcement, and of a North under siege by crowds from the South. Or the economistic approach, which highlights the contribution of migrants (especially in areas shunned by nationals) and the benefits that their relatives and the balance of payments of their countries of origin derive from remittances, the overall volume of which continues to increase. Caught between these two images, which are true but reductionist, the migration dynamics at work at the international level and in the countries of the South are rarely considered in all their scope, diversity, and complexity (Fig. 5.1).

New thinking about human mobility, the benefits that can be derived from it, and the exciting pilot experiments conducted in this field are too often ignored. The fact of the matter is that human mobility is growing slowly but steadily – migration has tripled in 40 years and there are now 250 million international migrants – and currently represents less than 4% of the world's population. These flows obey logics that may seem contradictory at first glance: sustained globalisation on the one hand (no country escapes this phenomenon) and undeniable regionalisation on the other: regional migratory systems that have sometimes existed for a long time have gradually come into being. Four out of five African migrants migrate from one country on the continent to another and two-thirds of European migrants move within Europe itself. While North America and Europe are still the main poles of attraction for migratory flows, South-South migration is now just as important.

We are also witnessing several changes, including the feminisation of migration flows (women now account for half of all migration flows, and more and

Exploring Hope: Case Studies of Innovation, Change and Development in the Global South, 35–38

Published under exclusive licence by Emerald Publishing Limited
doi:10.1108/978-1-83549-736-420241007

Fig. 5.1. A Boat of Migrants Fleeing Wars. *Source*: DNI 230641609 © Corradobarattaphotos | Dreamstime.com.

more of them are emigrating on their own, rather than just as part of a family reunion), the rejuvenation and aging of migrants (with the emergence of generations born abroad and the retirement of the first generations), and above all the development of the socio-cultural level of migrants: for example, nearly 20% of Moroccan emigrants now have a university degree (baccalaureate +6 years of university studies). But alongside these highly qualified skills, other new migrant profiles are emerging, including retired people from the North who live part of their retirement in southern countries, and unaccompanied minors who have become independent actors in the international mobility of adults.

On the political level, there are also many paradoxes. At the national level, public policies, especially in developed countries, swing between tightening the conditions of entry and residence of foreigners, as shown for example by visa policy, and selectivity. Behind the 'firm' rhetoric against immigration, most of these countries are engaged in fierce competition to hunt highly qualified skills (PhDs, engineers, researchers) or less qualified migrants, but who are in high demand in certain niches such as 'caregiving' jobs (services for the elderly, for example).

On a global level, governance of migration is proving difficult as demonstrated by the process of drafting the 'Marrakech Pact for Safe, Orderly and Regular Migration', adopted at an intergovernmental conference held in that city in December 2018. The United Nations deliberations on this Pact, which contain a set of non-binding principles calling for shared management among states of key migration issues, were more complex than expected, and participation in the international conference for its adoption caused political crises in several countries, pushing some governments to abstain from participating. The reluctance of many countries to engage decisively with the migration issue is revealed in the 'International Convention on the Protection of the Rights of All Migrant Workers and Members of Their Families' adopted on 18th December 1990. This treaty, which is an integral part of the instruments that make up the international human rights law of the United Nations, has been signed and ratified to date by only 20 countries, all of them from the South, but none from the North.

In this context, a minority of humanity moves freely on the planet while the immense majority is under 'house arrest'. When certain groups excluded from this freedom try to move, it is often at the cost of their lives or the violation of their fundamental rights, trapped by the rejection of governments, the mistrust of public opinion and victims of diverse types of exploitation of criminal human trafficking networks.

The problem of human mobility thus appears to be one of the fundamental issues of the 21st century, and if it seems difficult to imagine today a universal right to mobility. This perspective is easier to consider at the regional level. We are obviously thinking here of the freedom of movement and residence established within the European Union for the benefit of the nationals of the member countries only. But we can also mention the example of the Economic Community of West African States (ECOWAS), which is more difficult to implement but ambitious in its objectives. This geostrategic African bloc, which comprises 15 countries and a population approaching 350 million people, has set for itself since the last century the goal of creating a zone of free movement for the citizens of its member states.

In fact, all the regional economic communities that are part of the African Union have adopted legal instruments with a view to eventually establishing freedom of movement and settlement for their citizens. This objective, which heralds such freedom on a continental scale (a protocol of the African Union has been adopted on the matter), is far from being achieved. But it is a mobilising ambition that can give rise to multiple initiatives by public authorities in the South, but also by all other actors (entrepreneurs, NGOs, universities, etc.). It is therefore an issue of rehabilitating human mobility and encouraging any initiative that allows, as the Marrakech Pact proclaims, 'safe, orderly and regular migration', but beyond that, it is the entire approach to migration that needs to be revisited by relying on the resources and opportunities that diasporas offer.

The focus of the international debate on border management and irregular flows hides a more important reality: most migrants are regularly settled in the countries where they reside, and large segments of these populations not only take root in the 'host' societies but increasingly adopt their nationality. For the new generations, the integration process is even more obvious, despite the persistence of discrimination. An even more interesting phenomenon is that in all northern countries of immigration, many talents have emerged within the diasporas and enriched with their touch the cinema, literature, and music, of countries that are now also theirs. It is no longer only in sports that diversity manifests itself with talents. The European literature of recent decades, for example, can no longer be considered without the contribution of dozens of writers whose parents once came from elsewhere. All these creators illustrate the dual belonging that diasporas from the South assume without great difficulty, at different paces of course, depending on family histories, historical contexts between countries of origin and countries of settlement, geostrategic framework, etc. These processes of diaspora insertion are never obvious. They are often complex, painful, and sometimes impossible. But it is an overwhelming reality and an essential resource.

Fig. 5.2. African Migrants at the Street in Rome Next to the Group of the Local Residents. *Source*: DNI 266823255 © Taymuraz Gumerov | Dreamstime.com.

Many countries in the South today have large diasporas, divided between countries in the North and countries in the South. The shaping of these communities has varied historically, but one fact seems to cut across national particularities: these communities maintain diversified relations with the country of origin and take root in the countries of residence while maintaining multiple *heritages* in separate ways (Fig. 5.2). The dual attachment and belonging of these groups must be accepted and not rejected by governments and societies (*home* and *host*) and must not be forced to choose but considered as a common heritage that could be used to encourage international cooperation and the contribution of diasporas to the development policies of countries of the South.

Many countries have started to act in such a manner, by setting up institutions and public policies dedicated to diasporas. Nineteen countries have established an advisory council for their expatriate communities (Italy, Dominican Republic, Senegal, France, Portugal, Romania, Spain, Mali, Peru, Mexico, Brazil, Benin, Guatemala, El Salvador, Jamaica, Uruguay, Morocco, Nigeria, and Togo), and four others (Ivory Coast, Algeria, Guinea, and the Democratic Republic of the Congo) are preparing to do the same. These councils are spaces for maintaining and re-founding the link and forums for consultation and proposals. Other states have been working since the mid-1990s on experimenting with several ways for their emigrant compatriots, especially highly qualified skills, to contribute to investment, research, and development programs, etc.

After initially 'dreaming' of a return of the 'brains' of the diaspora, the tendency today is to adopt policies of mobilisation with a distance, implying circulation rather than a definitive return. If we also take into consideration the contribution that people of the realm of culture can make to creation on both sides, we will begin to see human migration differently, no longer as a risk of an invasion, but as a welcome blessing, despite the problems, necessarily temporary.

Chapter 6

Curbing Electoral Corruption: Two South Asian Civil Society Efforts to Build Robust Democracies

Anwesha Chakraborty

University of Bologna, Italy

India and Bangladesh are considered two of the fastest-growing economies in the world by various media outlets and financial institutions and global think tanks. Both are populous countries: India being the second-most populous, while Bangladesh the eighth, as per World Bank data from 2021. Both countries have robust republics, while India is a secular republic considered the world's largest democracy, Bangladesh is a people's republic with Islam as a state religion. Such settings provide the possibility to explore a rich landscape of political and legal systems intertwined with a densely populated civil society of various religious, cultural and political persuasions. In recent years, however, the governments of both countries have been accused by international think tanks of curbing the space for civil society to speak up against a variety of issues of public interest, especially those which implicate the ruling government directly (Freedom House, 2022a, 2022b). Both countries also continue to fall on the lower end of the Corruption Perception Index published annually by Transparency International (TI), a global think-tank which tracks corruption, indicating persistent problems of governance. According to a TI report from 2014, the South Asian region faces the scourge of corruption, which threatens its economic progress while giving rise to socio-economic inequalities.

The report calls corruption an epidemic in South Asia and says that it is caused by opaque public institutions, lack of protection for anti-corruption actors and widespread government interference in the work of anti-corruption watchdogs. According to TI's Global Corruption Barometer of 2013, the top four sectors which the public perceives to be most corrupt in South Asia include political parties, police, parliament and public officials, indicating endemic corruption in both the political establishments and the public sector. Goetz and Jenkins (2001)

Exploring Hope: Case Studies of Innovation, Change and Development in the Global South, 39–44

Published under exclusive licence by Emerald Publishing Limited
doi:10.1108/978-1-83549-736-420241008

noted, in the Indian context, that institutions linked to the public sector which should be responsible for monitoring government performances are often not open to citizens' inputs, leading to widespread dissatisfaction among sections of the public, which in turn provides a fertile ground for civil society-led monitoring initiatives to proliferate.

Speaking about citizen-led initiatives, it is important to note the importance of the Right to Information (RTI) Movement in India which had its origins in the 1980s and which has been sustained through collective efforts of activists across the country, in the history of citizen-led initiatives against corruption and greater transparency and accountability. It may be argued that anti-corruption action from the grassroots in India is primarily about gathering public data and making them available to the citizens, thereby contributing to citizens' efforts to monitor government activities. An important aspect characterising the RTI movement is rethinking democratic politics and participation through intense grassroots activism (Ghosh, 2018). It intended to make citizens aware that they have the power to demand answers from the government and that they should do so to ensure that those in power remain transparent and accountable to the public. The organisation which is known to have spearheaded the RTI movement in India, the Mazdoor Kisan Shakti Sangathan (MKSS) deserves a special mention in this context as it showed the way by empowering ordinary citizens in rural Rajasthan to seek, compile and share public expenditure data (Jenkins & Goetz, 1999). The citizens, through this process, were, and continue to be, empowered as they exercise their right to know about government action and participate in public audits of their representatives. The MKSS and associated activists deserve credit, alongside several prominent civil society activists, to have helped pass the RTI Act in India in 2005.

Like in India, the RTI Act is an important legal measure also in Bangladesh which, as the TI Bangladesh profile of 2019 notes, plays an important role in ensuring transparency and accountability in public office(s). The act, passed in 2009, has simplified the fees required to access information, has overridden existing secrecy legislation and has granted greater independence to the Information Commission, tasked with overseeing and promoting the law. However, Baroi and Alam (2021) suggest that because of its top-down implementation and little citizen involvement, the act has not managed to improve the corruption scenario of the country. While the RTI laws in both countries have their pitfalls, civil society activists and organisations have managed to utilise them to seek information and make the same available to the public. In this chapter, I present two such initiatives using data gathered from their websites as well as through interviews with key stakeholders.

Civil Society Organisations as 'Infomediaries' to Fight Corruption

That civil society is a key factor in the control of corruption has been argued by multiple scholars (Grimes, 2008; Kossow & Kukutschka, 2017; Mungiu Pippidi, 2013). The effectiveness of civil society in fighting corruption is highly predicated on the strength of institutions in societies. Civil society organisations (CSOs) comprise one such crucial institution which may work independently from public and private sector organisations and contribute to the creation of an active citizenry at the grassroots level (Kossow & Kukutschka, 2017). CSOs are prime examples of collective action as they are organisations which bring together individuals bound by common interests to address certain issues that affect (and afflict) the societies. In anti-corruption literature, they are acknowledged for their role in mobilising citizens to fight corruption.

Here I present two such examples which deal with one particular sectoral corruption, i.e. elections, whose goal is to empower people by furnishing information about elections (candidates, political party funding and electoral laws) so that citizens can make informed choices while selecting their representatives. These two initiatives are the Association for Democratic Reforms in India and Shujan (Citizens for Good Governance) in Bangladesh. Borrowing the word 'infomediaries', a portmanteau of information intermediaries from Fattah (2016), I argue that the two initiatives are instances of infomediaries in the South Asian context which intend to monitor election-related data as well as influence policymaking in the electoral arena, thereby aiding to mechanisms for horizontal accountability in places where vertical accountability is weak.

Association for Democratic Reforms, India

The Association for Democratic Reforms (ADR hereafter) is a non-partisan CSO born in 1999 due to collective efforts of academics from the Indian Institute of Management, Ahmedabad who decided to work towards tackling corruption and bringing in more transparency in the political process. Already in that year, the founders filed a Public Interest Litigation (to protect public interests) at the Delhi High Court to request electoral candidates to disclose their educational qualifications, financial assets and liabilities and criminal records. The voices of ADR's founders gained traction even if they were met with heavy criticism from political parties and parliamentarians. After three years, in 2002, the Supreme Court of India ruled in favour of the activists of ADR which made it compulsory for all candidates to disclose educational, financial and criminal background before contesting elections. Since then, the organisation has made large data sets about all national and state elections available to the public as comprehensive reports posted on its website and later, on its mobile app, My Neta (Chakraborty & Mattoni, 2023). The type of democratic intervention that the organisation envisages is twofold: on one hand, they expect the electorate to monitor the data shared by them to make informed choices in selecting transparent candidates. On the other, members of the organisation have in the past actively sought to reform the electoral system by acting as a pressure group; and they continue to do so with meetings and seminars conducted at regular intervals with a wide range of stakeholders from politicians to students to other civil society members. ADR's more recent work, especially in the last seven years, involves ensuring transparency in political party financing. ADR is able to continue to its work thanks to donations from individuals as well as grant-making bodies.

Shujan, Bangladesh

Founded in 2002, Shujan, also known as Shushasaner Jannya Nagorik (Citizens for Good Governance), calls itself a volunteer-based movement whose aim is to make citizens aware of electoral laws and practices, as well as the candidates seeking to be elected, so that they are able to make informed choices about their political representatives. The organisation is run by its members who work as volunteers and pay a nominal annual membership fee. The members cannot have any political affiliations.

Like ADR, Shujan can also be considered an infomediary as it makes election-related information such as laws, a list of political parties and their manifestos, candidates seeking to get elected, available to the public. One of its achievements includes converting the existing electoral roll into an online database in 2007, thereby creating the template for a transparent list to avoid duplication of names. Its website features election laws, a list of political parties and their manifestos plus a list of publications. Furthermore, like ADR, Shujan has also managed to positively influence electoral reforms, such as disclosure of antecedents by candidates, registration of political parties and ensuring 33% women's representation in committees of all political parties.

Non-Partisan Pressure Groups to Monitor (and Mobilise Against) Corruption

The two initiatives are examples of civil society watchdogs which utilise constant monitoring of data as the primary corruption-fighting mechanism. As mentioned before, they make a wide range of electoral data available to the public so that the potential voters can make informed choices about what kind of representative they want to elect. While these infomediaries make the collected data available online, they also carry out press conferences where they release reports to the media, and at times even work in tandem with newspapers, to reach out to larger audiences who do not have access to or may not access the internet. Because of the work that they do in country contexts which are not always sympathetic to their cause, the clause of remaining non-partisan, i.e. not tethered to any political party, is fundamental to their sustainability. Both initiatives were started by members of the civil society who belong to the upper echelons of their respective societies wielding great socio-cultural capital, and hence possessing a voice which would have a weight in places where social hierarchies reign supreme.

In both cases, the respondents were honest about their shortcomings recognising that endemic corruption was hard to combat. However, both initiatives have shown remarkable resilience to not only survive but even thrive in less than conducive environments, having taken on political establishments and made meaningful changes to the electoral system. In particular, ADR's work on party financing deserves mention here as the organisation, along with other civil society actors, managed to successfully petition at the Supreme Court, to strike down a law regarding electoral bonds as unconstitutional in February 2024.

More importantly, by making large data sets available to the public, they act as valuable infomediaries in raising awareness of citizens to participate meaningfully in the democratic process of choosing their representatives.

Table 1. Initiatives in comparison

	Shujan	**ADR**
Founded in	2002	1999
Mission	promoting democracy, decentralization, electoral reforms, clean politics and accountable governance	improving governance and strengthening democracy by continuous work in the area of electoral and political reforms
Anti-corruption/ pro-transparency mechanism	Monitoring data on electoral candidates; participating in mobilising electoral reforms through continuous engagement with public authorities and the media	Monitoring data on candidates and political party financing; participating in mobilising electoral reforms through continuous engagement with public authorities and the media
Funding	Self-funded through nominal membership fees	Donations (individual and institutions)
Primary dissemination strategies	Online dissemination: websites (www.shujan.org) and (www.votebd.org), online seminars and e-newsletters (started during COVID)	Online dissemination: websites (https://adrindia.org/ and https://myneta.info/), mobile application: My Neta, podcasts and online seminars
	Offline dissemination: regular meetings and interactions with media and the public	Offline dissemination: in-person meetings, press conferences and seminars are held at regular intervals to share data with the media and the public
Key outcomes	In 2007, Shujan submitted a draft proposal to the Election Commission indicating multiple reforms to amend the primary electoral law titled Representation of the People Order, 1972. Many of these suggestions were taken up by the Commission.	Between 2002 and 2003, ADR's petitions resulted in a landmark judgment by the Supreme Court of India which made it mandatory for candidates contesting national and state-level elections to file affidavits declaring full information regarding their criminal, financial and educational background.

Table 1. (*Continued*)

	Shujan	ADR
	In the same year, Shujan took up the task of digitising voter lists which helped identify millions of bogus voters. The two websites www.shujan.org and www.votebd.org) were launched.	In 2024, the Supreme Court passed a landmark judgment in favour of ADR by declaring the electoral bonds scheme passed by the Indian Parliament in 2017 as unconstitutional. This took place just a couple of months before the 2024 general elections and became one of the main discussed agendas in political debates in the country.

References

Baroi, H., & Alam, S. (2021). Operationalizing the Right to Information Act through E-Governance in Bangladesh: Challenges and opportunities. *International Journal of Public Administration*, *44*(8), 685–698. https://doi.org/10.1080/01900692.2020.1747489

Chakraborty, A., & Mattoni, A. (2023). Addressing corruption through visual tools in India: the case of three civil society initiatives and their Facebook pages. *Visual Studies*, *38*(5), 803–816. https://doi.org/10.1080/1472586X.2023.2239759.

Fattah, K. N. (2016). Right to information (RTI) legislation: The role of infomediaries in enhancing citizens' access to information. *Development in Practice*, *26*(1), 3–14. https://doi.org/10.1080/09614524.2016.1119248

Freedom House. (2022a). *Country profile: Bangladesh*. https://freedomhouse.org/country/bangladesh/freedom-world/2022

Freedom House. (2022b). *Country profile: India*. https://freedomhouse.org/country/india/freedom-world/2022

Ghosh, S. (2018). Accountability, democratisation and the right to information in India. *Asian Studies Review*, *42*(4), 626–647. https://doi.org/10.1080/10357823.2018.1516734

Goetz, A., & Jenkins, R. (2001). Hybrid forms of accountability: Citizen engagement in institutions of public-sector oversight in India. *Public Management Review*, *3*(3), 363–383. https://doi.org/10.1080/14616670110051957

Grimes, M. (2008). *The conditions of successful civil society involvement in combating corruption: A survey of case study evidence*. [Quality of Governance Working Paper Series, 22. University of Gothenburg].

Jenkins, R., & Goetz, A. (1999). Accounts and accountability: Theoretical implications of the right-to-information movement in India. *Third World Quarterly*, *20*(3), 603–622. https://doi.org/10.1080/01436599913712

Kossow, N., & Kukutschka, R. M. B. (2017). Civil society and online connectivity: Controlling corruption on the net? *Crime, Law and Social Change*, *68*, 459–476. https://doi.org/10.1007/s10611-017-9696-0

Mungiu Pippidi, A. (2013). Controlling corruption through collective action. *Journal of Democracy*, *24*(1), 101–115.

Part 2

Organising Territories and Infrastructures to Improve Life

Introduction

Samira Mizbar

National Assessment Body of the Higher Council of Education, Training and Scientific Research, Morocco

According to an organic process linked to the presence of human communities in a place and the activities they carry out there, the territory of the living spaces changes. Thus, the various development actions, whether they concern the territory or its infrastructures, are generated from the need to order living together, taking into account hygiene, mobility, security, economic framework, efficiency of networks and public facilities, protection and conservation of natural and built resources and many other considerations. As societies evolve, the territorial impacts of demographic, social, economic and technological growth diversify and change while generating more pressure on living environments and creating territorial inequalities. Alongside the negative effects, new social demands emerge, giving rise to trends that create new relationships between human activity and habitable space, and in which the great challenges of peoples' development are located. Poorly regulated, the various forms of growth, particularly demographics, have negative consequences that have a direct impact on the quality of life and the prospects for the evolution of spaces and societies. With the passage of time and political priorities, the countries of the global south face major development challenges so as not to hinder their evolution. This second chapter presents innovative, courageous and hopeful experiences as game-changers by relying on confidence in people and the desire to live better.

Clearly, development is not an operation to make public and private investments profitable. It is primarily at the service of the proper functioning of a society for individual and collective wellbeing, which must result in a balanced distribution of economic activity, employment and public services, thus bringing workplaces closer to places of residence, while advocating equal opportunities for all, regardless of where they live. The example of the Metrocable in Medellin (Colombia) is instructive. The project overcame the paradigms of the time for this type of transport, about technical challenges such as operation in the urban environment, with intermediate stations, integration with a metro and a very high intensity of use which operated in less densely populated areas, only seasonally or during restricted hours. In addition, it is an environmentally friendly system that increases the wellbeing of the neighbours with interventions that organise,

Exploring Hope: Case Studies of Innovation, Change and Development in the Global South, 47–51

Published under exclusive licence by Emerald Publishing Limited
doi:10.1108/978-1-83549-736-420241009

improve or increase the public space near its infrastructure and promote commercial, tourist and cultural interest in the surrounding areas. The Metrocable become an example of sustainable and inclusive mobility and a Latin American benchmark for mass transport systems.

While the occupation of the territory is marked by, on one hand, the economic and demographic hyper concentration on large cities and their peri-urban extensions, and on the other hand, the rural exodus, in recent years, we have witnessed the advent of a new trend: the relocation of companies and activities, the development of self-employment and remote work as the digital revolution has created large economic sectors free from concentration, and the settlement of families to the non-urban, the countryside and small towns, in search of better living conditions, or even to live differently. The coronavirus pandemic has accelerated this movement. Regions now offer alternative locations to the big city, both desirable and viable. The hyper-concentrated model of land use is now taking shape by the multipolar model mobilising the regional urban fabric. These long-neglected spaces are no longer organised on the margins but within modernity. This active and dynamic modernity is based on three pillars: metropolitan agglomerations, the network of small and medium-sized cities that polarise and irrigate territories, and the countryside that is redefining itself.

The experiment conducted in the peri-urban area of the city of Morelia illustrates an opportunity for the implementation of innovative schemes of socio-environmental inclusion in Mexico. The peri-urban area of Morelia is delimited by urban, urbanisable and agricultural areas, a wide strip surrounding the city centre where agricultural, livestock, industrial and commercial activities are mixed. It is a space in which rural livelihoods and ways of life subsist and are in the process of adapting to the reality generated by the new architectural and urban forms that are being built in their immediate surroundings. The interest of the inhabitants in maintaining agricultural activity on the areas of land they still have, and a certain degree of environmental awareness led to integration of this peri-urban area to preserve and respect the way of life of the rural population, the obtaining fresh food, the protection of the biodiversity of plants and animals and most of all, the fostering of a sense of belonging.

Also, the experience of the Andean peasants in Molinos (Argentina) shows us how a territory condemned because of its heavy historical past was reconverted into a dynamic territory with a strong positive identity. Constituted as the old *encomienda* of San Pedro Nolasco de Los Molinos, lands that were donated by the King of Spain to a receiver who had to populate, evangelise and domesticate its inhabitants within a determined period of time, this encomienda became *latifundios*, large private estates, inhabited by peasant and indigenous communities under different regimes of domination. Ten years ago, an experience was developed permitting the generation of new conditions for the autonomy of the population and the construction of their own development project. The change of identity and the work between technicians and peasant communities made it possible to build a new social territory that encouraged the inhabitants to leave the limits of the farm, the employer, the place, and turn a commonplace into a territory to fight for. In parallel with the communities' approach, work was done on the creation of new irrigation infrastructures, improvement of animal production, creation of rural housing, creation of new marketing mechanisms, creation of a local brand image, training, among many other actions for local improvement. An integral approach to the problems of the peasants, in a democratic and participatory manner, allowed for their political emancipation, overcoming their socio-historical condition of traditional dependence, contributing to the emergence of a peasant development model of their own in a context of globalisation.

In a situation of perpetual change, doing politics means at the same time orienting, valuing, framing, daring and protecting. It is necessary to maintain the human size of cities, but also of structures and bodies, which must not lose sight of the values for which they are responsible and the objectives that led to their creation. Formerly marginalised regions could become victims of their own success, so it is essential to be able to monitor their evolution and learn to recognise the warning signs of asphyxiation and how to intervene. The non-respect of the values of living together in order to optimise the wellbeing, health and quality of life of the population, while taking into account the issues related to sustainable development, or the exhaustion of these values in the face of the slogans of trickling down the benefits of economic growth leads to the collapse of the institutions and worldview of the societal group that gave rise to them. In those circumstances, chaos remains the only possible trend scenario. The city of Quito is an edifying example of a good practice: the capital of Ecuador concentrates on services and institutions of national importance, and at the same time is considered the most important point of national and international connectivity in the country, making it a city with a very marked central role. The historical and cultural city centre has suffered strong transformations and a deep deterioration through the years, with new constructions that do not respect the identity and heritage, with the incorporation of inadequate public transport systems, environmental pollution, informality and disorganisation in commerce, solid waste management and security issues, among many other problems. The reorganisation of the informal trade present in the colonial centre of Quito, turned this space into a 'large-scale popular market'. If the requalification of this space took years, the revaluation and reconstruction of the centre is an action that cannot be separated from public policy, security considerations and investment planning. Also, the demonstration has been made that change requires the active participation of the people who live and work in this space.

The issue of spatial planning and infrastructure is an essential lever for development. While these issues were very fashionable in the post-colonisation years, during the 1990s, several states faced financial difficulties and moved towards a gradual withdrawal from the infrastructure sector without being able to replace public financing with private investment. Yet, infrastructure should not be seen as individual resources, such as a hospital or a water supply network, but as parts of a system whose different elements, taken together, have considerable potential to strengthen the economic, environmental and social sustainability of states.

Another project in progress concerns Pakistan that emphasises the new infrastructure initiatives in regional connectivity and shows how enhanced regional connectivity can result in increased investment, trade and cross-border movement of people, goods and services. On account of Pakistan's geographical position, the country will play a vital role in connecting the routes to the Middle East, South Asia and Central Asia. Under the BRI umbrella, China is investing in the energy and transport infrastructure in Pakistan under the China–Pakistan Economic Corridor (CPEC). Also, after the country joined the CAREC Program in 2010, Pakistan has pursued this policy to overcome barriers to growth and to play a role and integrate Central Asian countries into global markets. In Pakistan, policymakers have labelled these economic corridors as 'game-changer' and 'fate-changer' for the region in terms of industrialisation, jobs' creation and upgradation of infrastructure. Once completed, these infrastructure initiatives can enable the region to usher in a new era of increased connectivity and trade and investments, creating a win-win situation for all actors.

By protecting the environment, land use planning and infrastructure play an essential role in conserving natural resources and reducing the effects of climate change. Thus, clean energy production facilities are fundamental to reducing dependence on fossil fuels and the rationalisation of the use of water resources has become an essential strategic issue to consider to ensure social justice. A new relationship with the environment is on the agenda with a rationalised use of available materials to reduce pollution, promote the renewal of resources and encourage the sustainability of living spaces.

An inspiring example is the evolution of building materials. A lot of Global South countries historically used noble and natural materials for the construction of their dwellings. In the 20th century, new technologies and the use of cement monopolised construction and infrastructure, relegating the use of natural materials to the poorest and most rural areas. Even if self-construction and the use of natural materials have suffered a certain loss of prestige because they are considered poor architecture, bioconstruction is emerging strongly, making it possible to solve infrastructure and housing problems in an original way, with greater sustainability and resource savings. The environmental factor is the key, as natural or recycled materials are used, minimising the high environmental impact produced by conventional construction. From the economic point of view, the savings are significant, due to the low cost of materials and also because of the energy savings achieved in all stages of the building's life cycle. In Latin America, this movement of awareness has allowed the creation of a lot of organisations that promote sustainable construction in the continent. There, it is now possible to construct legal buildings with natural techniques, thanks to the work carried out jointly by various organisations that have made it possible to carry out tests in official laboratories. Also, these projects, financed by major sponsors, involve the participation of local companies and associations and prestigious architectural firms.

The most important role of spatial planning and infrastructure is to improve people's resilience so as to withstand shocks and stresses during rapid changes, upheavals and extreme events. When equal access is ensured, spatial planning and infrastructure are beneficial to improving quality of life by significantly contributing to gender equality and the right to respect and dignity for all.

'Green infrastructure', which incorporates trees, plantations and forests into their design, can improve air quality and help remove carbon dioxide from the atmosphere or, in the case of mangroves, prevent flooding and soil erosion. In China, the slogan of building a people's city is to make the city suitable for business, living, entertainment and tourism. Two pilot projects are described in this chapter: the transformation of the traditional industrial line in Yangpu Riverside and the innovation of Gubei Civic Center. Yangpu Riverside of Shanghai has gradually transformed from an industrial coastline dominated by factories and warehouses to an ecological coastline and landscape full of parks and green spaces. The Gubei community, the first international community in China (a total of 32,000 residents and 51% of the residents are from more than 50 countries and regions) is a good example for investigating the construction of the Gubei International Community Citizen Center as an effective practice of implementing the new development concept based on innovative community governance with the use of innovation, coordination, green development and sharing social resources with the government departments. Renewal of Yangpu Industrial Area and Innovation of Gubei Civic Center are two good examples of urban planning, reflecting the new development concept of green development and people-centeredness, as well as the eclecticism and friendliness of Shanghai as an international metropolis to foreigners.

Sustainable spatial planning and infrastructure stimulate economic growth, while improving the quality of life and human dignity. Experiences from around the Big South show that other choices are possible and that they bear fruit.

Chapter 7

The Peri-Urban Area of the City of Morelia: An Opportunity for the Implementation of Innovative Schemes of Socio-Environmental Inclusion in México

Norma Angélica Rodríguez Valladares[a] *and Antonio Vieyra*[b]

[a]*Centro de Estudios en Geografía Humana de El Colegio de Michoacán A.C., México*
[b]*Centro de Investigaciones en Geografía Ambiental de la UNAM, México*

The growth of cities over their surrounding rural areas gives rise to the formation of extensive peri-urban areas where problems of insecurity, lack of services and infrastructure are manifested, which are related to the phenomena of residential segregation, social exclusion and environmental degradation present in Latin America's urban peripheries (Aguilar, 2021; Ávila, 2016; Cruz Muñoz, 2021; Poncela et al., 2015; Robles et al., 2021; Ruiz-López et al., 2021). The move of urban lifestyles towards the rural environment implies the gradual disappearance of primary activities such as agriculture and livestock farming, as well as the loss of rural ways of life (Méndez et al., 2016; Vieyra et al., 2016). Institutionalism promotes a policy of rupture and systematic territorial separation, with the issuing of disjointed plans and programmes that do not contemplate the connection of the city centre with the peri-urban spaces dedicated to the primary sector of the economy. There is no scheme of connected rural areas, which in turn preserves their independence, in the sense of safeguarding their ways of being, living and subsisting. On the contrary, political action takes for granted the gradual disappearance of the agrarian nuclei located on the periphery of the cities (Rodríguez, 2020).

For the purposes of this research, the peri-urban area of Morelia (Fig. 7.1) is delimited by urban, urbanisable and agricultural areas (Fig. 7.2). It is a wide strip surrounding the city centre where agricultural, livestock, industrial and

Exploring Hope: Case Studies of Innovation, Change and Development in the Global South, 53–58

doi:10.1108/978-1-83549-736-420241010

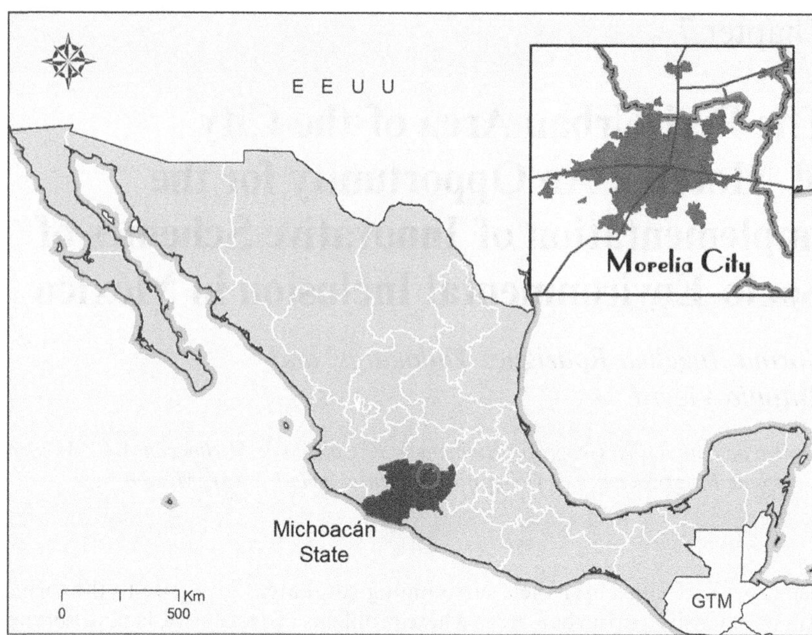

Fig. 7.1. Localisation of Morelia City. *Source*: Own elaboration.

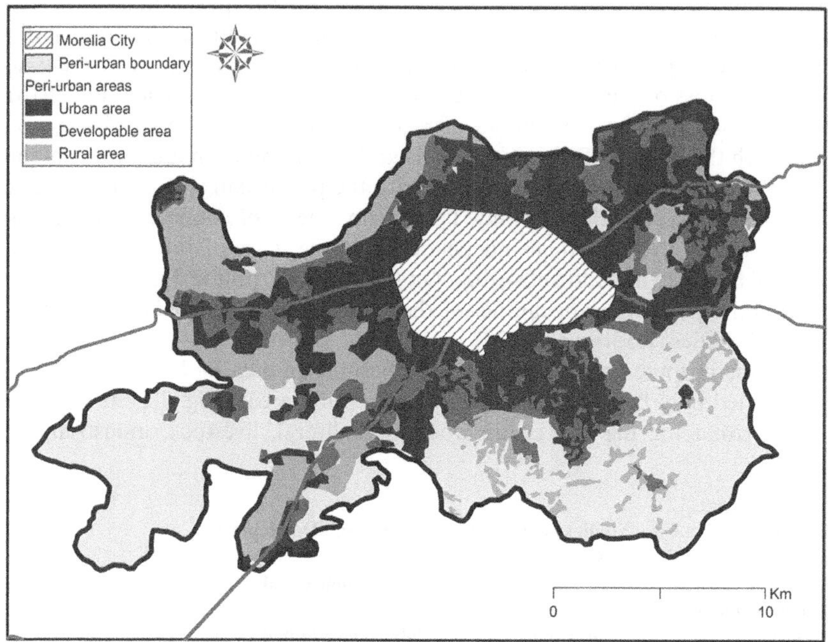

Fig. 7.2. Peri-Urban Area of Morelia City. *Source*: Own elaboration.

commercial activities are mixed. It is a space in which rural livelihoods and ways of life subsist and are in the process of adapting to the reality generated by the new architectural and urban forms that are being built in their immediate surroundings.

The peri-urban is a space of rural–urban interaction where it is possible to find *ejidos* and irregular settlements (Fig. 7.3), as well as real estate schemes that arise with the policies of financialisation of housing produced by the real estate market, in the framework of the implementation of neoliberal policies (Gasca Zamora, 2013; Harvey, 2001; Mattos, 2019; Olivera, 2014; Rodríguez et al., 2019; Santos, 2014). The interaction of the various actors living in this extended periphery, whose livelihoods and ways of life are different, leads to the emergence of new forms of social and environmental exclusion (Olivera, 2015). This is due to the unequal distribution of services such as drinking water, sewage and sanitation, as well as the construction and use of health, education and recreational infrastructure, in the context of a process of exclusion that favours some groups to the detriment of others. In this way, the interaction of gated housing developments, irregular settlements and rural localities with agricultural and livestock land uses, environmental protection areas and industrial zones tends to be competitive and conflictive.

Thus, rural localities with lifestyles that in many cases oppose urban culture are immersed in a process of construction of excluding and multidimensional spatialities articulated from segregated actions (Hidalgo et al., 2021). Thus, the population of San Juanito Itzícuaro, San Lorenzo Itzícuaro, San Nicolás Obispo, San Antonio Parangare and La Mintzita, ejidos whose livelihoods are based on agriculture and livestock, are faced with the need to abandon the activity they have developed throughout their lives and which represents their means of subsistence. Consequently, the gradual transformation of productive activities in rural localities is attributed to the increase in insecurity due to the

Fig. 7.3. The Peri-Urban Area of the City of Morelia. *Source*: Own elaboration.

arrival of new settlers, the loss of productive land after its sale to the real estate market, and the contamination of water used for agricultural activities due to the inadequate channelling of wastewater from new housing developments (interviews with residents conducted between July and August 2017). The city was not born with this scenario of socio-environmental degradation; in its origins, Morelia's peri-urban area was made up of rural villages, extensive natural areas and farmland (Fig. 7.4). The 1986 Urban Development Plan reveals the establishment of important areas of ecological preservation that would serve as buffer zones within the urban sprawl.

However, this urban planning proposal was not respected due to the dynamics of land commodification, derived from the implementation of neoliberal policies, which led to the positioning of the private real estate sector as the sole provider of housing and the authorisation of housing developments in areas previously set aside for ecological preservation. Thus, the scheme of an inclusive city, with significant areas of green spaces, was blurred. Nevertheless, it is still possible for innovative schemes to emerge in some areas of the city. The west of the city presents ideal conditions such as the existence of the protected natural area that houses the Mintzita spring and is recognised as a wetland of international importance, as well as the proposed extension of the spring's recharge area.

There is also an interest on the part of the inhabitants in maintaining agricultural activity on the areas of land they still have, and a certain degree of environmental awareness can also be perceived, in the sense that they share the importance of the rational use of natural resources, the conservation of the spring and the idea of establishing other forms of urbanisation that are environmentally friendly (interviews with the inhabitants carried out between July and

Fig. 7.4. The Panorama of Morelia in Mexico with Colourful Streets and Colonial Houses in the Historic Center. *Source*: ID 251340118 © Elovkoff | Dreamstime.com.

August 2017). Based on these peculiarities of the territory, it is viable to establish a proposal for rural–urban integration, which favours the inclusion of human settlements with dissimilar means and ways of life, in order to achieve a territorial balance and effective socio-environmental interaction. Proposals in this sense are recognised for other territorial, social and economic contexts, such as the plans of Amsterdam, London and Copenhagen which, in 1934, 1943 and 1947, respectively, considered the coexistence of rural and urban land uses in their planning instruments (López Goyburu, 2017). These are innovative experiences that, although they cannot be replicated in the Latin American context, they do provide elements for the harmonious integration of peri-urban areas.

The advantages of an integrated peri-urban area are the preservation of and respect for the way of life of the rural population, the obtaining of fresh food, the protection of the biodiversity of plants and animals (to which the consolidation of the proposed extension of the spring reserve area would contribute), the fostering of a sense of belonging (which could have positive effects on the prevention and eradication of delinquency). The urban–rural integration proposal would allow, in parallel, the fulfilment by governments, at different levels, of the stipulations of the Sustainable Development Goals, the UN-Habitat programme and the National Biodiversity Strategy (ENBioMex), among others, which call for urban-rural integration through connectivity and the development and implementation of instruments focused on the conservation and sustainable use of biodiversity in peri-urban and rural areas, the rescue of traditional knowledge and practices, as well as the rehabilitation and restoration of green areas through community strategies.

References

Aguilar, A. G. (2021). Institucionalidad y redimensionamiento urbano-regional en México. La Ley de Asentamientos Humanos de 2016 y las oportunidades perdidas. In J. Delgadillo Macías, A. Hildenbrand Scheid, & R. Garrido Yserte (Coords.), *Planificación Regional y Ordenación Territorial. Visiones Contemporáneas desde España y México* (1st ed., pp. 311–346). Universidad de Alcalá-España y Fondo de Cultura Económica-México.

Ávila, H. (2016). Periurbanización y gestión territorial. Algunas ideas y enfoques disciplinarios. In A. Vieyra, Y. Méndez, & J. Hernández (Coords.), *Procesos urbanos, pobreza y ambiente. Implicaciones en ciudades medias y megaciudades* (pp. 49–69). UNAM-CIGA.

Cruz Muñoz, F. (2021). Patrones de expansión urbana de las megaurbes latinoamericanas en el nuevo milenio. *EURE (Santiago)*, *47*(140), 29–49.

Gasca Zamora, J. (2013). Restructuración y polarización entre ciudades y regiones en México durante el neoliberalismo. In P. Olivera (Ed.), *Polarización social en la ciudad contemporanea* (pp. 21–53). Universidad Nacional Autonoma de México.

Harvey, D. (2001). *Espacios del Capital. Hacia una geografía crítica*. Akal.

Hidalgo, R., Rodríguez, L., Alvarado, V., & Paulsen Espinoza, A. (2021). La fragmentación en siete dimensione: la ciudad de Valdivia, Chile como laboratorio geográfico. In C. Rosas, A. Saldívar, & C. Ruiz (Coords.), *Territorios fragmentados. Posibles realidades latinoamericanas* (pp. 12–52). Universidad Nacional Autónoma de México.

López Goyburu, P. (2017). Miradas innovadoras sobre la interfaz urbano-rural: el plan de Extensión de Ámsterdam, los planes del Condado de Londres y del Gran Londres, y el plan Dedos de Copenhague. *EURE (Santiago)*, *43*(128), 175–196.

Mattos, C. (2019). Impactos de la financiarización inmobiliaria y la mercantilización de la metamorfosis urbana. In J. Gasca (Ed.), *Capital Inmobiliario. Producción y transgresión del espacio social en la ciudad neoliberal* (pp. 17–49). Instituto de Investigaciones Económicas de la Universidad Nacional Autónoma de México.

Méndez, Y., Vieyra, A., Guiza Valverde, F., & Hernández Guerrero, J. (2016). Relaciones sociales y expansión urbana: aplicación del enfoque de capital social en el análisis de la adaptación de los medios de vida agropecuarios a la periurbanización. In A. Vieyra, Y. Méndez & J. Hernández (Coords.), *Procesos urbanos, pobreza y ambiente. Implicaciones en ciudades medias y megaciudades* (pp. 89–107). UNAM-CIGA.

Olivera, P. (2014). Neoliberalismo en la Ciudad de México: polarización y gentrificación. In R. Hidalgo, & M. Janoschka (Eds.), *La ciudad neoliberal. Gentrificación y exclusión en Santiago de Chile, Buenos Aires, Ciudad de México y Madrid* (pp. 151–177). Serie GEOlibros.

Olivera, G. (2015). La incorporación de suelo social al crecimiento urbano de Cuernavaca y sus efectos en el desarrollo urbano formal e informal del suelo y la vivienda. In G. Oolivera (Coord.), *La urbanización social y privada del ejido: ensayos sobre la dualidad del desarrollo urbano en México* (pp. 149–196). Universidad Nacional Autónoma de México.

Poncela, L., Vieyra, A., & Méndez-Lemus, Y. (2015). Procesos participativos intramunicipales como pasos hacia la gobernanza local en territorios periurbanos. La experiencia en el municipio de Tarímbaro, Michoacán, México. *Journal of Latin American Geography*, *14*(2), 130–156.

Robles, M. S. R., Rodríguez, N., & Dattwyler, R. H. (2021). De la periferia y el periurbano al margen: comprendiendo el espacio de expansión de la ciudad latinoamericana. *Ateliê Geográfico*, *15*(2), 6–26.

Rodríguez, N. (2020). Marcos legislativos, racionalidades político-económicas y ordenamiento territorial: La desarticulación sectorial y multinivel en México. *Revista de Geografía Norte Grande*, (77), 11–29. http://dx.doi.org/10.4067/S0718-34022020000300011

Rodríguez, N., Vieyra, A., & González, O. (2019). El periurbano y los grandes proyectos inmobiliarios: los casos de Altozano y Tres Marías en Morelia, Michoacán. In G. Jose (Ed.), *Capital inmobiliario. produción y transgresión del espacio social en la ciudad neoliberal* (pp. 299–318). Universidad Nacional Autónoma de México.

Ruiz-López, C., Vieyra, A., & Méndez-Lemus, Y. (2021). Segregación espacial en Tarímbaro, municipio periurbano de la zona metropolitana de Morelia, Michoacán, México. *Revista de Geografía Norte Grande*, (78), 237–257.

Santos, M. (2014). *A naturaleza do espaço* (4a ed.). Edusp.

Vieyra, A., Méndez, Y., & Hernández, J. (2016). *Procesos urbanos, pobreza y ambiente, implicaciones en ciudades medias y megaciudades*. Universidad Nacional Autónoma de México.

Chapter 8

Emancipation and the Construction of New Development Models: The Experience of Andean Peasants in Argentina

Paula Lucía Olaizola

Instituto Nacional de Tecnología Agropecuaria, Argentina

The Department of Molinos, in the Province of Salta (Fig. 8.1), and more precisely in the Calchaquí Valleys, was constituted as the old encomienda of San Pedro Nolasco de Los Molinos, lands that were donated by the King of Spain to a receiver who had to populate, evangelise and domesticate its inhabitants within a determined period of time (Fig. 8.2). This *encomienda* became *latifundios*, large private estates, inhabited by peasant and indigenous communities under different regimes of domination.

This system of life and production was maintained for centuries, with traditional forms of domination that can be considered as a functional situation for its subjugation or disappearance. It can be affirmed that it is a complex, unequal and inequitable rural world that is naturalised by a large part of the population, with clear complicity at the different levels of the national state, which contributed to consolidating these rural structures, and which has also favoured the advance of land concentration. However, 10 years ago, a team of extensionists from INTA and a local NGO, Red Valles de Altura, began to develop an experience that allowed them to generate new conditions for the autonomy of the population and the construction of their own development project. From the outset, the technicians introduced the concept of *community*, with a strong sense of identity, solidarity and reciprocity. The intervention process has meant that, 16 years later, young people from these areas do not hesitate to call their places *communities*. The change of identity and the work between technicians and peasant communities made it possible to build a new social territory that encouraged the inhabitants to leave the limits of the farm, the employer, the place, and turn a common place into a territory to fight for. In this way, from the approach to communities, work was done on the

Exploring Hope: Case Studies of Innovation, Change and Development in the Global South, 59–62

doi:10.1108/978-1-83549-736-420241011

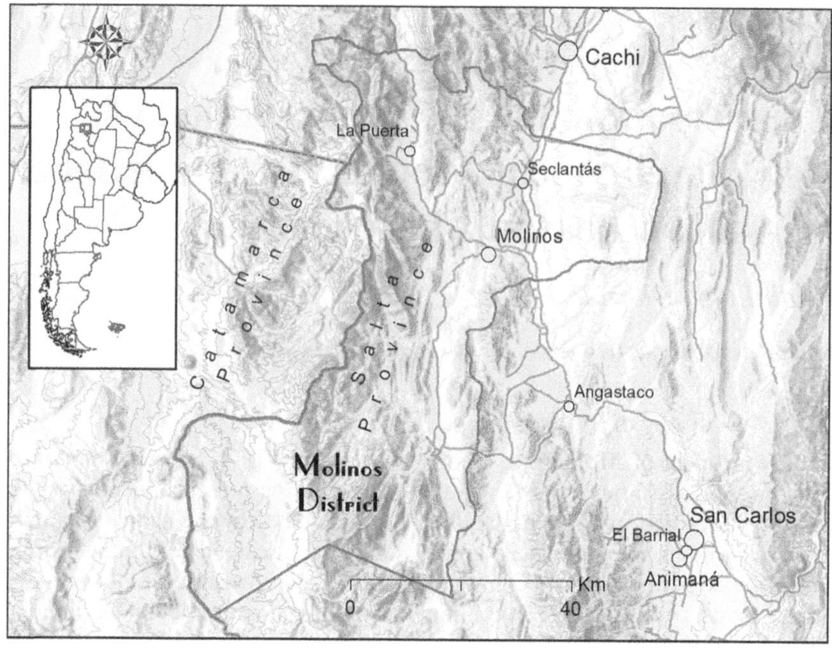

Fig. 8.1. Department of Molinos in the Province of Salta, Argentina.
Source: Own elaboration.

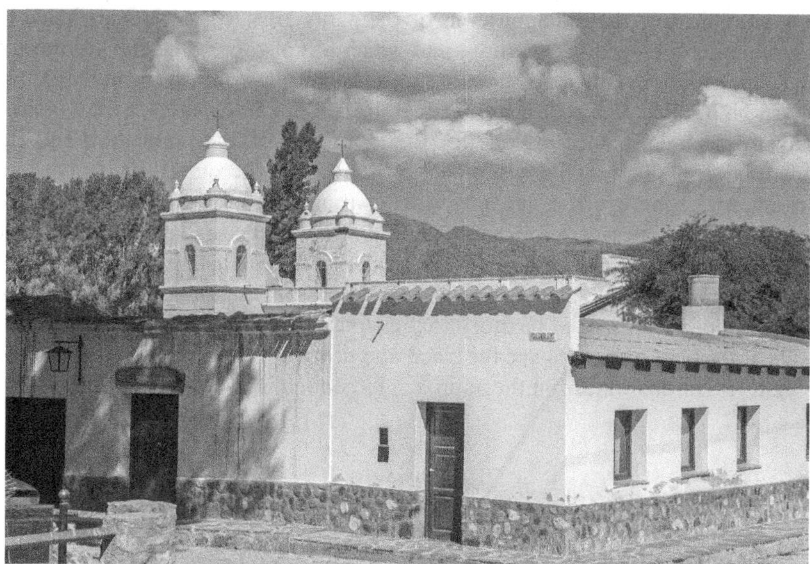

Fig. 8.2. Colonial Heritage in Seclantas, Department of Molinos.
Source: ID 38905195 © Anibal Trejo | Dreamstime.com.

creation of new irrigation infrastructures, improvement of animal production, creation of rural housing, creation of new marketing mechanisms, creation of a local brand image, training, among many other actions for local improvement.

In this context of work, community meetings began to appear as the culminating space for decision making, from where the management of financing was endorsed or not, roles were distributed, conflicts were dealt with, and therefore it was in these spaces where a community project began to take shape. This integral approach to the problems of the peasants, in a democratic and participatory manner, allowed for their political emancipation, overcoming their socio-historical condition of traditional dependence, contributing to the emergence of a peasant development model of their own.

A concrete action that originated in this transformation process was the gestation of a new political actor, the 'Community of Los Molinos', which was the birth of an emancipated peasant organisation that began to intervene in the region, building a new territory and a new discourse, where peasants and technicians, from their different institutions or roles, converge in a common and overcoming purpose that demarcates a new peasant condition. The emergence of this new way of constructing the development of rural territories is the result of the convergence of four major dimensions, from which different actions are generated. New forms of knowledge construction, with peasant schools, participatory methods, exchanges, on the other hand, innovative marketing processes, with peasant markets, collective branding, thirdly by promoting changes in local and provincial public policies and finally with a strong process of emancipation of the actors, with the organisation of the communities.

The awareness of inequalities has been the starting point for a strong destructuring and change in the communities. Andean communities have become protagonists of their future (Fig. 8.3), which has allowed them to discover that there is a concrete possibility of achieving the political emancipation of oppressed peasants. They have succeeded in transforming the traditional organisational model in which they were immersed into a new model of citizen (emancipated) territorial organisation. These processes have contributed to the emergence of a peasant development model in the context of globalisation. Experience shows that the mere presence of peasant communities with Andean logics of production and reproduction within private farms was enough to build resistance to the hegemonic model. But resisting is not synonymous with transforming, let alone guaranteeing equity, justice or social change.

From Hannah Arendt's approach, what is called gathering power has been observed, whereby the form of articulation between them resides in opposition to some instance external to them. In the power of assembly, Di Pego (2006) says:

> there is a cohesion between people based on shared opposition or resistance to some instance external to that multitude (which can be either a government or some other social group). In the power of assembly, people pursue a common goal, but one that does not arise from a concerted dialogue, but rather from a widely disseminated and shared opposition.

Fig. 8.3. Seclantas Landscape, Department of Molinos. *Source*: ID 38905195 © Anibal Trejo | Dreamstime.com.

Resistance is therefore often about enduring, remaining, or surviving in order not to disappear, but does not necessarily build an alternative.

> Participatory democracy assumes that the institutions of our representative democracies can be complemented by the creation of public spaces where citizens can act by introducing novelty into the world. To make this deepening of democracy concrete requires innovation and foundation, the former supposes a space where people can exercise freedom, and the latter supposes the institutionalisation of that space in our form of government. (Di Pego, 2006, p. 120)

In this sense, the Communities of Molinos managed to overcome their condition of resistance and made progress in the meeting spaces, encouraging them to be free, to build new dynamics and a new model of development. The commitment lies in taking advantage of the opportunities offered by action, seen as the only way, beyond structures, that allows us to risk taking some degree of freedom for action.

Reference

Di Pego, A. (2006). Poder, violencia y revolución en los escritos de Hannah Arendt: Algunas notas para repensar la política. *Argumentos (México, DF)*, *19*(52), 101–122.

Chapter 9

Metrocable: Public Transport for Urban and Social Transformation in Medellín

Beatriz Garcés Beltrán

Engineer and philosopher, Medellín, Colombia

Orfa Rojas arrived in Medellín in the 1980s from Santa Rosa de Osos, a town in the north of the Department of Antioquia, when she was beginning her secondary studies. She found a home in the Santa Cruz neighbourhood, on the slopes of the north-eastern hills of the Aburrá Valley, overpopulated by the arrival of the so-called 'displaced people' in search of opportunities to live; an area hit by poverty, violence and abandonment. Orfa vividly remembers the skirt of her school uniform fluttering in the wind like a flag as she travelled to her school in a small informal transport vehicle, so full of passengers that often the only place she could find was 'hanging on a door'. The vehicle would speed down the steep little streets, always a long, tortuous and unsafe journey.

When construction began on the Santo Domingo Metrocable, the first of the entire Metro System, Orfa, like the other inhabitants of the sector, could not believe that the city administration had 'set its sights on such a poor community, invisible in so many ways… We were overjoyed'. Her house would be close to the second Metrocable station, Andalucía, so the cable became her means of transport from its inauguration. For Orfa, as for her neighbours, the arrival of the Metro System via the cable meant much more than saving time and money. It was a total change in their landscape and in their way of getting around, thinking, living and relating to other city dwellers.

> We visualised ourselves… we didn't know how poor we were, or how many of us there were, how big the area was… we also realised, and showed the world, that we weren't so bad, that we weren't so poor; a lot of manpower came from there for the whole city of Medellín.

Exploring Hope: Case Studies of Innovation, Change and Development in the Global South, 63–68

Published under exclusive licence by Emerald Publishing Limited
doi:10.1108/978-1-83549-736-420241012

Both tourists and Medellín residents from other sectors arrived en masse to the area and got to know the other side of the city. 'We learned from each other', says Orfa, because for the locals, with the arrival of the Metrocable, 'the world opened up'.

A History of Integration

The Andes, the magnificent mountain range that crosses South America from south to north, splits into three branches – Western, Central and Eastern – as soon as it reaches Colombian territory. The Aburrá Valley, nestled between two ranges of the Cordillera Central, is the last inter-Andean valley of this mountain branch, just before its last foothills die out near the Caribbean coast. Located in the centre of the department of Antioquia, the Aburrá Valley is long, narrow and steeply sloping. Its approximate length is 60 km, its average width is 6 km and its irregular topography has altitudes between 1,300 and 2,800 m above sea level. The valley forms the basin of the Medellín River, which crosses it from south to north and acts as a structuring axis for the urbanisation of the 10 municipalities established on its lands, which are home to a population of approximately 4 million inhabitants. Among these municipalities is Medellín, the capital of the department and the second most populated city in Colombia, with 2.5 million inhabitants.

By 1995, Medellín had almost 1.9 million residents, settled both on its lower, relatively flat terrain and on its steep mountain slopes, on which numerous rural migrants were gradually and rapidly building their homes. Immigration generated informal settlements of chaotic growth, difficult access and disconnected from the city centre, complex conditions for its population and conducive to illegal activities and criminality. In the same year, the Metro de Medellín transport system (Fig. 9.1), a public company set up by the Department of Antioquia and the Municipality of Medellín, began operating. The system began with an elevated electric metropolitan train, which ran on Line A, parallel to the river. Line B was soon added, connecting the centre with the west of the city. But the real revolution was yet to come.

In 2004, the Santo Domingo line (Line K) came into operation, a cable that runs for 2.1 km from Acevedo station, located in the north of the valley, to the east, up an average gradient of 20%. This was the inauguration of what is known as Metrocable, the first massive aerial cable system designed for urban, non-tourist use in the world. The project overcame the paradigms of the time for this type of transport, overcoming technical challenges such as operation in the urban environment, with intermediate stations, integration with a metro and a very high intensity of use, unlike tourist cables, which operated in less densely populated areas, only seasonally or during restricted hours. The Metrocable became an example of sustainable and inclusive mobility (Fig. 9.2). The inhabitants of the steep north-eastern slopes – who now number 240,000 – were given the opportunity to integrate spatially, socially and economically with the rest of the city. By 2022, it was the busiest cable car: on a typical working day, it moved 46,000 people.

Fig. 9.1. Medellin Metro Cable Cars. *Source*: ID 39446233 © Jesse Kraft | **Dreamstime.com**.

Fig. 9.2. The Metrocable Is the Permanent Rapid Transit System of the Cable Car Type for the Urban Mobilisation of Passengers in Medellín. *Source*: ID 190399097 © Alexander Canas Arango | **Dreamstime.com**.

The system continued to grow. In 2008, the second Metrocable, San Javier (Line J), began service from the station of the same name, located in the centre-west of the valley, running 2.7 km to the north and benefiting 120,000 inhabitants. La Aurora, its last station, is located in the Pajarito sector, inhabited by low-income families who had previously suffered acute violence in their territory. The Mayor's Office of Medellín established that Pajarito would be land for urban expansion, which became a reality through the South American Games that were held in the city that same year: the Villa Suramericana was built in the sector and was subsequently destined for families benefiting from social housing programmes, who perhaps would not have ventured to live in a place that was difficult to access from the city centre, had it not been for the existence of this means of transport. The travel time of the cable car between San Javier and La Aurora is only 12 min. By 2022, on a regular working day, this line carried 32,000 people. Subsequently, in 2010, the longest and first tourist cable line was inaugurated, the Arví Cable (Line L), which starts at the Santo Domingo station – the last station of the Metrocable Line K – and extends eastwards for 4.8 km, rising to an altitude of 2,500 m. The last station is located in the Arví Park, an open public reserve of 18 million m^2 of native forests and plantations. This line linked the system to the township of Santa Elena, one of the five rural areas of Medellín.

The Metro System included a comprehensive project for the benefit of 450,000 inhabitants of the central-eastern part of the city, consisting of a tramway and two cable lines. In 2016, the Ayacucho Tramway (Line T) began operating, leaving from San Antonio station, where Lines A and B converge. A metrocable (Line H) departs from its last station, which came into operation that same year. This cable continues its route along the steep eastern slopes to La Sierra, one of the city's most marginalised working-class neighbourhoods, with its difficult topography, high population density and few narrow streets. The metrocable Line H covers a length of 1.4 km and has a gradient of 187 m. In 2020, it carried 5,000 passengers per day. The integration of the inhabitants of the eastern neighbourhoods was complemented in 2019 with the delivery of the Miraflores cable line (Line M), which links the tramway station of the same name and the Trece de noviembre neighbourhood. This cable, with a length of just 1 km, is the shortest, but also one of the steepest, with gradients of more than 30%. Since 2020 it has been carrying around 8,000 passengers a day. It has an electric motor, a more advanced technology than the previous cables, so it is quieter and does not emit pollutants into the atmosphere. The system's newest cable, the sixth, is the Metrocable Picacho (Line P), which has been in service since June 2021. This line operates from Acevedo station on Line A and runs west to the El progreso neighbourhood on the slopes of Picacho Hill, benefiting 420,000 inhabitants of the north-western part of the valley. It is the aerial cable with the highest installed capacity and speed in the country, in fact, by 2022, it was the second cable that transported more users daily: 40,000 people on average per working day, only 6,000 less than Line K, the oldest.

At present, the Metro System is a multimodal network covering more than 80 km on its 12 lines. The Metrocable covers 15 km, which are covered by 500 cable cars. The network has direct influence in six municipalities in the Aburrá Valley: Bello, Medellín, Itagüí, Envigado, Sabaneta and La Estrella, and has integrated bus routes to other nearby municipalities. It transports up to 1.5 million passengers on a typical working day.

An Urban But Also a Social Transformation

The Metrocable, Metro de Medellín's overhead cable system, allows the integration and connection of the population of the hillsides – a topography that is difficult to access by other means – with the flat area of the Aburrá Valley, materialising a sustainable, inclusive and equitable mobility proposal that favours the quality of life of all the region's inhabitants. In the Metrocable, as in the entire Metro System, thousands of users travel daily with comfort, safety, speed and economy. In addition, it is an environmentally friendly system that increases the wellbeing of the neighbours with interventions that organise, improve or increase the public space near its infrastructure and promote commercial, tourist and cultural interest in the surrounding areas.

The money saving for users is embodied in the fare integration: with a single payment, for 90 min the passenger can use the entire system – except for the Arví Cable. During the same period, only a portion of the fare of the integrated bus routes arriving or departing from the stations is paid. Fares range from 0.3 to 0.8 USD and are differentiated for occasional and frequent users, students, senior citizens and persons with disabilities. It should be noted that all stations in the system have accessibility features, promoting social inclusion.

The time savings for Metrocable users have been considerable. The hillside neighbourhoods used to have only a few buses to navigate their steep and narrow streets, the rest was informal transport with reduced timetables and long walks. For example, an inhabitant of the Santo Domingo Savio neighbourhood might need 90 min to reach the city centre, a time that has been reduced to 30 min thanks to the integration of the Line K cable and the rest of the Metro System.

In terms of environmental impact, one of the principles of the Medellín Metro is sustainable mobility, based on the use of clean energy. The Metrocable has made it possible to reduce atmospheric emissions of pollutants by replacing the use of old vehicles, or those in poor condition, which served as the only means of transport on the hillsides. In 2018, the emission of 36,000 tonnes of CO_2 and 1,100 tonnes of other pollutants, such as nitrogen oxides and particulate matter, was avoided. In addition, many elements of the system have electric mobility, from the trains, the tram and the M and P cables, to more than 60 buses. The city has been able to finance part of the System's operating costs through emissions trading. For example, in 2019, the Metro recorded positive externalities valued at USD 790 million, thanks to travel time savings, as well as avoided pollution and accidents. The effects on the economy, safety and culture of the areas connected by the mobility solution that makes up the Metro System are driven by the intervention of the public space adjacent to its infrastructure. In the first instance, the surrounding public space is recovered with road and pedestrian corridors. The favoured space is equipped with libraries, sports facilities, playgrounds, parks and viewpoints. Among the more specialised facilities are the digital literacy rooms and the Bibliometros, where users are accompanied and trained in the use of technological tools free of charge.

Political consistency has been key to the success of the Metro System, which has been supported by successive local and regional governments in Medellín and

Antioquia in its planning, construction and development. Urban problems have been approached in a comprehensive manner, which has included active social management to raise community awareness and win community support. This management implies a presence in the territory from the planning phase, so that the neighbours become familiar with the project and know its benefits. Strategies include user education and training to ensure the development of a sense of ownership in the community. A valuable intangible gain has been the eradication of the stigma of exclusion in the marginalised sectors, who have begun to feel part of the city and recognised by their fellow citizens. The impacted areas have become tourist attractions, and their inhabitants have been able to feel proud to live there.

By virtue of the social and urban transformation it has achieved, its associated coexistence model and its pioneering and innovative character, the Metrocable has become a Latin American benchmark for mass transport systems. Cities such as Bogotá (Colombia), Santo Domingo (Dominican Republic) and Rio de Janeiro (Brazil), among others, have replicated this experience. The cable cars going up and down the slopes of the Aburrá Valley have become an icon of Medellín and a symbol of its regeneration, of the resilience with which it has been able to overcome its most difficult moments.

Chapter 10

Revaluing Heritage and Managing Conflicts Over Land Use in the City of Quito

Rosa Cuesta and Martha Villagómez

Instituto Geográfico Militar, Ecuador

The city of Quito, the capital of Ecuador, is located at an altitude of 2,850 m above sea level. Historically, it was the centre of organisation for the entire Andean region, and a bastion of Spanish colonisation in Ecuador. By 2022, the city, according to population projections, has 2,781,641 inhabitants and extends over the valley and the slopes of the neighbouring mountains, including large volcanoes, which directly affects its linear growth extending north and south, however, if there is the occupation of the slopes and spaces unsuitable for urban growth.

The city of Quito can be seen from various points of view, since its character as the capital concentrates on services and institutions of national importance, and at the same time it is considered the most important point of national and international connectivity in the country, making it a city with a very marked central role. An additional consideration is the historical character of this metropolis, so much so that the historic centre of Quito (CHQ) was declared a World Heritage Site in 1978 by UNESCO, as a testimony to the existence and persistence of cultural and historical values, as well as for having one of the highest densities of heritage historical centres in Latin America (Carrión, 2001). The city has gone through several stages, always retaining its mysticism and history, this area contains the largest and best preserved colonial case of the entire southern cone. In addition, it has an area of 373 ha (Parroquia Centro), its houses, squares and parks, which, at first sight, show a façade that transports us to colonial times (Figs. 10.1 and 10.2), and upon entering each building, we can better appreciate the physical state of the buildings and their very particular architecture, generally the colonial houses have a pool in their central patio and long corridors adorned with balconies, these buildings are distributed over cobblestone streets that form a very striking urban fabric.

Exploring Hope: Case Studies of Innovation, Change and Development in the Global South, 69–73

doi:10.1108/978-1-83549-736-420241013

Fig. 10.1. Streets of the Historic Centre of Ecuador. *Source*: ID 265581592 © Atosan | Dreamstime.com.

Fig. 10.2. Calle La Ronda: Typical Colonial Street in the Historic Centre of Quito Ecuador. *Source*: ID 265581878 © Atosan | Dreamstime.com.

This historical and cultural area has suffered strong transformations and a deep deterioration through the years, with new constructions that do not respect the identity and heritage, with the incorporation of inadequate public transport systems, environmental pollution, informality and chaos in commerce, solid waste management and security issues, among many other problems. These problems have been treated differently by the local governments in power, where the lack of a long-term vision and the desire for true conservation of the colonial case is not perceived by the Quiteños, and where local management is weak and poorly articulated with the actors of real change, which are the inhabitants of the CHQ.

Faced with all these problems, the municipality of Quito, in recent decades has tried to promote several initiatives that aim to restore the quality of life of the inhabitants of the CHQ and return to domestic and foreign tourists a safe space, with quality services and easy mobility (Fig. 10.3). In this sense, one of the most ambitious projects undertaken in the 1990s was the reorganisation of the informal trade present in the colonial centre of Quito, which turned this space into a 'large-scale popular market'. This trade was carried out under two modalities, one that was located in fixed spaces (pavements of the historic centre) and the second that was carried out in an itinerant manner within the influence of CHQ (approximately 22 blocks). 200 informal traders were relocated to popular commercial centres located in the historic centre (Valdivieso Ortega, 2009).

This process of relocation of informal traders in the CHQ was not a simple process, as there were many private interests that hindered the mayor's intentions to reorganise public space. Between the 1980s and 1990s, several actions were carried out, mainly the creation of institutions and specific regulations in order to lay the legal and institutional foundations, which made the relocation

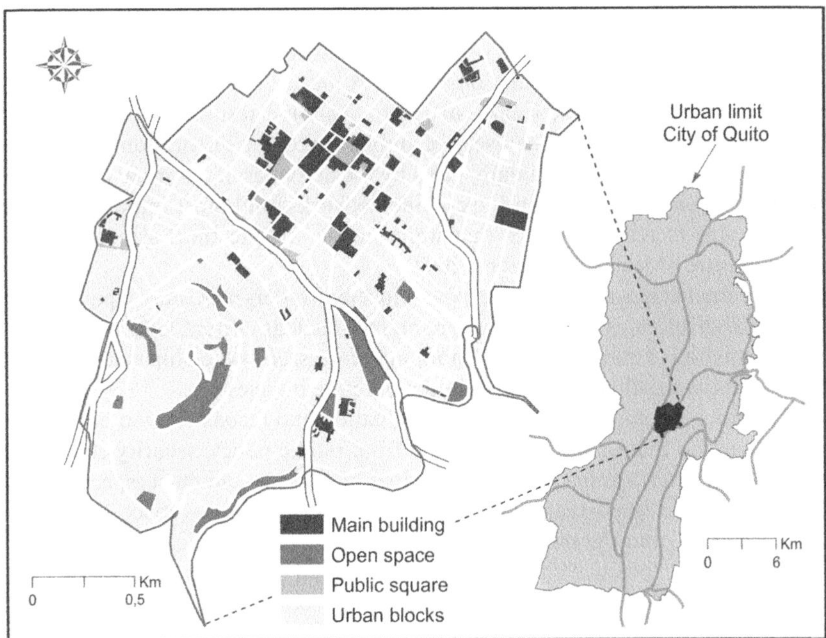

Fig. 10.3. Location of the Historic Centre in Relation to Quito's Urban Area. *Source*: Own elaboration.

of informal traders feasible, In 1994, the Quito Metropolitan District Law was approved, which created administrative zones, including the one corresponding to the Historic Centre, and in the same year the Quito Historic Centre Development Company (ECH) was created, whose main objective was to promote the comprehensive rehabilitation of the historic centre area, made up of around 154 blocks. Similarly, a series of municipal ordinances were published that referred to specific regulations for the control and issuing of permits for the operation of commercial activities in the historic centre (Valdivieso Ortega, 2007).

At the same time, international loans were arranged in order to finance the construction and adaptation of six popular shopping centres, spaces that would be occupied by informal traders who were trading on the public highway. Throughout this process, emphasis was placed on community participation, dialogue was encouraged with key actors (traders and residents of the CHQ), a strong campaign was carried out for the appropriation of Quito's space, and economic alternatives were sought to finance the acquisition of the spaces in the various shopping centres, with the Municipality of Quito subsidising 50% of the total value of the commercial premises.

Between 1999 and 2000, there was a change of authorities in the Quito City Council. It is important to note that the incoming mayor continued with the work carried out by the outgoing authorities regarding the relocation of informal commerce and created other municipal departments to further promote the project implemented in previous years.

In 2003, after several years of intense conversations, negotiations and agreements established with the various traders' associations that until then had been present in the CHQ, the process of relocating informal traders began. This process was regulated by the Regulations for the Allocation of Commercial Premises to Retailers in the Historic Centre of Quito, The first results of this relocation were, in the first instance, a recovery of public space, the restoration of heritage assets that were affected on a daily basis by the activities of informal commerce, the readjustment of energy and telephone networks, and most importantly, the city was able to recover spaces that were mostly 'architectural symbols of the historic centre' (Monsalve Herrera, 2007).

In the final stage of this project, the relocated traders were accompanied and advice was given on issues of common interest, such as current legal regulations, the administrative management of shopping centres, co-ownership rules and fundamental issues such as advertising and marketing policies.

This process demonstrates that the revaluation and reconstruction of the centre is an action that cannot be separated from public policy, security considerations, investment planning among other areas of interest, and most especially that it requires the active participation of the people who live in this space, the 'neighbours' or 'vecis' and the traders who directly participated and can be considered as true agents of positive change, promoting the idea that it is necessary for the historic centre to once again be a meeting place, where a number of services and socio-cultural attractions can be enjoyed.

It took about six years under the administration of two mayors, Roque Sevilla (1998–2000) and Paco Moncayo (2000–2009), to make the proposal to relocate informal traders in the CHQ a reality, with the aim of recovering a space to be enjoyed by locals and foreigners alike. The changes were very important, more than 5,000 traders were regularised, important agreements were reached regarding the use of public spaces for commercial purposes, important ordinances were created to provide a legal basis that allows this whole process to be maintained over time, and something worth highlighting is that when there is a political decision and a real desire to contribute to a positive change in the city, no matter the political tendencies or rivalries, the important thing is to continue with a project of change that was really necessary for the CHQ.

Almost 20 years have passed since the day when the streets of Quito's historic centre regained their functionality and became spaces conducive to facilitating the mobility of passers-by who visit this space so representative of the city on a daily basis, and which holds an immense cultural and scenic wealth. The current authorities have a very important challenge, which is to keep these spaces free of informal and itinerant commerce, a difficult challenge, as the socio-economic conditions resulting from a pandemic and world crisis have once again forced people to resort to commerce in the streets in order to earn a living, This constant struggle invites the authorities on duty to think and build new commitments with the traders and neighbours, to develop new alternatives such as the creation of 'trade corridors' in the CHQ, to deliver more permits for the operation of businesses, among other strategies, approaches that are currently in the design process. The municipal authorities have a very hard but necessary task if they want to safeguard all the work developed for several decades, always looking for the CHQ to be a space of peaceful coexistence and admiration for locals and strangers alike.

References

Carrión, F. (2001). *Centros Históricos de América Latina y el Caribe*. FLACSO Ecuador.

Monsalve Herrera, F. A. (2007). *Políticas municipales y memoria de actores colectivos en el proceso de reubicación del comercio minorista del sector de Ipiales en el Centro Histórico de Quito* [Master's thesis, Universidad Andina Simón Bolívar, Sede Ecuador]. https://repositorio.uasb.edu.ec/bitstream/10644/812/1/T469-MEC-Monsalve-Políticas municipales y memoria de actores colectivos en el proceso de reubicación.pdf

Valdivieso Ortega, N. (2007, April). Modernización del comercio informal en el Centro Histórico de Quito. In *Simposio URB-1*. Quito: Flacso. *Electronico document:* http://www.reseau-amerique-latine.fr/ceisal-bruxelles/URB/URB-1-VALDIVIESO.pdf

Valdivieso Ortega, N. R. (2009). *Reubicación del comercio informal en el centro histórico de Quito: conflicto y resolución* [Master's thesis, Quito, Ecuador: Flacso Ecuador]. https://repositorio.flacsoandes.edu.ec/bitstream/10469/2483/6/TFLACSO-2009NRVO.pdf

Chapter 11

The Emergence of New Paradigms of Sustainable Construction

Juan José García Pérez

Fundación CÍCLICA (Fundación para el desarrollo colectivo y autónomo del hábitat Cíclica), Chile

Latin America is a continent that historically used noble and natural materials for the construction of its dwellings. In the 20th century, new technologies and the use of cement monopolised construction and infrastructure, relegating the use of natural materials to the poorest and most rural areas. Thus, although self-construction and the use of natural materials are part of Latin America's identity, in recent decades these techniques have suffered a certain loss of prestige because they are considered poor architecture or inferior to contemporary construction techniques that have been displacing them.

However, bio-construction is emerging strongly in the region, making it possible to solve infrastructure and housing problems in an original way, with greater sustainability and resource savings (Figs. 11.1 and 11.2). The environmental factor is key, as natural or recycled materials are used, minimising the high environmental impact produced by conventional construction; from the economic point of view, the savings are significant, due to the low cost of materials and also because of the energy savings achieved in all stages of the building's life cycle.

Since the beginning of the 2010s, the processes of training, experimentation and construction of housing and infrastructure based on biomaterials have been developed in the region, driven by various actors with experience in the region and in Europe. This led to the creation of the *Red Chilena de Construcción con Fardos de Paja (Chilean Strawbale Building Network)* (which has given rise to other networks in different Latin American countries), the *Gremio de Bioconstrucción de Chile (Chilean Bio-construction Gathering)* and other organisations that promote sustainable construction in the continent.

The work within these networks has been basically the recovery of ancestral techniques and the proposal of new sustainable technologies, revaluing them and giving them back their lost prestige. The key to the success of this process has

Exploring Hope: Case Studies of Innovation, Change and Development in the Global South, 75–78

doi:10.1108/978-1-83549-736-420241014

Fig. 11.1. Exterior of a Sustainable Construction. *Source:* The Author.

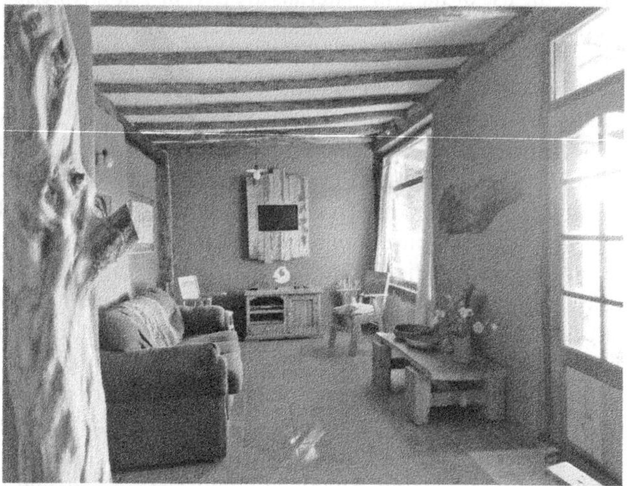

Fig. 11.2. Interior of a Sustainable Construction. *Source:* The Author.

been the combination of the rescue of artisanal work and the research and certification of technologies. Thus, it is now possible to construct legal buildings with straw bales, wattle and daub (known as "quincha", "bahareque" or "fajina" in different Latin American countries) or other natural techniques, thanks to the work carried out jointly by various organisations that have made it possible to carry out tests in official laboratories. This is especially important in countries with high seismic activity such as Chile. A major milestone was the validation process of straw bale construction, led by the *Manzana Verde* collective and joined by the *Red Chilena de Construcción con Fardos de Paja* (Chilean Straw Bale

Construction Network) and other entities, which made it possible to determine values for fire resistance, thermal and structural resistance of the construction system. Subsequently, similar processes have been carried out, such as the one carried out on the pallet quincha system by the SEMBRA Association in collaboration with the Universidad de La Frontera (UFRO) and other entities, those carried out by *Estudio Tribal* and *Arquitecturaenfardos* using different techniques of metallic wattle and daub and others mainly oriented towards prefabricated panel systems.

Thanks to these initiatives, it has been possible to carry out multiple social projects such as those developed throughout the country by the SEMBRA Association, an NGO that has an Ecotechnology Exploratory Camp in the town of Nogales, where prototypes made with various techniques can be visited and inhabited, and thus be perfected in order to implement them in various programmes in other regions. Projects such as social centres, workshops, housing and other buildings constructed with local earth, straw, pallets, scraps of clothing and other materials, would not have been possible otherwise. What gives real sustainability to these projects is the training of the community that takes part in the design and execution processes, and the possibility of doing it in a legal way, with building permits, which guarantees their stability and durability (Fig. 11.3).

Other similar projects, carried out in collaboration with other entities, have made it possible to build social housing incorporating bio-construction techniques, which would not have been possible without the prior validation processes of construction systems. Thus, after the collaboration between the SEMBRA Association and the UFRO for the development of insulating materials with low environmental impact, the impulse of the public administration (Ministry of Housing and Urbanism – MINVU) and private companies that participated in the implementation process, more than 50 houses could be built with a design

Fig. 11.3. A Woman Building Sustainably. *Source:* The Author.

especially suited to the needs of its inhabitants (rural and primarily indigenous population). One of the most interesting points of this project called *Vivienda Origen* is the incorporation of two walls based on the traditional technique of 'wattle and daub (known in the region as "quincha")', which reconnects the inhabitants with the land, improves the comfort of the house through a low-tech system and takes advantage of local resources, among other advantages. Through on-site training processes, the beneficiaries themselves were able to participate in the execution of the plasters, becoming part of the process and being trained in its maintenance without having to depend on third parties. This initiative has been of particular interest to MINVU as it is a project with sustainable construction attributes and is especially emblematic as it involves social housing, which tends to be very conservative in terms of the choice of materials and construction systems.

These experiences have been expanding throughout the continent. In Uruguay, for example, a network of sustainable schools was created in 2016. Other organisations have joined in the region, carrying out projects in Uruguay, Argentina, Chile, Ecuador, Colombia, Peru and other countries. These projects, financed by major sponsors, involve the participation of local companies and associations, prestigious architectural firms such as EARTHSHIP BIOTECTURE (USA), ALBORDE (Ecuador) or PLAN B (Colombia), the beneficiary community and hundreds of volunteers and students from different countries who sign up for the sustainable construction course that is carried out in parallel to each construction. The result of each project is a sustainable school that functions efficiently with bioclimatic design, non-conventional renewable energies (NCRE), water management systems, farming and crops spaces and other devices that are themselves educational resources for the school programme.

There are many more emblematic projects throughout Latin America, some very ambitious and others that owe their high value to their simplicity.

Chapter 12

China's New Development Concept and the New Model of 'People's City' in the Context of Globalisation – Renewal of Yangpu Industrial Area and Innovation of Gubei Civic Center in Shanghai as an Example

Zhongshi Yuan and Jingting Zhang

School of European and Latin American Studies, Shanghai International Studies University, China

The Fifth Plenary Session of the 18th Central Committee of the Communist Party of China (CPC) adopted the Proposal of the CPC Central Committee on Formulating the 13th Five-Year Plan for National Economic and Social Development, which puts forward the new development concept of innovation, coordination, green, openness and sharing. People's City, as it means, is built by the people and is for the people. In China, building a people's city is to make the city suitable for business, living, entertainment and tourism. Shanghai, as one of the largest cities in the world, has taken people-oriented values as the core orientation to promote urban development. In this chapter, we use two case analyses in order to summarise two initiatives and the relationship between these initiatives and China's new development concept. One is the transformation of the traditional industrial line in Yangpu Riverside and the other is the innovation of Gubei Civic Center. The Yangpu Riverside was originally an industrial site with abandoned factories and rusted facilities. While the industrial area faced closure in the process of globalisation and urbanisation, Yangpu Riverside is a successful example of Shanghai's early urban planning in turning industrial parks into public parks, while Gubei New District was transformed from a farmland village house to an international community of the first generation in the 1980s, according to the Shanghai Urban Master Plan. These two cases are excellent examples

Exploring Hope: Case Studies of Innovation, Change and Development in the Global South, 79–84

Published under exclusive licence by Emerald Publishing Limited
doi:10.1108/978-1-83549-736-420241015

of Shanghai's urban construction. Through case studies and literature analysis, this chapter will use them to discuss how Shanghai solves urban management problems, implements the new development concept and meets both the modernisation of the city and the real needs of the people through spatial planning. It is also hoped that this case study will provide feasible solutions and hopes for other cities around the world in terms of development issues and urban planning.

We conducted a three-month qualitative survey from November 2021 to January 2022, including: visits to important planned buildings in Yangpu Riverside and Gubei New Area; interviews with relevant people, nearby residents and tourists, questionnaires and semi-open-ended interviews; community research, selecting several important communities for in-depth interviews, which are not limited to residents' daily life, urban emotions, problem feedback, surrounding traffic, environment, cultural conditions, etc. We distributed 80 questionnaires, 73 valid questionnaires and interviewed 21 visitors, residents and related staff. The following analysis will be based on the results of our survey.

Industrial Coastline Becomes Urban Public Space

Yangpu Riverside has witnessed a period of modern industrialisation of Shanghai because of taking advantage of the geographical convenience of water transportation and forming a developed connection with overseas and now this industrial coastline has to face the decline crisis. Big industrial buildings are abandoned and have become obstacles to making urban space. Some people insist on removing them, others consider these plants as industrial heritage which cannot be pulled down. After many discussions, the Shanghai Government decides to rebuild some plants, conserve their important parts to protect industrial heritage and transform other parts into urban public spaces (Fig. 12.1).

> My husband worked in the factory here before, but after he retired, the place became more and more dilapidated and the factory was abandoned. The factory witnessed our young days, so we always felt sorry for it. I never thought that after the renovation it would now have a different look and vitality. (Retired worker, 75 years old)

The former mechanical warehouse of the Shanghai Tobacco Co. Ltd. now becomes the Green Hill covered with green plants. It is a complex public transportation, an urban infrastructure, an office, an exhibition hall, a coffee shop and an urban park (Xu, 2015). 'I live nearby and come here for a run every weekend, and I love the modern artistic feel of this old building for a change' (journalist, 31 years old). The designer who was involved in the design of the Green Hill team, said

> The former tobacco company blocked the city road plan, but it was difficult to demolish it, so we chose to cut the facade of the former tobacco company and transform it into a multifunctional urban complex that combines municipal transportation, parkland and public services. (Designer, 51 years old)

Fig. 12.1. Cranes at Yangpu Port, Hainan, China. *Source:* ID 215658159 © Yongnian Gui | Dreamstime.com.

Green development addresses the issue of harmony between humans and nature. It is a realm pursued by the Chinese. Green water, green mountains and beautiful countryside have always been the aspiration. A beautiful environment and safe food are the expectations of the present generation, and sustainable development is the responsibility of future generations. This is also an important embodiment of the new development concept of ecological harmony.

This project seems to be a good example of maximising the way in which the rivers should be returned to citizens and providing citizens with social space and greens. Founded in 1913, Yangshupu Power Plant was the first thermal power plant in the Far East and it is now the Yangshupu Power Plant Relic Park, its design has won the Rosa Barba Audience Prize Winner in the International Biennial of Landscape Architecture of Barcelona in 2021; the nearly 100-year-old Shanghai Soap Factory has turned into a soap dream space where the citizens can feel the historical context of the soap factory and experience the soap making process in this unique space. Wing On Storehouse was converted into a WorldSkills Museum.

> These big buildings used to be rented out. I know they may be full of stories as Wing On Company was founded more than one hundred years ago, but this house is incompatible with the riverside. Now it is a museum and World Skills Competition will be celebrated here in 2026. I'd like to participate in it. (Technical school student, 20 years old)

Shanghai's riverside is where an inch of land is worth an inch of gold. With an area of nearly 2 square kilometres, which some estimate to have a market value of over 100 billion yuan, however, Shanghai use it to build parks and green spaces for citizens and visitors to walk and rest. This is precisely the practice of the important concept of people's city. What Shanghai wants to build is a city of socialism with Chinese characteristics, not a replica of foreign cities.

> I live in the neighbourhood and I know how expensive it is and how hard it is to pay the mortgage every month. I can't believe that the government has built such a large area of landscaped lines and green spaces. My family and I go for a walk here every night. The children are also very happy. (Housewife, 38 years old)

All of the above cases are old buildings rejuvenated in urban planning, and most of them are non-profit buildings and venues to serve the lives of citizens. Yangpu Riverside has gradually transformed from an industrial coastline dominated by factories and warehouses to an ecological coastline and landscape full of parks and green spaces. 'People's city built by the People, People's city for the People' is what President Xi Jinping said about Shanghai's urban development during his visit to Yangpu Binjiang in November 2019. Building a city of the people is a reflection of the people-centred ideology in urban work.

Gubei Civic Center Upgrades Its Service

The Gubei community is the first international community in China and a good example for investigating the construction of an international community. In 1986, the State Council determined that Gubei's new district would be mainly inhabited by overseas people, foreign experts, Hong Kong, Macao and Taiwan compatriots, etc. Now as a large-scale high-standard international community in Shanghai, there lives a total of 32,000 residents and 51% of the residents are from more than 50 countries and regions. It is known as the 'Little United Nations'. Some foreign residents may not understand Chinese well. How to help the foreigners participate in the community and solve their problems by appropriate means? How to encourage more people to participate in local community governance? The local government sets up a civic centre with multiple functions.

> My family and I came to live in Shanghai 20 years ago, I'm Dutch and we didn't speak Chinese very well when we arrived, but there were many young Chinese volunteers who helped us and many restaurants where you can even order in English. There are also a lot of neighbours from other countries here and I feel very international. I really like the atmosphere here. (Financial practitioner, 55 years old)

Gubei Civic Center is a comprehensive service platform which aims at gathering wisdom and strength from the people and offering convenience with four parts: business, service, cultural integration and co-governance. In the centre, there are catering, medical, legal and other professional service offices, as well as a foreign personnel service place. In 2020, the business office upgraded with five new sites for overseas people, foreign specialists, immigrants, bilingual tax payments and one net service. It also provides Chinese and foreign cultural exchange projects such as libraries, cultural salons, theatres, etc. The centre provides residents with colourful cultural services every month, so that residents living in Gubei can feel the warmth of home. When discussing matters, representatives from home and abroad share the same opportunities and rights to express their ideas and to participate in governance. 'I'm Spanish and I'm retired, but I still want to continue living here and don't want to go back to my country. Because it makes me feel warm, there are often rich activities and the food is delicious' (Engineer, 68 years old).

The construction of the Gubei International Community Citizen Center is a good research sample and an effective practice of implementing the new development concept. We can observe some notable features, such as: innovation, based on advanced technology; informatisation, which is firmly promoted as a basic project of innovative community governance; coordination, which unites many members for more precise community governance and green development, which let the concept of 'green, low-carbon and environmental protection' be deeply rooted in the hearts of the people and sharing. The centre integrates more extensive social resources with the government departments and also helps form a positive community public spirit. In this way, the community residents' autonomy develops in an orderly manner.

The questionnaire was designed to measure the satisfaction of residents and visitors to Yangpu Binjiang and Gubei New District, including service, environment, traffic and culture. The satisfaction rate was 94.5%, and the main reasons for dissatisfaction were the high cost of living and the high price of housing.

Values of New Development Concept for the International Community

China is a deep participant and an important contributor to global development, and the development problems it faces are global. China's new development concept is a summary of China's development experience and a reflection of its general problems. In response to the current global fatigue of an overall slowdown in world economic growth and the challenge of economic growth deviating from the goal of human development, the five development concepts of innovation, coordination, green, openness and sharing, in concert, can enlighten the world to understand and solve specific development challenges from a new perspective, and have given a systematic answer full of practical value in multiple dimensions (Zhi, 2020).

China's new development philosophy is essentially based on its judgement of the international political situation and the international economic situation, and is closely linked to and organically integrated with the building of a community of common destiny (Han, 2018). Among the five elements of the new development concept, open development is directly related to economic relations with other countries; shared development means the principle of mutually beneficial international economic and trade relations; green development confirms the direction of the international community's efforts to promote sustainable development; and innovative development transcends the spell of natural resources and strikes at the fundamental issue of development dynamics and has universal significance. Renewal of Yangpu Industrial Area and Innovation of Gubei Civic Center are two good examples of urban planning, reflecting the new development concept of green development and people-centeredness, as well as the eclecticism and friendliness of Shanghai as an international metropolis to foreigners. Many cities in the world are now facing problems in the development process, and the Shanghai case also brings hope for its solution, especially Shanghai provides a feasible reference sample regarding the renovation of old buildings, ecological issues and internationalisation.

References

Han, L. (2018). China's new development concept and international rule leadership. *Journal of Social Sciences of Jilin University*, *58*(6), 46–59.

Xu, H. (2015). The Rebirth of "Industrial Rust Belt": A case study of the Waterfront Region in Shanghai Yangpu District. *Huazhogn Arquitecture*, *33*(10), 99–102.

Zhi, J. (2020). The world value of China's new development concept in the new era. *Social Science Front*, *2020*(1), 247–253.

Chapter 13

Pakistan and Trans-regional Connectivity: Infrastructure for Regional Transformation

Murad Ali

Department of Political Science, University of Malakand, Pakistan

This chapter examines the role of new infrastructure initiatives in regional connectivity, and how enhanced regional connectivity can result in increased investment, trade and cross-border movement of people, goods and services. To this end, the chapter first briefly highlights the geographical significance of Pakistan for regional connectivity. It is followed by a discussion of new infrastructure initiatives and their role in achieving the dream of regional connectivity and bringing socio-economic benefits to the region.

Pakistan: A Bridge Between South Asia and Central Asia

As shown in Fig. 13.1, Pakistan is geographically situated at the converging pivot of three regions: South Asia, Central Asia and the Middle East. The country's prized geographical location has enabled Pakistan to play a key role in events of global significance such as the Cold War and recently in the US-led 'war on terror'. Due to its strategically vital position, Pakistan is poised to play a critical role in the successful implementation of President Xi's signature foreign economic plan: the Belt and Road Initiative (BRI). Under the BRI umbrella, Beijing is investing over 62 billion USD in the energy and transport infrastructure in Pakistan under the China–Pakistan Economic Corridor (CPEC). With the upgradation of infrastructure, Pakistan expects to emerge as a hub for regional trade and investments. Hence, on account of its geography as well as demography, being the 5th most populous country in the world, Pakistan has emerged as one of the largest BRI beneficiaries (Fig. 13.2).

Exploring Hope: Case Studies of Innovation, Change and Development in the Global South, 85–90

Published under exclusive licence by Emerald Publishing Limited
doi:10.1108/978-1-83549-736-420241016

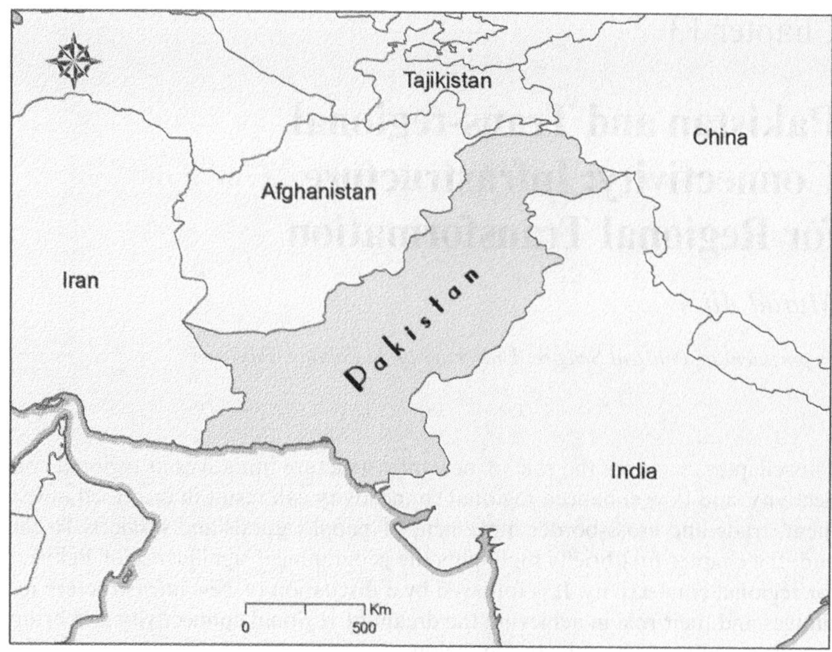

Fig. 13.1. Geographical Map of Pakistan. *Source*: Own elaboration.

Fig. 13.2. Settlement, Karakoram Highway, Highest International Highway, Pakistan. *Source*: ID 122622736 © Mortenhuebbe | Dreamstime.com.

CPEC and Trans-regional Connectivity

There is significant potential to connect energy-rich Central Asian states with heavily populated energy-starved South Asian countries. In various policy documents, Pakistan has underlined to utilise the country's geography as a connector in the region. In its long-term plan, Pakistan Vision 2025, the government identified regional connectivity as a key element. The policy document specifically mentioned that CPEC plays a vital role in achieving the potential of regional connectivity and trade with member states of the Central Asia Regional Economic Cooperation (CAREC, including Afghanistan, Azerbaijan, China, Georgia, Kazakhstan, Kyrgyz Republic, Mongolia, Pakistan, Tajikistan Turkmenistan and Uzbekistan) and the Economic Cooperation Organization (ECO, including Afghanistan, Azerbaijan, Iran, Kazakhstan, Kyrgyzstan, Pakistan, Tajikistan, Turkey, Turkmenistan and Uzbekistan) besides South Asian countries. Similarly, Pakistan's first-ever National Security Policy 2022–2026 has stated that Pakistan's location offers a unique opportunity to make the country 'a hub for connecting important economic and resource-rich regions' (Government of Pakistan, 2022a, p. 35). The same policy document asserts that Pakistan's geo-economic pivot is focused on enhancing trade and economic ties through connectivity that links Central Asia to Pakistan's warm waters. Under its 'Vision Central Asia', Pakistan has long desired to deepen and expand its ties with the region in multiple domains including political, cultural, trade, energy and connectivity, security and defence and people-to-people connections. 'Pakistan offers shortest land route to CARs (Central Asian Republics) for access to the Arabian Sea for their trade; 2600 km via Afghanistan as compared to Iran (4500 km) or Turkey (5000 km)' (Younus, 2021, p. 6). To this end, the government has stated that based on its cherished geo-strategic locale Pakistan certainly 'offers the most effective, economical and viable transit routes throughout the seasons to the land locked Central Asian countries and other neighbouring states while providing them a very convenient trade corridor' (Government of Pakistan, 2022b, p. 241).

With the enlargement of CPEC beyond Pakistan, Afghanistan and the region would certainly gain from the initiative. With the expansion of CPEC, landlocked Central Asian countries would diversify their trade routes. Central Asia is the largest landlocked area of the world which has suffered from poor access to global markets. Being landlocked, almost every sphere of life including foreign policy, national security, and economy is affected by their location. According to Idan (2018), the typical GDP of landlocked economies achieves only 57% of their maritime neighbours. The author explains that in contrast to maritime countries, landlocked nations incur an additional 10% on their exports and imports, which makes them less competitive in the global trade markets. The combination of geographic location, trade and economic growth explains the cost of being landlocked. Due to these factors, such non-coastal countries experience about 30% impediment vis-à-vis their maritime counterparts. These geographical shortcomings can be effectively offset if shorter and cheaper alternative routes like CPEC are developed.

In its comprehensive study titled 'Belt and Road Economics: Opportunities and Risks of Transport Corridors', the World Bank has estimated that through enhanced inter-regional connectivity, integration, trade and growth, 'at the global level, BRI-related investments could lift 7.6 million from extreme poverty [less than 1.90 USD a day]... 4.3 million in Belt and Road corridor economies and 3.3 million in non-Belt and Road countries' (World Bank, 2019, p. 59). The same report asserts that the 'largest spatial impacts from BRI investments are likely to be in Central Asia (including Kazakhstan, the Kyrgyz Republic and Tajikistan), South Asia (Pakistan)' (World Bank, 2019, p. 89). Reduction in transport cost, increased internal mobility of people, goods and services and enhanced connectivity between the more isolated rural areas and the better connected urban and commercial centres within these countries as well as among these countries would result in a tremendous economic turnaround in the region and beyond. For instance, among all the BRI economies, countries such as 'Pakistan and the Kyrgyz Republic are expected to experience the largest gains in real income, respectively 10.5 and 10.4 percent higher than the baseline' (World Bank, 2019, p. 57), as these countries will have improved access to national and international markets. Overall, there are significant prospects to connect Central Asian states having vast energy reserves with South Asian countries looking eagerly for energy resources to fulfil the demands of their expanding economies and growing population.

Non-CPEC Initiatives for Regional Connectivity

In addition to infrastructure projects under the CPEC framework, Pakistan has completed several infrastructural projects (construction of roads) to enhance its connectivity with Afghanistan and beyond. These include the Peshawar-Torkham road, Torkham-Jalalabad road, the D.I. Khan/South Waziristan-Angoor Adda road and North Waziristan-Ghulam Khan road connecting to Paktika and Khost in Afghanistan. Also, Pakistan has started work on the construction of Khyber Pass Economic Corridor (KPEC). Known as the Peshawar-Kabul expressway which is considered the Gateway to Central Asia, it is a 4-lane, 'access controlled, 281 Km long stretch of the motorway connecting Peshawar, the capital city of Khyber-Pakhtunkhwa (KP) Province in Pakistan with Kabul, the Capital city of Afghanistan' (National Highway Authority, 2018, p. 11). This infrastructure project is expected to create up to 100,000 new jobs and over 70 million people, trade between Pakistan and the Central Asian Republics (CARs) is minimal with an expected annual potential of 1.5 billion USD (KPEC, 2022). Thus, in addition to several projects under the CPEC initiative, Pakistan has been investing in connectivity projects to further increase its trade and investment with the Central Asian economies.

Projects Under the Framework of the CAREC

As discussed earlier, in all its policy plans, Pakistan has given substantial importance to the idea of increased connectivity with Central Asian countries. After the country joined the CAREC Program in 2010, Pakistan has pursued this policy to overcome barriers to growth and to play a role and integrate Central Asian countries into global markets. As per its long-term plan, 'CAREC 2030 envisages focus on five operational clusters going forward: (i) economic and financial stability; (ii) trade, tourism, and economic corridors; (iii) infrastructure and economic connectivity; (iv) agriculture and water; and (v) human development' (Asian Development Bank, 2017, p. iii).

In line with these goals, CAREC has invested in infrastructure projects in Pakistan to upgrade its national road corridors, which serve as routes to the Middle East and South Asia for the country's northern neighbours. In 2021, about US$1.74 billion was invested in Pakistan via CAREC projects. The main objectives are to establish a modern transport and energy infrastructure that will allow the region to fully benefit from its vast physical and human resources. In the long run, these corridors will eventually be part of a streamlined land transport network stretching from Azerbaijan, in the west, to the People's Republic of China in the east, and north to Kazakhstan and beyond.

Another significant infrastructure project to which three neighbouring countries, Pakistan, Uzbekistan, and Afghanistan, have agreed upon, is the 600-km long US$5 billion (estimated cost) Trans-Afghan Railway Line. In a high-level trilateral meeting held in 2022, these three countries in Tashkent agreed to a roadmap for the construction of a 600-km-long rail project connecting Pakistan, Uzbekistan and Afghanistan (Mazar-i-Sharif-Kabul-Peshawar railroad). 'This Trans-Afghan Railway project is the most economical and shortest route connecting Central Asia with Pakistani ports of Karachi, Gwadar, and Qasim', stated by Muhammad Azfar Ahsan, Minister of State and Chairman of Board of Investment (BOI) while speaking at the Trilateral Working Meeting in Uzbek city of Termez. He underscored that its geography makes Pakistan the shortest, most economical, and easiest land route for Central Asia to access the Arabian Sea. It must be noted that Afghanistan's first railroad, the ADB-funded Hairatan to Mazar-e-Sharif Railway Project connecting Afghanistan with Uzbekistan's southern city of Termez was also completed under the CAREC program. As per the ADB, 'more than 7 million people have benefited from the new railway through jobs and increased trade. This has included freight operators, traders, businesses, and local communities served by the railway' (Asian Development Bank, 2014, p. 7).

Conclusions

On account of Pakistan's geographical position, the country can play a vital role to connect South Asia with Central Asia. There is unprecedented optimism regarding how the envisaged infrastructure projects under the CPEC as well as projects implemented under the CAREC program and those initiatives funded by Pakistan can help in the transformation of the region. In Pakistan, policymakers have labelled these economic corridors as 'game-changer' and 'fate-changer' for the region in terms of industrialisation, jobs' creation and up gradation of infrastructure. Once completed, these infrastructure initiatives can enable the region to usher in a new era of increased connectivity, trade and investments, creating a win-win situation for all actors.

References

Asian Development Bank. (2014). *Together we deliver: 10 stories from ADB-supported projects with clear development impacts*. Asian Development Bank. http://hdl.handle.net/11540/60

Asian Development Bank. (2017). *CAREC 2030: Connecting the region for shared and sustainable development*. Asian Development Bank. http://dx.doi.org/10.22617/TCS179132-2

Government of Pakistan. (2022a). *National Security Policy of Pakistan: 2022–2026*. National Security Division.

Government of Pakistan. (2022b). *Pakistan Economic Survey 2021-22*. Ministry of Finance.

Idan, A. (2018, May 1). *China's Belt and Road Initiative: Relieving Landlocked Central Asia*. The Central Asia-Caucasus Analyst. Retrieved June 15, 2022, from https://www.cacianalyst.org/publications/analytical-articles/item/13510-chinas-belt-and-road-initiative-relieving-landlocked-central-asia.html

KPEC. (2022). *Khyber Pass Economic Corridor (KPEC): About*. Retrieved June 15, 2022, from https://kpec.org.pk/Home/about

National Highway Authority. (2018). *Khyber Pass Economic Corridor Project: Environmental and Social Impact Assessment for Peshawar-Torkham Expressway* (Component I). National Highway Authority (NHA).

The World Factbook. (2022). *Pakistan – Details*. Retrieved October 20, 2022, from https://www.cia.gov/the-world-factbook/countries/pakistan/map

World Bank. (2019). *BELT AND ROAD ECONOMICS: Opportunities and Risks of Transport Corridors*. World Bank.

Younus, M. (2021). *Potential of Preferential Trade Agreement (PTA) between Pakistan and Afghanistan*. Trade Development Authority of Pakistan (TDAP).

Part 3

Revitalising the Economy with a Sustainable Approach

Introduction

Marcelo Sili

CONICET, Universidad Nacional del Sur, Argentina

International experiences show very clearly that there are success factors for economic and productive development. Thus, much of the literature reinforces the idea that it is necessary to promote policies that support the development of small and medium-sized enterprises (SMEs), which are key drivers of job creation and economic growth. This can be done through access to finance, training and mentorship programs, as well as policies that promote the participation of SMEs in value chains and international trade. In addition, it is necessary to promote innovation and technology transfer, which can help to create new industries, increase productivity and reduce environmental impact. This can be done through the establishment of research and development centres, the promotion of public–private partnerships, and policies that support the commercialisation of innovation. International experience also shows that in order to ensure economic development, it is necessary to promote social inclusion, which means ensuring that economic growth benefits all sectors of society. This can be achieved through policies and programs that promote access to education, healthcare and social protection, as well as policies that promote gender equality, youth employment and the participation of marginalised communities in economic decision-making. In recent decades, international literature as well as development and cooperation agencies has also placed emphasis on the care and protection of the environment. Thus, it is argued that another key challenge in dynamising the economy with a sustainable approach is to ensure that economic growth is environmentally responsible. This means promoting the transition to a low-carbon, resource-efficient and resilient economy. This can be achieved through policies and programs that promote renewable energy, energy efficiency, sustainable transport and the circular economy.

On balance, the international literature concludes that dynamising the economy in countries of the Global South with a sustainable approach is a complex and multifaceted task. It requires policies and programs that promote economic growth, job creation and investment, while also ensuring that this growth is socially and environmentally responsible. By promoting innovation, entrepreneurship and social and environmental sustainability, it is possible to create a more prosperous and equitable future for all.

Exploring Hope: Case Studies of Innovation, Change and Development in the Global South, 93–98

doi:10.1108/978-1-83549-736-420241017

However, beyond these conditions, the reality of the countries of the Global South is substantially different, as there are key elements that affect their development, such as cultural factors, approaches or simply the availability of resources. In view of this, it is necessary to change the way in which economic and productive problems are thought of and what kind of solutions are needed, without falling into old dichotomous views or approaches, as has tended to be the case. In fact, many countries of the Global South have constructed in the last century, perhaps as a product of the economic matrix and the history of dependency, grand images and discourses on economic and productive development which, by resorting to rigid oppositions and sometimes over-ideologised formulas, have not helped them to overcome situations of backwardness, poverty and marginality, but have given rise to contradictory and generally sterile dynamics, and the consequent squandering of resources and time. One of these images, much more orthodox, emphasises the production of goods and services at any price, without social or environmental limitations, with the aim of generating the resources necessary to escape poverty, following the guidelines and models of developed countries. Another image points to a revaluation of the local, an idyllic version, based on the discourse of living with what is ours, tied to the conditions of each town and country.

Despite the pre-eminence of this dichotomous view of economic and productive development, there are processes of change in the countries of the Global South that give hope for new paths of economic and productive development. Three factors should be highlighted.

- First, there is a process of technological change that is revolutionising communications, mobility and production systems and clearly affecting the economies of the Global South, generating new opportunities (Sili, 2018).
- Secondly, there is a profound change in the nature–society relationship, driven above all by increased awareness of the environmental problems generated by unsustainable production logics.
- Finally, there are new forms of consumption and changes in consumer preferences, which stimulate the production of new products under more sustainable logics, which becomes an immense opportunity for the countries of the Global South.

These three major trends are driving the generation of initiatives that could reconfigure the dominant productive models, giving rise to new forms of production, employment generation and economic development. The main idea of this part is to show, through different experiences and reflections in the Global South, how these three major dynamics of global change could be harnessed to break out of this dichotomous approach and generate processes of economic and productive development, with sustainability, capable of contributing to overcoming situations of backwardness, poverty and marginality. Our hypothesis is that it is possible to recognise in the countries of the Global South, authentic processes of innovation, understood in a broad sense. These processes include the generation of new products, but also new processes, services or forms of management, and creative solutions to the problems faced by societies. In this part, we present several innovative processes that support this hypothesis.

An example of a productive and organisational innovation process is the Alliance for Sustainable and Holistic Agriculture in India. This experience shows numerous groups are increasingly engaging in a number of grassroots activities and social innovations that extract agriculture from the exploitative calculation of productivity and economic growth and embed it into a post-growth imaginary of culturally rich practices and relationships of care. This initiative shows that in order to consolidate virtuous development dynamics in rural areas, it is necessary to maintain a holistic view of productive processes, linking them to the ethical, cultural and environmental conditions of the people and their places. Thus, this experience shows that economic and productive development should not only be an opportunity to generate income, but also an opportunity for human development, for personal and collective fulfilment. When production is linked to and values the social and cultural heritage of a society, it guarantees coherence and sustainability in long-term economic growth, because growth is organic to a society or human group.

The case of the Brazilian Cerrado is also an innovative experience. It involves the development of bio-economic activities and a clear contribution to reducing deforestation and building more sustainable environmental scenarios. Brazil's experience shows that for the countries of the Global South, with its huge biomass availability, the bioeconomy represents an opportunity to overcome the historic opposition between agricultural and industrial development strategies and to achieve a more balanced territorial development. The bioeconomy emerges as a new set of activities based on the use of biological resources. It mainly rests on three pillars: the intensive and diverse use of products of biological origin (biomass); the intensive use of innovative knowledge; and the development of a wide range of new products derived from these biological resources. The promotion and consolidation of the bioeconomy, the generation of new products and the enrichment of value chains are underpinned by the region's socio-biodiversity, which, as the authors state, represents the hope for the future of the region of changing the Cerrado's fate for the better in socially inclusive ways through genuine sustainable development.

Another innovative experience with the capacity to transform the economic and productive dynamics of a territory is the emergence of agroecology as a sustainable and inclusive mode of production, very different from the agroexport model that has historically organised the economy and territories of many countries in the Global South. The experience of agroecology in Argentina shows how productive economic development can be sustained by reducing conflicts and environmental problems, while at the same time sustaining the population structure of rural areas and generating healthier food that is in greater demand in global markets.

A good lesson learned about economic and productive development, and the need to improve people's quality of life, is the need to think about development from a perspective of encounter, of collective action among many actors, and not only from an individual perspective. The productive experiences of Bolivia and Mexico allow us to think that economic and productive development alternatives are not only the result of individual action in a world of perfect market competition, but can also be the result of collective action where multiple actors converge in the construction of opportunities, which necessarily require shared action. The experiences of joint production and commercialisation of Quinoa, in close relationship with globalised markets, is a good experience that shows how it is possible to build solutions for economic and productive development in marginal areas. In the same way, the construction of cooperative spaces such as Yomol A'Tel in Mexico shows how, in a context of strong economic competitiveness, communities can build productive alternatives that respect their roots and their relationship with nature.

Innovation is also present in the resolution of historical problems of insertion in global value chains. Thus, the experience of palm production in Indonesia and its international commercialisation is extremely useful to see how innovative mechanisms can overcome the duality between global and local markets, or between large enterprises and small local companies, observing that more appropriate governance mechanisms can be found or established that respect differences and scales of production, within a framework of environmental sustainability.

Other experiences show that innovation processes, technological change and training, are clearly adapted to local conditions and are undoubtedly necessary for production and productivity improvements to take place. The experience of Sri Lankan banana producers shows how innovation processes built with producers, and centred on their cultural realities and needs, are a powerful driver of change, and thus capable of generating greater growth and productive development.

Beyond emerging innovative initiatives and processes, economic and productive development requires infrastructure, equipment, logistics and skilled human resources, i.e. production factors without which it is not possible to think about the valorisation of natural resources, industrial transformation or the provision of quality services. Developed countries have been able to solve these problems through dense networks of infrastructures and facilities in their territories, but this has not been possible in the countries of the Global South, which continue to suffer from a lack of them. However, some experiences show how it is possible to generate strategies for the concentration of infrastructure, facilities and quality services in some territories, creating special economic zones or poles of greater competitiveness capable of generating development dynamics in the medium and long term. These good experiences also highlight the need to consolidate political and administrative governance mechanisms to ensure the proper functioning of these zones and especially to guarantee that these experiences can generate a greater spillover effect on the rest of the territories and do not remain productive enclaves for foreign companies that only use these zones or special territories as a simple productive platform.

It is important to understand that all these initiatives that are being generated in the countries of the Global South, generating new products, management innovation and the creation of infrastructures, are being supported by multiple actors based on new expectations and visions of development, driven by a growing concern for the environment, new ways of relating to nature, new consumption patterns and the search for production and employment opportunities. These initiatives feed off each other and generate systemic loops, which in many cases trigger virtuous processes of varying scale and complexity (Sili, 2019). A central element that we are interested in highlighting is that these innovation processes do not remain as niche elements, but are scaled up and integrated into the current model of production and territorial organisation and modify it over time, strongly influencing the organisation of the economy and territories (Geels, 2002; Horlings & Marsden, 2014; Sili, 2005). In this way, these initiatives should be seen, in short, as innovative processes that would allow the creation of other logics of development of the territories (Santhanam-Martin et al., 2015), more diversified, with more innovative processes of valorisation of socio-biocultural resources, with more respect for diversity and environmental sustainability and with a strong capacity for local anchoring of income and generation of new employment opportunities.

The review of the experiences that we have recovered allows us to draw two clear lessons that should be taken into account in order to find more promising paths for productive development. The first lesson is that the cycles of nature and the temporal rhythms of societies must be respected. Building a transition towards more sustainable production models requires time, which is different for the different social groups that make up a region or a country. It is necessary to move away from the hegemonic temporal logic, on which the current economy is built, and make room for more diverse temporal logics, especially the one that governs natural processes, because without respect for nature's time, there is no possibility of sustainability. This is even more valid in societies that are strongly linked to the production of goods derived from natural resources, where nature imposes rhythms that the market ignores.

The second lesson is that we must keep a broad perspective on innovation, understood as a continuous improvement of existing production techniques, but more than anything else as a permanent process of adaptation to the new global realities in continuous evolution. In this way, innovation is not only the invention of a product, but the construction of solutions to the problems of our societies, or the transformation of models instituted under a logic of dependence, towards models that are more sovereign and more respectful of the societies of the Global South.

References

Geels, F. W. (2002). Technological transitions as evolutionary reconfiguration processes: A multi-level perspective and a case-study. *Research Policy*, *31*(8–9), 1257–1274. https://doi.org/10.1016/S0048-7333(02)00062-8

Horlings, L., & Marsden, T. (2014). Exploring the "New Rural Paradigm" in Europe: Eco-economic strategies as a counterforce to the global competitiveness agenda. *European Urban and Regional Studies*, *21*(1), 4–20. https://doi.org/10.1177/0969776412441934

Santhanam-Martin, M., Ayre, M., & Nettle, R. (2015). Community sustainability and agricultural landscape change: Insights into the durability and vulnerability of the productivist regime. *Sustainability Science*, *10*(2), 207–217. https://doi.org/10.1007/s11625-014-0268-2

Sili, M. (2005). *La Argentina Rural. De la crisis de la modernización agraria a la construcción de un nuevo paradigma de desarrollo de los territorios rurales. (INTA)*. INTA.

Sili, M. (2018). Gobernanza territorial. Problemáticas y desafíos de la planificación y la gestión territorial en el contexto de la globalización. (M. Sili, Ed.) (Perspectiv). Universitá del Salento. https://doi.org/10.1285/i26113775n2

Sili, M. (2019). La migración de la ciudad a las zonas rurales en Argentina. Una caracterización basada en estudios de [Migration from the City to Rural Areas in Argentina. A characterization based on Case Studies]. *Población & Sociedad*, *26*(1), 90–119. https://doi.org/10.19137/pys-2019-260105

Chapter 14

A Toolkit for Hope (ASHA): Farmers' Sovereignty and Holistic Agriculture in India

Poonam Pandey[a] *and Kavitha Kuruganti*[b]

[a]*Post-Growth Innovation Lab, University of Vigo, Spain*
[b]*Alliance for Sustainable and Holistic Agriculture, India*

The sustainability of agri-food systems is a major concern worldwide in relation to the changing climate, resource depletion and biodiversity loss (FAO, 2018). Civil Society Organisations (CSO) are often seen in polar opposition to the state-corporate coalition when it comes to concerns related to ownership of resources such as land and seeds (Peschard & Randeria, 2020). There is a lot of growing scholarship on the ways in which civil society groups and networks, especially in the global south, engage in long, confrontational, legal battles with corporate entities (Peschard & Randeria, 2020; Silva Garzón & Gutiérrez Escobar, 2020). However, within this scholarship and the activist circles, there is a growing concern that legal battles and confrontational protests are not enough to engage with the skewed power dynamics in favour of big corporations and neo-liberal policies (Pottinger, 2017; Silva Garzón & Gutiérrez Escobar, 2020). As a result, CSO groups are increasingly engaging in a number of grassroots activities and social innovations that extract agriculture from the exploitative calculation of productivity and economic growth and embed it into a post-growth imaginary of culturally rich practices and relationships of care (McGreevy et al., 2022; Puig de la Bellacasa, 2015). In this chapter, we will discuss the vision of holistic and sustainable agriculture developed and materialised through the network – Alliance for Sustainable and Holistic Agriculture (ASHA). ASHA is a large, volunteer-driven informal network of civil society groups, farmers and like-minded individuals that are concerned about the ongoing crisis in agriculture, the plight of farmers, the destruction of biodiversity and environment and the corporate takeover of agriculture enabled by neo-liberal policies. Based in India, the network came into being in 2010 to collectively build a platform to engage with these pressing

Exploring Hope: Case Studies of Innovation, Change and Development in the Global South, 99–103

doi:10.1108/978-1-83549-736-420241018

concerns. In this chapter, we will discuss three innovative ways – *Kisan Swaraj Yatra* (Farmers' Sovereignty March), *Kisan Swaraj Niti* (Policy for Farmers' Sovereignty) and *Beej Utsav* (Seed Festivals) – through which ASHA is co-crafting and mobilising the vision of a sustainable and holistic agricultural future.

Mobilising for Farmers' Sovereignty: Kisan Swaraj Yatra (Farmers' Sovereignty March)

On 2 October 2010, on the birth anniversary of Mahatma Gandhi, a *Kisan Swaraj Yatra* was initiated from *Sabarmati Ashram* in Gujarat. Sabarmati Ashram (also known as *Satyagraha* Ashram) was established by Mahatma Gandhi as his workplace. Satyagraha means 'staying firm and insisting in support of truth in a peaceful non-violent manner'. The Ashram has a lot of ideological significance for social movements and people interested in non-violent dissent and peaceful mobilisation. The initiation of the Kisan Swaraj Yatra from Sabarmati at Gandhi's birth anniversary was symbolic of the commitment of the movement towards Gandhian ideals of Swaraj and Satyagraha. Where Swaraj insists on farmers' autonomy and sovereignty in decisions related to agriculture, Satyagraha is a non-violent movement that registers peaceful dissent towards the existing policies and insists on the truth of the people (here farmers and workers allied to agriculture) to be actualised through policies. The *Yatra* travelled through 20 states and 100s of places in India for 70 days (till December 2010) to culminate in Raj Ghat, a memorial dedicated to Gandhi.

The aim of the march was three-fold. First, the march aimed at demonstrating to the Indian Government that a large number of rural and urban people are concerned about the ongoing crisis in agriculture that has led to indebtedness and suicides of farmers, degradation of the environment and health issues for the consumers. Through the peaceful procession, ASHA wanted to draw the attention of the politicians and policy-makers to focus on farmer- and environment-friendly policies rather than a pro-corporatist agenda. Second, the procession aimed at mobilising like-minded individuals and groups by providing them a platform to join their voices and articulate their concerns. Third, the procession provided the opportunity for a diversity of people to discuss and debate the vision of ASHA on a 'new path for agriculture' that eventually materialised into the four-pillared policy proposal known as the *Kisan Swaraj Niti* (Policy for Farmers' Sovereignty).

Co-Creating the Vision for the Future of Agriculture: *Kisan Swaraj Niti* for Sustainable and Holistic Agriculture

The *Kisan Swaraj Niti* (Policy for Farmers' Sovereignty) emerged as one of the outcomes of 70 days of Kisan Swaraj March and multiple deliberations with farmers, consumers and people allied to agriculture. The policy has four pillars that include (1) income security for farmers; (2) ecological sustainability of agriculture; (3) people's control over resources like land, forests, water and seed; and (4) access to safe, healthy, sufficient food for all (Fig. 14.1).

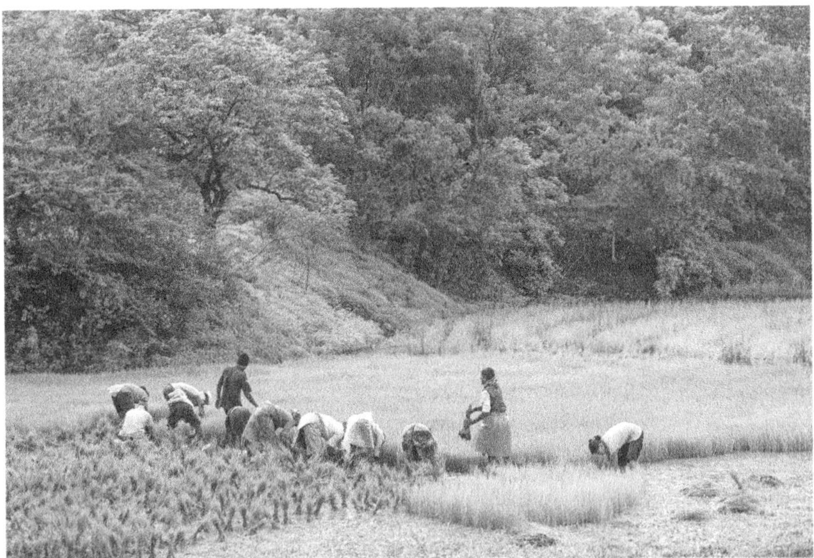

Fig. 14.1. Farmers Working in the Field. *Source*: DNI 223358881 © Harshal Sathe | Dreamstime.com.

A holistic vision of agriculture requires that different networks of relations that make agriculture possible are respected and nurtured. These include, to name a few, the relationships between (1) seeds and their environment (i.e. soil, microbes, animals and humans), (2) food and nutrition (i.e. mechanisms of growing, processing, cooking, consuming and preserving food) and (3) farmer and consumer. In order to think about sustainability, it is crucial that consumers are re-connected to the materiality and tangibility of their food systems. *Kisan Swaraj* literally translates into farmers' autonomy. Autonomy for farmers means not just the freedom but also the space and capability to make their own decisions. This means the choice to make decisions on what to grow, when to grow, how to grow and where to market their produce. To enable Kisan Swaraj, policymaking has to ensure that different alternative visions of agriculture (be it high-tech or low-tech) receive a symmetrical treatment from the government and have equal opportunities to flourish and find their space in the market. In ASHA's vision, the path of sustainable and holistic agriculture can only be imagined if the farmers have the freedom to use resources, knowledge and skills as per their own wisdom (Fig. 14.2).

Bringing Culture Back to Agriculture: *Beej Utsav* (Seed Festivals) and Community Engagement

From a civilisational point of view, agriculture is seen as a worldview where human life is organised around the cultivation of crops. In this imaginary, nature is a life-giving force and agriculture and human life need to be harmonised with the rhythms of nature so much so that work and leisure are tied to the cycles

Fig. 14.2. Farmers Are Cultivating Paddy in Their Own Ground in India.
Source: DNI 186756908 © Arbind Ekka | Dreamstime.com.

of nature (Tyagi & Kumar, 2020). In this set-up seeds, technology (all agricultural equipment), animals, soil (and its microfauna) and humans are all relationally and ritualistically tied to experience and perform agriculture. Agricultural festivals, which are still celebrated in different parts of India, are the ritualistic celebration of how the relational bringing together of technology, environment (soil, rain), humans and more than humans (microbes and animals) make agriculture possible. Tapping on relational and ritualistic aspects of agricultural festivals, ASHA organises *Beej Utsavs* (seed festivals) which attempt to revive the fast-disappearing relationship between different actors that collectively constitute agriculture. For example, the relationship between food producers, biodiversity and consumers.

Though Beej Utsavs have seeded as a central component, all its relational dimensions (and the politics that hides these relations) are beautifully demonstrated and experienced. For example, ASHA organised multiple seed festivals that focused, among other seeds, on millets. There are numerous varieties of millets that were and still are traditionally grown in India. Millets is one of the most sustainable solutions for the problem of food and nutritional security in the face of resource depletion and climate change. However, within the dominant monocropping, resource-intensive paradigm that centres around wheat and rice, millets rarely find any space. The seed festival hosted organisations from different parts of India that have developed a rich diversity of organic seeds of different kinds of millets. The festival had people who talked about recipes of how to consume and preserve different food items made from millets and people who sang songs and told stories about the cultural significance of these grains. The seed festivals become sites where consumers come in direct contact with bio-diversity and the producers and conservers of such biodiversity. Here, the consumers simultaneously learn about the expertise and skills of the producers as well as the hardships and challenges they face in producing and preserving nutrition for the consumers. The relational encounter between the food producers, consumers, the ritual of food making, consuming and preserving becomes a site where the politics of agri-food system and how it affects producers, consumers and the environment become apparent.

Conclusions

Rather than focusing on the confrontational aspects of CSOs, in this chapter, we looked at the creative ways ASHA employs to tap into civilisational and moral aspects of agriculture to build alliance, solidarity and trust among different actors concerned with sustainable agri-food systems. We focused on three features – ASHA's vision and *Kisan Swaraj Niti* (Policy for Farmers' Sovereignty), *Kisan Swaraj Yatras* (Farmer Sovereignty March) and *Beej Utsav* (Seed Festivals) to demonstrate the creative power of CSO networks. We observed that ASHA engages with a vision of agriculture that is not disconnected, but rather more situated within the contemporary politics of agri-food systems. Laced by the feminist care ethics that nurture relationality, subjectivity and narrative affects (Preston & Wickson, 2016), ASHA creatively transforms the distant and disconnected nodes of agri-food systems (e.g. production and consumption) into sites of solidarity and collective action.

References

FAO. (2018). *Transforming Food and Agriculture to Achieve the SDGs: 20 interconnected actions to guide decision-makers* (Technical Reference Document). Food and Agriculture Organization of the United Nations.

McGreevy, S. R., Rupprecht, C. D., Niles, D., Wiek, A., Carolan, M., Kallis, G., Kantamaturapoj, K., Mangnus, A., Jehlička, P., Taherzadeh, O., Sahakian, M., Chabay, I., Colby, A., Vivero-Pol, J.-L., Chaudhuri, R., Spiegelberg, M., Kobayashi, M., Balázs, B., Tsuchiya, K., Nicholls, C., … Tachikawa, M. (2022). Sustainable agrifood systems for a post-growth world. *Nature Sustainability*, 1–7.

Peschard, K., & Randeria, S. (2020). 'Keeping seeds in our hands': The rise of seed activism. *The Journal of Peasant Studies*, *47*(4), 613–647.

Pottinger, L. (2017). Planting the seeds of a quiet activism. *Area*, *49*(2), 215–222.

Preston, C. J., & Wickson, F. (2016). Broadening the lens for the governance of emerging technologies: Care ethics and agricultural biotechnology. *Technology in Society*, *45*, 48–57.

Puig de La Bellacasa, M. (2015). Making time for soil: Technoscientific futurity and the pace of care. *Social Studies of Science*, *45*(5), 691–716.

Silva Garzón, D., & Gutiérrez Escobar, L. (2020). Revolturas: Resisting multinational seed corporations and legal seed regimes through seed-saving practices and activism in Colombia. *The Journal of Peasant Studies*, *47*(4), 674–699.

Tyagi, B. B., & Kumar, R. (2020). The future of farming: To what end and for what purpose? *Science, Technology and Society*, *25*(2), 256–272.

Chapter 15

Agroecological Experiences from Argentina

Rodrigo Tizón

Instituto Nacional de Tecnología Agropecuaria (INTA), Argentina

Agroecology is an approach to sustainable rural production that has grown in recent years, providing answers to many of the problems created by industrial agriculture (Fig. 15.1). In Argentina, this phenomenon is given by soya cultivation, i.e. the implementation of soya monoculture or very simplified sequences, which extend beyond the Pampean region (original formation of temperate grassland on very fertile soils). After several years of this degrading process of socio-ecosystems, many of the producers lost part of their capital or sold their farms outright, losing more than 40% of their capital in the last 20 years. Against this backdrop, alternative, more diversified models of production have begun to appear, with a view to regenerating soils, reducing the use of agrochemicals and proposing the return of people to the countryside (reterritorialisation). Thus, hundreds of farms with family experiences such as *El Mate* and *Laguna Blanca*, which we will present in these lines, have become beacons to follow due to their success and continuous teaching-learning in the agro-ecological transition.

El Mate Farm

El Mate is a family farm near the town of Adelia María, department of Río Cuarto, province of Córdoba, Argentina. The Vasquetto family began the agroecological transition in 2013 from a soybean farming system, at first specialising in rational Voisin grazing (PRV) of cattle and sheep, and then adding the production of double-breasted chickens and agroecological eggs, integrated into the general rotation.

This experience, like many others, began in a degraded agro-ecosystem, from a productive, environmental and social point of view. This meant that soils were

Exploring Hope: Case Studies of Innovation, Change and Development in the Global South, 105–108

Published under exclusive licence by Emerald Publishing Limited
doi:10.1108/978-1-83549-736-420241019

Fig. 15.1. Organic Fruit and Vegetable Crates with the Word Agroecology Written on Them. *Source*: ID 263132030 © Carolina Jaramillo | Dreamstime.com.

very compacted, with little life, productive biodiversity eroded and human capital was reduced as a result of years of an industrial system that did not need labour. Regenerating the matrix of sustainability is complex, but opportunity disturbances appear to initiate the transition, a very important one being motivation and enthusiasm. Of course, on the basis of good technologies and with the support of people who are eager to improve systems.

The PRV, in addition to reintroducing the animal into the system, proposes perennialisation with grassland and rotational/rational grazing management that redistributes the grazing. *El Mate* opted for alfalfa-based pastures (with clover, lotus, fescue, barley, bentgrass, ryegrass and phalaris), all species that make up polyphytic pastures of high nutritional quality. The owners recommend using 'pampean' seeds and less improved seeds than found, as they are adapted to harsher weather and animal trampling. The farm's production is certified by the Asociación Grassfeed Argentina, among others.

The family emphasises that the agro-ecological roof is still a long way off, a path initiated by the dissatisfaction with the agricultural paradigm and the crippling debts. From the 300 ha, they saved from the previous system, a monoculture of soya, they moved on to a virtuous model without debts (350 to 500 kg of meat/ha/year). As if this were not enough, they learned about the management of other species, poultry and by-products.

Broiler chickens and laying hens, also entered into a rational grazing system, besides being great fertilisers, pest and weed controllers, thus avoiding slaughter areas where peladales, odours and flies are produced. This is a low-investment business scheme, which can start generating income 65 days after the start of rearing or 6 months in the case of laying hens. It quickly transforms energy and protein (from weeds and insects) into high-quality, value-added feed for direct sale to the consumer.

Laying hens can lay up to 290 eggs per year (Hy-line, Isa Brown, Negrita INTA breeds), with a peak laying rate of 85% in spring-summer and up to 60% in winter. Eggs produced under this system have better colour, texture and nutrition (6 times more vitamin E and beta carotene, 40% more vitamin A and half the cholesterol).

Farm Laguna Blanca

The *Laguna Blanca* farm is located in the municipality of Tres de Abril, department of Bella Vista, province of Corrientes, Argentina. The agroecological transition on the farm was initiated by the Fleita family in 1998, after going through a conventional stage since 1993. Fiscal pressure, low prices and floods favoured a process of transition to another form of production. The first stage began with the reduction of inputs and the progressive incorporation of biopreparations (supermagro, green manures, home-made preparations) and the incorporation of multifunctional species, reaching 2002 with a mature agroecological reconversion, only 4 years after the beginning of the transition (e.g. 2 to 3 sprays per week against whitefly and moth).

The production system of *Laguna Blanca* is mainly oriented towards lemons, sowing crops (sweet potato, manioc, corn, maize, beans, peanuts, pumpkin, etc.), cattle and beekeeping. They also grow other crops for self-consumption and sale of surpluses, such as vegetable gardens, fruit trees (pink grapefruit, white grapefruit, tangerine, quinoto, orange, banana, Brazilian mango, avocado, peach, plum, pear, mamon, walnut, etc.), chickens and broiler chickens (eggs and meat) and processed products (baked goods, sweets, cheese). The production obtained is destined for family consumption and direct sales (agroecological products fair, sales on demand, home sales) and for the conventional market (lemon and animals).

The lemon sales system is divided between differentiated direct sales (at events or by order in the city of Corrientes), fresh on the conventional market and some to industry. Although they do not use agrochemicals, they do not sell in a differentiated way to the industry. In 2013, they incorporated beekeeping for self-consumption and sale at the fair or on demand. They have always kept chickens and sometimes they make batches of broiler chickens.

The farm supports 60 cattle that are fed on natural pasture and sugar cane, silage and grass. They have incorporated maize, sorghum and sugar cane to make silage for the winter (approximately 5 tons). Grazing is semi-intensive rotational grazing, by means of plots with cattle herds. The system is highly developed in agro-ecological management practices: natural pest and disease control, associations, crop rotations, production and use of organic fertilisers (manure, compost, and earthworm humus), biofertilisers, rotational grazing, fodder silage, etc.

The family participated in the formation of the Las Tres Colonias Agroecological Group in 1998, although it was formally created in 2007 (Fig. 15.2). They are actively involved in the community of San Pablo, where they donated land for the construction of a chapel.

Fig. 15.2. Meeting of a Group of Producers from the 'Tres Colonias' Agroecological Group. *Source*: The author.

Conclusions

Successful experiences such as those described above are multiplying throughout Argentina, with their own particularities and non-linear transitions. The families and communities that approach the agroecological transition face challenges on different scales: those of the subsystem itself (farm and estate) to that of a whole paradigm that crosses political-institutional instances at the territorial, regional and national levels. Agroecology is proposed as an approach for the resolution of situated problems, conceptualising transition as the restoration of the functions and resilience of the socio-ecosystem, which weaves global solutions locally.

Chapter 16

Trade as a Driver of Sustainability Pathways: Insights from the Palm Oil Sector in Indonesia

Ahmad Dermawan[a,d] *and Otto Hospes*[b,c]

[a]*Center for International Forestry Research and World Agroforestry (CIFOR-ICRAF), Bogor, Indonesia*
[b]*Public Administration and Policy, Wageningen University, Wageningen, the Netherlands*
[c]*IPB University, Bogor, Indonesia*
[d]*School of Business and Economics, Norwegian University of Life Sciences, Ås. Norway*

The role of trade is like a double-edged sword. On the one hand, economics literature acknowledges trade as a driver for economic development. On the other hand, there are concerns that trade also drives ecological degradation. The case of palm oil in Indonesia presented here highlights that trade-related initiatives can also improve positive outcomes and reduce adverse effects.

Oil Palm: A Flex Crop

Oil palm (*Elais guineensis*) has been arguably the most debated crop concerning development outcomes and associated impacts. Oil palm is the most productive vegetable oil crop. The palm oil trade contributes to 40% of the total global volume of vegetable oil trade. Indonesia, Malaysia and Thailand produce approximately 95% of global palm oil (Shahbandeh, 2022).

One factor that drives the increasing demand for palm oil is its versatility (Pacheco et al., 2020). Palm oil has many uses, from food and energy to several industries. Crude palm oil (CPO) is the leading industrial product of palm oil. CPO uses several processes to produce many derivative products: food, oleochemical and energy. There has also been an increasing demand for empty fruit bunches for power plants or bioethanol. Palm oil has served as a critical feedstock for biofuels. Even palm oil methane effluent, one of the residues of CPO production, has become a source of biogas for electricity production.

Exploring Hope: Case Studies of Innovation, Change and Development in the Global South, 109–113

Published under exclusive licence by Emerald Publishing Limited
doi:10.1108/978-1-83549-736-420241020

Impacts of Palm Oil Development

For Indonesia, palm oil makes significant economic contributions: high government revenues, foreign exchange, and employment make palm oil the engine of growth. In 2020, Indonesia exported 25 million tons of palm oil worth USD 17.4 billion (Bank Indonesia, 2022). Palm oil also involves millions of smallholders and workers at plantations and mills, downstream industries, and other related sectors (Pacheco et al., 2020).

On the other hand, rapidly increasing oil palm expansion has brought undesirable ecological and social footprints (Fig. 16.1). Environmental impacts of palm oil expansion include deforestation and associated biodiversity loss, pollution, soil erosion, greenhouse gas emissions and loss of ecosystem services and forest ecosystem functions (Meijaard et al., 2018). Moreover, countries with corporations dominating oil palm production often have poor social impacts of oil palm expansion, such as a lack of smallholder involvement in large-scale oil palm projects and poor working conditions for labourers. In summary, the palm oil sector has three significant performance challenges: (i) conflicts over land and benefit

Fig. 16.1. Two Trucks Loaded with Oil Palm Fruits Bunches in the Plantation. *Source*: ID 182324519 © Riefza | Dreamstime.com.

flows associated with the expansion of industrial plantations; (ii) the large yield gap between smallholders and company plantations; and (iii) detrimental environmental impacts (Pacheco et al., 2020).

The Rise of Different Governance Arrangements

The positive and – particularly – the negative impacts of palm oil have become a subject of debate. However, the problems with oil palm are more about how actors plant and grow the crop than its inherent characteristics. Several initiatives aim to minimise the negative impacts and enhance positive impacts (Dermawan & Hospes, 2018). Driven by the realisation that public authorities lacked the capacity to enforce their regulations, non-governmental organisations (NGOs) drove the rise of *private regulation* or *industry* self-regulation governing sustainable palm oil. The Roundtable on Sustainable Palm Oil (RSPO), launched in 2007, is the private regulatory authority on sustainable palm oil production. Four years later, in 2011, the Government of Indonesia launched the Indonesian Standard for Sustainable Palm Oil (ISPO), the *public mandatory sustainability regulation* for producers operating in Indonesia.

Despite the increasing adoption of the RSPO and ISPO, the amount of certified sustainable palm oil trade is still relatively small. Moreover, deforestation induced by oil palm expansion is still a major global problem (Austin et al., 2019). In addition, some consumer countries do not require certified sustainable palm oil. To respond to the challenges, NGOs engage directly with the actors along the palm oil supply chains. Due to these engagements, several major palm oil companies have embraced *corporate self-regulation* since 2013. The companies set out rules for themselves in individual commitments to become deforestation-free palm oil producers (Dermawan et al., 2022). The emergence of various regulatory systems to govern sustainable palm oil in Indonesia has marked the rise of a plural system regulating the sustainability of oil palm production (Pacheco et al., 2020).

Governance Arrangements and Sustainability Pathways

While not all governance arrangements (public, private and self-regulations) mentioned above are about the palm oil trade, their implementation modalities come from trade. For example, while the ISPO regulates palm oil production, it is promoted by the Indonesian government to partner countries to gain market acceptance for its palm oil. In addition, imports from several consumer countries require compliance or conformity to RSPO. Moreover, corporate self-regulation is mainly a value chain arrangement that uses trade as the instrument of interfirm coordination.

These governance arrangements aim to deal with the performance challenges and create sustainability pathways. Sustainable pathways can be conceptualised as trajectories that connect technical, environmental and governance practices that reinforce each other. They consist of actors at different levels that regulate, manage, implement and monitor these practices towards sustainable production (Dermawan & Hospes, 2018; Hospes et al., 2017). Sustainable pathways have three components: (1) aspiration to achieve sustainability (the endpoint); (2) a variety of practices that support each other (practices); and (3) governance by actors at different levels with different roles (actors and interactions).

There is no single pathway towards achieving sustainable palm oil. Existing governance arrangements may complement or conflict with each other. However, competing governance arrangements also trigger a race to the top. For example, corporate self-regulation on zero-deforestation palm oil production has triggered the public and private authorities to improve their standards for sustainable palm oil.

Several actionable steps can help achieve the sustainability pathways. First, find common ground and identify shared principles of sustainability. Second, define the actor-practice connections that reinforce the technical, land use and governance practices. Third, improve one arrangement by learning from the others using the principle of continuous improvement. Fourth, acknowledge the diversity of authorities and regulatory systems and, simultaneously, seek mutual recognition.

Implications for Trade Measures on Palm Oil for Indonesia

The dynamics of governance arrangements as sustainability pathways would help public and private authorities, and civil society finds actionable options on palm oil-related issues. For example, the European Union (EU) is arguably the most active region promoting sustainable palm oil use. In 2019, the EU issued a Green Deal to support a commitment to making the EU climate neutral in 2050. The EU also issued a regulation on deforestation-free products, suggesting the prohibition of commodities produced on land subject to deforestation after 2020 from entering the EU market. While the EU has issued policies and actions for the EU territory, they have implications for producing countries such as Indonesia.

The EU measures provide challenges as well as opportunities for Indonesia. Indonesia has prepared by strengthening domestic infrastructure and intensifying engagement with external actors. Internally, the Government of Indonesia strengthens the ISPO regarding the regulatory framework and the process. Indonesia has put ISPO as a cross-sectoral regulation to gain uniform support from all sectoral ministries. In addition, Indonesia also developed a national action plan for sustainable palm oil, maintained the policy to stop the issuance of new oil palm concession licences, reduced deforestation and forest fires, and increased domestic absorption of palm oil by promoting biodiesel.

Meanwhile, Indonesia intensifies its engagement at bilateral and multilateral forums. Indonesia and Malaysia established the Council of Palm Oil Producing Countries, which voices the concerns of palm oil-producing countries on the global platform. Indonesia is also active in ensuring the importance of palm oil in achieving Sustainable Development Goals. Indonesia also involved in lengthy discussions and negotiations with their trade counterparts bilaterally to increase acceptance of ISPO as the sustainability standard for Indonesian palm oil. One focus is learning from the success in the timber sector, where Indonesia and the EU established a Voluntary Partnership Agreement using Indonesia's Timber Legality Verification System as a compatible mechanism.

Conclusions

Using the sustainable pathways concept, the EU and Indonesia have a *common agenda* to achieve climate change and development goals and the role of sustainable palm oil in achieving them. Then, existing platforms and *governance arrangements* can reinforce the common agenda without undermining each other, such as the Sustainable Development Goals. Additional initiatives may provide good *learning* for a bilateral agreement with the ISPO as a compatible mechanism. The EU could also appreciate and support the processes to strengthen the ISPO. Finally, the EU and Indonesia could seek *mutual recognition* of existing governance arrangements in certifying sustainable palm oil.

References

Austin, K. G., Schwantes, A., Gu, Y., & Kasibhatla, P. S. (2019). What causes deforestation in Indonesia? *Environmental Research Letters*, *14*, Article 024007. https://doi.org/10.1088/1748-9326/aaf6db

Bank Indonesia. (2022). *Volume of non-oil and gas export by commodity* (V.14.). https://www.bi.go.id/id/statistik/ekonomi-keuangan/seki/Default.aspx#headingFour

Dermawan, A., & Hospes, O. (2018). Sustainability pathways in oil palm cultivation: A comparison of Indonesia, Colombia and Cameroon. In A. Rival (Ed.), *Achieving sustainable cultivation of oil palm* (pp. 33–48). Burleigh Dodds Science Publishing Limited.

Dermawan, A., Hospes, O., & Termeer, C. J. A. M. (2022). Between zero-deforestation and zero-tolerance from the state: Navigating strategies of palm oil companies of Indonesia. *Forest Policy and Economics*, *136*, Article 102690. https://doi.org/10.1016/j.forpol.2022.102690

Hospes, O., Kroeze, C., Oosterveer, P., Schouten, G., & Slingerland, M. (2017). New generation of knowledge: Towards an inter-and transdisciplinary framework for sustainable pathways of palm oil production. *NJAS-Wageningen Journal of Life Sciences*, *80*, 75–84.

Meijaard, E., Garcia Ulloa, J., Sheil, D., Wich, S. A., Carlson, K. M., Juffe-Bignoli, D., & Brooks, T. M. (2018). *Oil palm and biodiversity. A situation analysis by the IUCN Oil Palm Task Force*. IUCN.

Pacheco, P., Schoneveld, G., Dermawan, A., Komarudin, H., & Djama, M. (2020). Governing sustainable palm oil supply: Disconnects, complementarities, and antagonisms between state regulations and private standards. *Regulation & Governance*, *14*(3), 568–598.

Shahbandeh, M. (2022, March 15). *Vegetable oils: Production worldwide 2012/13-2021/22, by type*. Statista. https://www.statista.com/statistics/263933/production-of-vegetable-oils-worldwide-since-2000/

Chapter 17

Bioeconomy and Local Value-Chain Development as a Hedge Against Deforestation in Brazil's Cerrado

Mairon G. Bastos Lima

Stockholm Environment Institute, Sweden

Brazil's Cerrado is South America's second-largest biome after the Amazon, an expanse of savannah, grass and woodlands which has been historically undervalued (Figs. 17.1 and 17.2). It suffered continuous clearing for pasture and monoculture expansion, and by the late 2010s, it had lost about half of its original coverage (Rausch et al., 2019). However, the Cerrado is a global biodiversity hotspot – the world's most biodiverse savannah – and plays vital hydrological functions, besides being home to numerous local communities and traditional cultures (Russo Lopes et al., 2021; Strassburg et al., 2017). In the past, neglect for those actors fuelled misconceptions about the Cerrado as a vacant wasteland (Bastos Lima & Kmoch, 2021), but such communities increasingly have shown that local value-chain development – along with forms of convivial conservation – can both address poverty and form a powerful hedge against unsustainable land-use change.

Many Cerrado communities have resisted being driven off the land by coalescing around so-called sociobiodiversity chains (*cadeias da sociobiodiversidade*). These are agricultural or non-timber forest product (NTFP) value chains. They are built to recognise and valorise not only the local biodiversity but also ethnic and cultural diversity, social identities linked to particular territories, and extensive traditional knowledge around native products. As local development enhances the economic viability of their livelihoods, those communities stay on the land and help with the survival of the Cerrado biome along with their own cultural maintenance. Such local communities, alongside civil society organisations, have long sought to promote biodiversity-based local value chains. Such efforts gained special momentum through Brazil's National Plan for the Promotion of

Exploring Hope: Case Studies of Innovation, Change and Development in the Global South, 115–120

Published under exclusive licence by Emerald Publishing Limited
doi:10.1108/978-1-83549-736-420241021

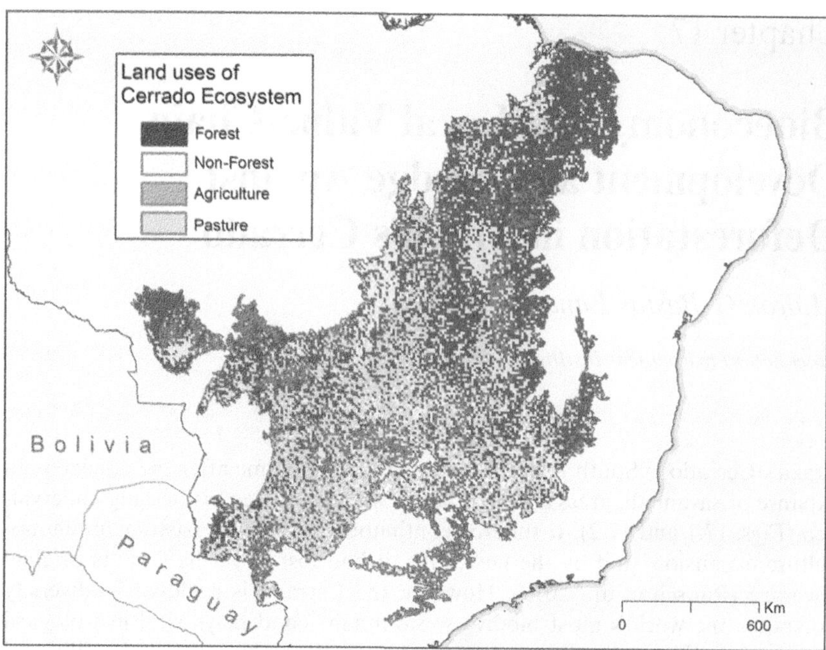

Fig. 17.1. Brazil's Cerrado Ecosystem and Its Key Land Uses. Various Forms of Native Vegetation Are Here Aggregated as 'Forest', Whereas 'Agriculture' Corresponds Mostly to Rotated Soy and Corn Monocultures. *Source*: Own elaboration.

Fig. 17.2. Brazil's Cerrado Landscape. *Source*: ID 253201094 © Ángela Macario | Dreamstime.com.

Sociobiodiversity-Chain Products (*Plano Nacional de Promoção das Cadeias de Produtos da Sociobiodiversidade*), launched in 2009 by the Ministry of Agrarian Development. It weaved together several incentives in the forms of agricultural technical assistance, research and development tuned to smallholder needs, dedicated credit lines at public banks and support for accessing institutional markets (e.g. school meals and public hospitals). That program has led to numerous success stories as well as the recognition of persistent challenges and lessons learnt over the years. Recently, under a bioeconomy umbrella, such efforts to promote sustainable development based on conserving rather than replacing native vegetation have then gained additional momentum (Abramovay et al., 2021; Bastos Lima, 2022).

Numerous native products have served as the focus of value-chain development efforts. They include staple food crops such as cassava as well as others harvested mostly for market value. The latter group includes baru nut (*Dypterix alata*) and babaçu (*Attalea* spp.), which are native nut types, and typical Cerrado fruits such as bacupari (*Garcinia gardneriana*), murici (*Byrsonima crassifolia*), mangaba (*Hancornia speciosa*), pequi (*Caryocar brasiliense*), turu palm fruit or bacaba (*Oenocarpus bacaba*), moriche palm fruit or buriti (*Mauritia flexuosa*) among others (Fig. 17.3). Various fruits are often used for making frozen organic fruit pulp, which Brazilian consumers regularly utilise. Beyond that, the idea is to emulate the success of certain Amazonian goods such as Brazil nut or açaí palm fruit, now established with large market value and which have helped promote local economic development through standing forests. There is a growing understanding that, while most bioeconomy efforts have historically focused on biofuels and other forms of bioenergy, communities may earn and benefit substantially more by adding value to local products as foods or for the cosmetics industry (Bastos Lima, 2022).

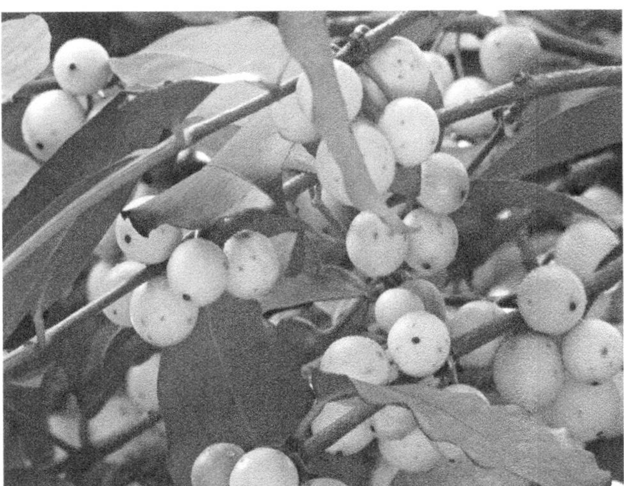

Fig. 17.3. Bacupari *(Garcinia gardneriana)* – Close-up. *Source*: DNI 253630636 © Passion4nature | Dreamstime.com.

Baru nut, for example, has long been artisanally used by local communities as a fruit and for handicrafts. However, the coveted hardwood of its tree rapidly threatened the species. The counterforce to that has been the sustainable utilisation of its nuts, with increasing value-added by producing vegetable oil, vegan butter and a protein-rich flour from its crushed nut turned into meal (Carrazza & Ávila, 2010). Baru meal has been used, for instance, to nutritionally enrich ice cream in Brazil, helping promote food security and the economic viability of local livelihoods (Pinho et al., 2015).

Simpler forms of value-added that have lower technological (and thus financial) requirements also remain useful, such as to produce dehydrated fruit. Buriti, is now processed and sold both in dehydrated form and as frozen pulp by multiple rural communities in the Cerrado. Meanwhile, higher-value goods have also surfaced. They include the Cerrado's native variety of vanilla (*Vanila edwalli*), increasingly sought by chefs in Brazil's high-end restaurants (Garcia et al., 2022), and cumaru (*Dypterix odorata*), a native bean utilised for its aromatic properties in the cosmetics industry that offers significant returns (Benevides Júnior et al., 2020).

From a sustainable development viewpoint, two concepts are key to understanding the importance of such sociobiodiversity chains. The first one is that of bio-based value webs, instead of single-product value chains, as the same product can enter several distinct pathways to meet the demands of different downstream markets (Bastos Lima, 2021; Scheiterle et al., 2018). That framing allows for conceiving – and planning for – multiple goods and benefits coming out of one species or product. Many market avenues can exist alongside local uses for livelihood maintenance and biodiversity conservation (Fig. 17.4).

The second concept is that of biorefinery, which suggests industrially processing (i.e. refining) biomass to extract and separate its various compounds. Besides *in natura* products that obtain good market value (e.g. the Cerrado's vanilla) or cases of simple mechanical processing (e.g. as with baru nut), biotechnology and adequate capacity enhancement can allow these native products to underpin increasingly

Fig. 17.4. A seller with a pequi stand at the fair. *Source*: DNI 231776943 © Ángela Macario | Dreamstime.com.

advanced bioeconomy developments. That can include bio-based substitutes for goods today made primarily from oil, such as solvents or lubricants, and they may also produce low-volume high-value chemicals for the food and pharmaceutical industries (Langeveld et al., 2010). Biorefineries thus present an enormous potential to renew the industrial base – moving away from fossil resources and towards biological ones – while creating more development opportunities.

For these socio-economic benefits to be accrued, there is a need for a just transition towards an inclusive and biodiverse bioeconomy (Bastos Lima, 2022). Such sociobiodiversity chains offer a clear pathway forward, but they still have challenges to overcome. For one, smallholders in the Cerrado and elsewhere typically lack legal expertise or formal managerial and accounting skills that may be critical for agri-entrepreneurship. Guéneau et al. (2020) reveal that a lack of sufficient support for local communities on that, alongside excessive dependence on government purchases for institutional markets, still leaves Brazilian rural communities only with informal or semi-formal supply arrangements and vulnerable to political changes that may dismantle public support policies and leave them unable to continue on their own (Niederle et al., 2022). Much in terms of business capacity enhancement remains needed, particularly for local value-added, which often ends up captured by intermediaries or private companies not linked to the communities.

Conclusions

As the Cerrado continues to be gradually deforested for pastures and plantations that also drive people off the land, such sociobiodiversity value chains offer a potent way forward. They represent the hope of changing the Cerrado's fate for the better in socially inclusive ways through genuine sustainable development. The world's most biodiverse savannah offers plenty of resources for that, while its communities have their cultures embedded in the land that can help develop it sustainably. How to scale up these efforts and overcome persistent challenges – such as local technological and financial gaps for value addition or improved market access – remain key questions, but experience to date points to a way ahead. As the bioeconomy becomes an increasingly set paradigm, the opportunity that the Cerrado's sociobiodiversity value chains provide becomes an imperative for Brazil and may offer inspiration for other developing regions of the world. Unsustainable practices may be, after all, best fought through sustainable development promotion for these critical landscapes.

References

Abramovay, R., Ferreira, J., Costa, F. D. A., Ehrlich, M., Castro Euler, A. M., Young, C. E. F., & Villanova, L. (2021). The new bioeconomy in the Amazon: Opportunities and challenges for a healthy standing forest and flowing rivers. *The Amazon We Want*, Chapter 30. http://theamazonwewant.org/

Bastos Lima, M. G. (2021). *The politics of bioeconomy and sustainability: Lessons from biofuel governance, policies and production strategies in the emerging world*. Springer International Publishing.

Bastos Lima, M. G. (2022). Just transition towards a bioeconomy: Four dimensions in Brazil, India and Indonesia. *Forest Policy and Economics, 136*, Article 102684.

Bastos Lima, M. G., & Kmoch, L. (2021). Neglect paves the way for dispossession: The politics of "last frontiers" in Brazil and Myanmar. *World Development, 148*, Article 105681.

CARRAZZA, Luiz Roberto; ÁVILA, João Carlos Cruz e. *Ma- nual tecnológico de aproveitamento integral do fruto do baru*. Brasília: ISPN, 2010.

Garcia, J. P., Zaneti, T., Diniz, J., & Gueneau, S. (2022). Dinâmicas Alimentares Alternativas e Gastronomia: Consumo de Produtos Locais em Restaurantes de Brasília. *Revista Grifos, 31*(57), 01–18.

Guéneau, S., Diniz, J. D. A. S., & Passos, C. J. S. (Orgs.) (2020). *Alternativas para o bioma Cerrado: Agroextrativismo e uso sustentável da sociobiodiversidade*. IEB Mil Folhas, Belo Horizonte.

Júnior, A. Y. B., de Souza Gama, B. T., Bezerra, T. T. C., da Silva, D., & Kieling, A. C. (2020). Prospecção Tecnológica do Cumaru (Dipteryx odorata). *Cadernos de Prospecção, 13*(4), 1103–1103.

Langeveld, J. W. A., Dixon, J., & Jaworski, J. F. (2010). Development perspectives of the biobased economy: A review. *Crop Science, 50*, S-142-151.

Niederle, P., Petersen, P., Coudel, E., Grisa, C., Schmitt, C., Sabourin, E., … Lamine, C. (2022). Ruptures in the agroecological transitions: Institutional change and policy dismantling in Brazil. *The Journal of Peasant Studies*, 1–23. http://doi.org/10.1080/03066150.2022.2055468

Pinho, L., Mesquita, D. S. R., Sarmento, A. F., & Flávio, E. F. (2015). Enriquecimento de sorvete com amêndoa de baru (Dipteryx alata Vogel) e aceitabilidade por consumidores. *Revista Unimontes Científica, 17*(1), 39–49.

Rausch, L. L., Gibbs, H. K., Schelly, I., Brandão Jr, A., Morton, D. C., Filho, A. C., … Meyer, D. (2019). Soy expansion in Brazil's Cerrado. *Conservation Letters, 12*(6), Article e12671.

Russo Lopes, G., Bastos Lima, M. G., & dos Reis, T. N. (2021). Maldevelopment revisited: Inclusiveness and social impacts of soy expansion over Brazil's Cerrado in Matopiba. *World Development, 139*(C), Article 105316.

Scheiterle, L., Ulmer, A., Birner, R., & Pyka, A. (2018). From commodity-based value chains to biomass-based value webs: The case of sugarcane in Brazil's bioeconomy. *Journal of Cleaner Production, 172*, 3851–3863.

Strassburg, B. B., Brooks, T., Feltran-Barbieri, R., Iribarrem, A., Crouzeilles, R., Loyola, R., … Balmford, A. (2017). Moment of truth for the Cerrado hotspot. *Nature Ecology & Evolution, 1*(4), Article 0099.

Chapter 18

The National Association of Quinoa Producers in Bolivia (ANAPQUI): An Experience of Collective Action and Participation in Globalised Market Chains

Elizabeth Jiménez

CIDES-UMSA, Universidad Mayor de San Andrés, Bolivia

It is only in recent times that the consumption of Quinoa has attained the large global popularity it has today. In 2013, UNESCO named Quinoa the 'perfect' food for humanity because of its many nutritional characteristics and attributes. In terms of food value, Quinoa has an ideal balance of fat, starch, oil and protein and a high quotient of amino acids. Such qualities have led to the characterisation of Quinoa as a critical grain for the world's future food supply (Healy, 2001).

Royal Quinoa is a kind of Quinoa that only grows in the southern Bolivian Highlands (Fig. 18.1), in an ecosystem characterised by a very arid environment: high mountains with extreme cold and more than 200 days with frost a year. Quinoa's growing areas are located at elevations that range between 3,650 and 4,200 m above sea level (Winkel et al., 2015), and it is about the only crop that has not only successfully adapted to these ecological conditions but also contributed to the biodiversity of the region. According to the Bolivian Institute of Agricultural and Forestry Innovation (INIAF), there are about 25 varieties registered of Quinoa, 10 of which are considered Royal Quinoa types.

Royal Quinoa has been cultivated in this region for over 3,000 years in small- to medium-scale family farms that largely depend on family labour and that traditionally have combined the production of Quinoa with the raising of camelids, llamas and alpacas that ensure access to organic manure which is used for land fertilisation (Fig. 18.2).

Production was largely aimed at fulfilling the producer's household consumption needs with small margins for commercialisation. Internal demand for Quinoa

Exploring Hope: Case Studies of Innovation, Change and Development in the Global South, 121–126

Published under exclusive licence by Emerald Publishing Limited
doi:10.1108/978-1-83549-736-420241022

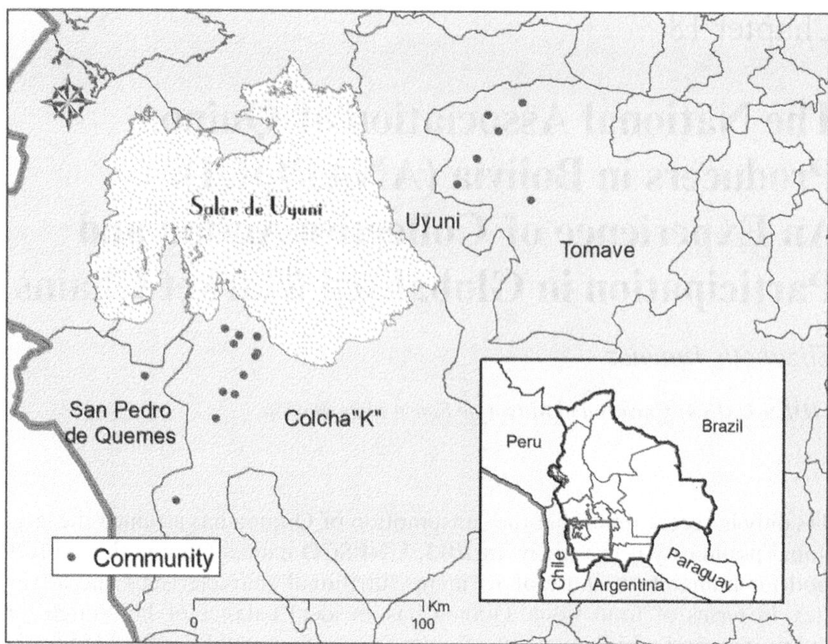

Fig. 18.1. Map of Bolivia's Southern Altiplano. *Source*: Own elaboration.

Fig. 18.2. Farm in the Mountain at Torotoro, Bolivia. *Source*: DNI 165559170 © Jef Wodniack | Dreamstime.com.

was very limited. Quinoa's nutritional properties had been largely ignored both; by urban Bolivian consumers as well as by the government that showed no interest in the crop. Commercialisation was usually carried out by intermediaries who, taking advantage of their position, paid very low prices for this crop – the price of Quinoa fluctuated around one-third of the price of rice. The most important market was Peru, where Quinoa collected in Bolivia was gathered and shipped to markets overseas (Laguna, 2011).

Starting in the 1970s, a growing need to increase production levels and aim at greater margins of commercialisation led to a partial-mechanisation of the production process. Tractors were introduced to expand the production fields raising production levels and allowing for greater commercialisation margins (Laguna, 2011). Yet, engaging actively in commercialisation itself was very difficult.

Associations for Commercialisation: The Experience of ANAPQUI

The National Association of Quinoa Producers (ANAPQUI) origin began in the early 1970s, when a group of Belgian missionaries tried to introduce economic alternatives to improve people's livelihoods by encouraging local organisations of producers (Laguna, 2011). After various not very successful experiences, it became clear that the comparative advantage of the region was indeed the production of royal Quinoa and thus what was needed was to raise production levels, increase commercialisation and gain from large-scale sales (Fig. 18.3).

To gain from Quinoa production, there was a need to commercialise collectively in order to access foreign markets, reach fair prices and avoid intermediaries. There was a need to go beyond Peru, and reach markets in the US and Europe, where awareness of Quinoa's benefits was growing and where higher prices could lead to economic benefits. Establishing contacts with distant buyers and retailers was key.

In 1983, the ANAPQUI emerged with the aim to represent and work for all Quinoa producers in the region. The emergence of ANAPQUI coincided with the rise of syndicalism and the organisation of a single representative union federation of peasants in the Southern Bolivian Highlands (FRUTCAS). It was precisely in a meeting of FRUTCAS that the ANAPQUI emerged as the so-called *economic arms* of the regional peasant's federation. The *economic arms* emerged as Peasant Agricultural Corporations (CORACAS). They were part of the peasant's federations national strategy to organise *parallel structures* whose functions were to provide technological and logistic support for improving agricultural production, transformation and commercialisation across peasant communities (Laguna, 2011; Laguna et al., 2006).

ANAPQUI's initial structure had two significant features. On one hand, it kept the political nature and interests of the peasant's regional federation that led to its organisation. As such, it become more than a mere economic organisation in search of profits and utilities. On the other hand, ANAPQUI's structure took after the traditional Andean Ayllu structure. Traditionally, communities in this region had been organised in Ayllus, a particular form of territorial and political

Fig. 18.3. Raw Quinoa Seeds. *Source*: ID 37432582 © Tashka2000 | Dreamstime.com.

organisation of local populations. Ayllus included a group of communities that shared a common identity, managed land communally and, among other features, had a structure of political representation that ensured equal participation.

Initially, ANAPQUI took advantage of the interest and support that grassroots organisations received from international donors and from the emerging community of fair-trade companies and organisations. Throughout its consolidation as the most important Quinoa export-led grassroots organisation, ANAPQUI has shown remarkable adaptation capacities to the opportunities and challenges of a very uncertain global market (Winkel et al., 2015). Following the *Ayllu* structure, ANAPQUI was conceived as an organisation managed and run by Quinoa producers themselves. Thus, all leadership and managerial positions had to be shared by all community representatives that is Quinoa producers with little to no training in such activities. The organisation sponsored a series of training activities including the provision of scholarships for young and promising leaders to enrol in public universities.

A very important step was taken in 1988 when the Program for Research and Technical Assistance was created (PIAT). Initially, the objective was to link traditional Andean knowledge with the so-called 'scientific' knowledge in order to produce sustainable practices and technologies that will suit better the needs of Quinoa production. In practice, such an ambitious objective was very difficult to attain. ANAPQUI's experiences in the introduction of new appropriate technologies remain one of the organisation's main challenges.

Starting in 1991 the organic production of royal Quinoa has become ANAPQUI's trademark. In 1994, PROQUINAT, a specific program to institutionalise organic practices throughout the production process, was implemented for research, experimentation and technical assistance. Organically produced Quinoa involves a series of restrictions including only the use of organic pesticides and fertilizers. To these restrictions ANAPQUI added the need to ensure sustainable practices, limiting the intensive use of land and maintaining Llamas and Alpacas to ensure access to organic manure. All these restrictions implied the use of highly labour-intensive practices. In a context where the opportunity cost of labour is high and market uncertainty is also present, it has become difficult to maintain high organic and sustainable production standards.

The Lessons

Throughout the 1990s ANAPQUI became the biggest and most important instance for exporting organically produced Quinoa from Bolivia (Laguna, 2003). In 2000, as a result of greater competition with the emerging private companies, ANAPQUI lost this number one position. Currently, competition with the 22 Quinoa exporting companies remains a key feature. In addition, there are more than 200 countries worldwide that are currently producing and/or experimenting with the production of Quinoa (Alandia et al., 2020). Despite worldwide competition, ANAPQUI remains a key central actor in the production and commercialisation of Quinoa in Bolivia. Most importantly, it is indeed the most important organisation that is run by producers themselves and whose interests go beyond benefiting only from commercialisation and higher prices.

Starting in 2005, ANAPQUI's efforts have included the industrialisation of the grain and the commercialisation of transformed products. It has also managed to increase Quinoa's consumption in the internal market, by actively participating in some food-transfer social programs, such as school breakfasts and food support for pregnant mothers.

Overall, ANAPQUI has shown a remarkable capacity to adapt to the shifting opportunities and demands of the market (Winkel et al., 2015). A thorough economic analysis of the organisation points out at some failed commercial agreements and a lack of needed forecasting of long-run market trends (Laguna, 2003). All of which could be expected given the nature of the organisation (i.e. organised and run by Quinoa producers). As expected, the organisation's shortcomings are largely related to a lack of entrepreneurial skills and experience.

The need for less labour-intensive organic and sustainable practices has to do with research, innovation and adaptation of better-fitted technologies. Something along the lines of what ANAPQUI's funders envisioned as the articulation of traditional with useful scientific knowledge can only be achieved by successful institutional arrangements among various actors, including universities, research organisations, and the state; as the most important facilitator that provides the incentives for virtuous arrangements to take place (Mazzucato, 2011).

Conclusions

The experience of ANAPQUI is the story of struggle in the process of building up a grassroots organisation that allows small to medium-scale agricultural producers to participate and gain from globalised market opportunities. It fundamentally shows that collective action together with determination and leadership, has worked in Quinoa producers' attempts to capture economic opportunities for the commercialisation of this grain.

References

Alandia, G., Rodriguez, J. P., Jacobsen, S. E., Bazile, D., & Condori, B. (2020). Global expansion of quinoa and challenges for the Andean region. *Global Food Security*, *26*, Article 100429.

Healy, K. (2001). *Llamas, weavings and organic chocolate: Multicultural grassroots development in the Andes and Amazon of Bolivia*. University of Notre Dame Press.

Laguna, P. (2003). La Cadena Global de La Quinua: Un Reto Para La Asociación Nacional de Productores de Quinua. In C. Romero Padilla & E. Peluppessy (Eds.), *La Gestión Economica-Ambiental En Las Cadenas Globales de Mercancías En Bolivia*. Tilburg University and Universidad Mayor de San Simon.

Laguna, P. (2011). *Mallas y flujos: acción colectiva, cambio social, quinua y desarrollo regional indígena en los Andes Bolivianos*. Wageningen University and Research.

Laguna, P., Cáceres, Z., & Carimentrand, A. (2006). Del Altiplano Sur Bolivariano hasta el mercado global: Coordinación y estructuras de gobernancia de la cadena de valor de la quinua orgánica y del comercio justo. *Agroalimentaria*, *11*(22), 65–76.

Mazzucato, M. (2011). The entrepreneurial state. *Soundings*, *49*(49), 131–142. https://doi.org/10.3898/136266211798411183

Winkel, T., Alvarez-Flores, R., Bommel, P., Bourliaud, J., Chevarria-Lazo, M., Cortes, G., … Vieira Pak, M. (2015). *The southern altiplano of Bolivia. State of the art report on quinoa around the world in 2013*. Centre de coopération internationale en recherche agronomique pour le développement; Food and Agriculture Organization of the United Nations.

Chapter 19

Yomol A'tel and its Struggle for Lekil Kuxlejal (Buen Vivir)

José Andrés Fuentes

Consejo Directivo del Grupo Cooperativo Yomol A'tel, México

We know that we live in a world in crisis. The COVID-19 pandemic and climate change are symptoms of a civilisational crisis with very deep roots, going back to the origin of civilisation, some five to six thousand years ago, and to the imposition of patriarchal and colonial domination over human societies, women, Nature and reality itself.

Hence, it is important to recognise what exists outside this collapsing world. That is to say, of the *alternatives*; many are under construction, but many, many others that already exist. These other possible worlds of which we speak are constructed from *these other worlds that are already* – yes, incomplete, with their contradictions and limitations, but that already exist. The experience of *Yomol A'tel* may be one of those alternatives, one of those little lights of hope.

Yomol A'tel is a group of cooperatives and solidarity economy enterprises in Chiapas, Mexico. It began its work in 2002 when coffee prices hit historic lows. For an indigenous region, impoverished and economically dependent on the sale of the bean, this was a devastating context. This prompted the creation of a small cooperative of 22 producers to organise the joint sale of their coffee.

Twenty years later, the group is made up of 4 cooperatives and 2 social enterprises, including more than 400 families from 115 indigenous Tseltal communities, and more than 70 workers located in Chiapas and in the cities of Mexico City, Guadalajara and Puebla. We mainly work with coffee (roasted and in our coffee shops called *Capeltic*) and honey (packaged and in products for personal hygiene). We also have processes within the territory, such as micro-finance – for family needs and small enterprises, agro-ecological work – which seeks an integrated management of the plot of land – or the organisational work necessary for the construction of our autonomy. We highlight the consolidation of the women's cooperative *Jun Pajal O'tanil* – harmony in the heart – whose *Xapontic*

Exploring Hope: Case Studies of Innovation, Change and Development in the Global South, 127–131

Published under exclusive licence by Emerald Publishing Limited
doi:10.1108/978-1-83549-736-420241023

Fig. 19.1. Ritual (*altar maya*) of welcome in the last General Assembly of Yomol A'tel.

products have achieved economic inclusion and have grown from 35 to more than 90 women members.

Yomol A'tel are two Tseltal words meaning *organisation* and *work*. And that is what we do: we organise ourselves on the basis of our work, not only as *employment*, but as the *action* of working and building the alternative with our own hands (Fig. 19.1). We seek, from the solidarity economy, to establish economic-productive processes that allow us to ensure the means of subsistence for our families and to defend our territory and Tseltal culture. All of this in order to be able to continue building our *Lekil kuxlejal* (*Buen vivir* in Spanish, eventually translatable into English as Good Living).

To achieve this, we must ensure a minimum economic income, and to this end, we work on products and services that can be sold *abroad*. But it is just as important, if not more important, to take care of our consumption and the spending of that money, because if we do not reorganise it, it will continue to leak like water in a barrel with holes in it. That is to say, no matter how much we get the best price for coffee or honey, or sell tons of products, or increase all our salaries; if there is no sense of *sufficiency* and a construction of autonomy in what we spend that money on, it will be like continuing to pour water into that leaky barrel.

We define solidarity economy not as a fairer channel to generate and distribute income, but from its political dimension that seeks to build autonomy and defend the Tseltal way of life and spirituality. Without romanticising – as this takes place amidst tensions and contradictions – we seek to generate relationships of solidarity and mutual support between people – producers, workers, suppliers, advisors, clients – and also with our Mother Earth and the world of the sacred. The latter can be seen in many organisational practices, for example, starting and ending meetings with a collective prayer and a particular greeting between participants. Or in the ritual of *sembrar la cruz* (planting the cross) before any construction – such as the coffee production plant – where permission is asked from the Earth by dancing and making offerings, a cross is placed in the ground and people eat, drink and celebrate. Or, as in the strategic planning days that we hold every three or four years, where we fast, pray, work, dance, discuss, plan, for 24 hours (Fuentes, 2022; Pieck & Vicente, 2019). These practices are our own and do not have to be the same for other solidarity economy organisations: each one has its own ways and forms.

As this is an economic-productive process, we must ensure the financial sustainability of the group in order to operate at a profit, or at least without losses. Resorting to international cooperation has allowed us to supply the seed capital to start ventures, but in the long run we know that this generates dependence. For this reason, we are committed to building our financial autonomy, so that we can stop depending on philanthropic support and dedicate it to financing new initiatives.

We have opted for strategies such as the appropriation of the coffee value-added chain: controlling the production, processing and commercialisation of the bean all the way to the consumer. Thus, we created the *Bats'il Maya* coffee roaster – which markets around 100 tonnes of roasted coffee annually – and later the *Capeltic* coffee shops – which offer the service of selling cups of coffee to final costumers. With this strategy we have been able *to build our own coffee price*, which no longer depends on the stock market, but on our own financial viability. In general, our price is between 20% and 50% above the intermediaries (Fuentes, 2022), although there are other times – such as the 2022 collection – when, due to high international prices, they have overtaken us. But we know that this will not last long before they come down again; we have seen it before.

The democratic process of participatory governance is pursued through representative bodies of producers and workers, such as the Boards of Directors of the cooperatives or the Regional Community Assemblies. Also, in order to ensure relevant business management, we have management spaces, such as the Executive Committee – composed of those who coordinate each area – or the Board of Directors – with external expert advisors and from the group itself – or the Steering Committees of each cooperative or enterprise. These spaces seek to ensure the proper operation of each area and its economic profitability.

This, as well as the group's own cultural diversity – with workers and advisors in the cities and families in the Tseltal communities – has led us to face various intercultural challenges, which we try to address through dialogue and the Tseltal cosmovision, through understanding and the dissolution of conflict. On the other hand, this cultural diversity has also led us to open a fruitful dialogue of knowledges; between Tseltal and academic-scientific knowledge there are many interesting things that emerge in day-to-day operations (Fig. 19.2). This is embodied in the multi-stakeholder model, from which we seek to walk together – with universities, other organisations, advisors and allies – to venture into new, unknown processes – from looking for clients to improving our production facilities.

Finally, the training strategy we follow is based on the Tseltal pedagogy of *learning by doing*. We understand our cooperatives and enterprises as schools,

Fig. 19.2. Meeting Places for Farmers and Advisors. *Source:* José Andres Fuentes.

where young people can learn what we work on while participating in the process itself – from roasting coffee, to brewing it in a cup, to generating accounting policies and exporting. To date, more than 45 young people have been trained in this methodology, 18 of whom are currently working at *Yomol A'tel*. This is essential to ensure sustainability over time, as well as territorial relevance. We are now building a Solidarity Economy Centre for Sustainability, which aims to be a production and learning centre with productive modules that are economically sustainable and that function as training spaces in productive, agro-ecological, financial activities, etc. This is fundamental for the construction of our autonomy, a process that is as important as the economic results of the group. These allow us to subsist as cooperatives and enterprises and generate a necessary income, while agroecology, organisation and autonomy set us on the road to building our *Lekil kuxlejal* as *Buen vivir*.

Conclusions

In the face of the civilisational crisis we are going through, solidarity economies can serve as intermediate steps for this historical juncture, so that we can build the possibility of increasingly detaching ourselves from the industrial system and money. From Tseltal knowledge and the spirituality of the Earth, the dialogue can be opened up to other forms of knowledge – such as post-normal science, political ecology or transformative economies – in order to discover the enormous epistemic and pragmatic potential that exists in this dialogue of knowledges. On the basis of epistemic reciprocity and complementarity, we will be able to construct relevant alternatives for our times, both in our economic-productive work and in the reproduction of life in harmony and community. On this path, we can consolidate alternative economies that invite us to imagine alternatives to the economy in order to go through this process of transition that has already begun and will accompany us in the coming decades.

References

Fuentes, J. A. (2022). *Alternativas en tiempos de crisis civilizatoria*. CdMx: CIIESS-Universidad Iberoamericana.

Pieck, E., & Vicente, R. (Coords.) (2019). *Voces de Yomol A'tel: una experiencia de economía social y solidaria*. Editorial IBERO.

Chapter 20

Development Facing the Challenge of Territorial Organisation: The Case of Special Economic Zones in West Africa

Idrissa Yaya Diandy

Université Cheikh Anta Diop de Dakar, Senegal

In Africa, and more particularly in West Africa, Special Economic Zones (SEZs) are on the increase. These development models, which were first observed in East Asia, are areas where economic activities are hosted and aim to offer a set of infrastructures and services that ensure the best conditions for companies to carry out their activities. One of the most famous examples, because of its success, is the city of Shenzhen, in China.

Although SEZs offer a lot of hope through the alternative model advocated for developing countries, the expected economic effects are not always guaranteed, as shown by the varied fortunes of the various experiments around the world. In order to better understand the issues at stake, this chapter will investigate the dynamics that guide the relationship between territory and development, and then review the SEZs in West Africa before highlighting the constraints posed by this model.

History of the Relationship Between Territory and Development: From the Industrial District to the SEZ

The idea of the Industrial District is inspired by the British model of organisation that existed towards the end of the 19th century. However, Marshall is credited with the concept, which he began to develop in 1890. The Industrial District is a grouping of interdependent, geographically defined companies, which are respectively involved in the different stages of production of a homogeneous good. These districts explain a large part of the performance of the English economy at the time.

Michael Porter's analysis is a continuation of Marshall's investigation. Above all, it was Becattini who, at the end of 1970, studied how, in the region between

Exploring Hope: Case Studies of Innovation, Change and Development in the Global South, 133–137

Published under exclusive licence by Emerald Publishing Limited
doi:10.1108/978-1-83549-736-420241024

Genoa, Milan and Turin, small- and medium-sized enterprises that were geographically close to each other and operating in the same sector of activity achieved remarkable performance in terms of growth, exports and employment thanks to the original relationships they had forged between them. In the same period, American researchers perceived that the concentration of innovative companies in very dynamic sectors, by reducing the transaction costs between firms, was at the root of the economic boom of certain American metropolises, as in the case of the success stories of the Hollywood film industry, the computer industry in Silicon Valley and the microelectronics industry on Route 128 in Boston.

Territorial economic development models from developing countries are more recent. These are Industrial Free Zones (IFZs) or Export Processing Zones (EPZs), which are generally defined as geographically located industrial parks in which all constraints are relaxed (installation conditions, availability of infrastructure, etc.) and the regulatory and fiscal legislation is sufficiently attractive. In Asia, the IFZs have been set up along the coastal cities, giving rise to large industrial mega-cities which will attract populations, but also capital and training structures. Very quickly, the coastal cities became the focus of economic activity and attracted populations, thus creating large megalopolises. This Japanese model of enhancing the value of the maritime façades by imitation effects was followed by all the countries with such a space (Lorot & Schwob, 1986).

As for the EPZs, the SEZs are parts of the territory where the economic conditions are more favourable than in the rest of the country. However, SEZs are larger than the free trade zones found in other Asian countries in that they span entire cities, and include business, residential and commercial areas, recreational facilities and a wide range of services and spin-offs that contribute to the dynamism of the area. There are 700 SEZs in Southeast Asia, and over 2,500 in China.

SEZs in West Africa, a Model for Territorial Development

As many Asian countries have demonstrated, SEZs can be tools for industrial development (Fig. 20.1). This explains their recent success in the South. To attract foreign investment, these zones benefit from significant tax advantages and better infrastructure (electricity, transport, telecommunications, etc.). Indeed, the installation of a large number of companies and workers on a given territory allows public authorities to provide modern infrastructures, as well as facilities adapted to the particular needs of companies. Since a dense infrastructure network can be shared by a large number of users, its financing becomes easier as the tax base that supports it expands. Today, there are an estimated 237 SEZs in Africa (UNCTAD, 2021). Successful examples can be found in Africa. One example is the Tangier Med industrial-port complex in Morocco. Automobile, aeronautics and food processing were rapidly growing industries. By 2018, Morocco had become the second largest African producer of automobiles with a total annual production of 430,000 automobiles (UNCTAD, 2021).

West African countries were relatively late to engage in this model compared to other regions of Africa. In 2021, only Nigeria leads with 38 SEZs (UNCTAD, 2021). Senegal, which had already experimented with IFZs in the 1970s (with

Fig. 20.1. Industrial Building. *Source*: ID 9680928 © Sebastián Czapnik | Dreamstime.com.

mixed results), has firmly established the SEZ model. The country now has three SEZs: the Diamniadio Industrial Park, the Diass Special Integrated Economic Zone and the Sandiara Special Economic Zone (Fig. 20.2). Since 2017, the country has had a legal framework that frames the creation and operation of SEZs (Law No. 2017-06 of 06 January 2017). Concerning the Diamniadio industrial platform, eligible activities are assembly and packaging, agri-food, building materials, ICT, electricity and electronics and logistics. The facilities include offices and workshops.

In Côte d'Ivoire, the Information Technology and Biotechnology Village (VITIB) is a new free zone dedicated to the development of ICT in Côte d'Ivoire. It is the only example of a free zone initially focused exclusively on ICT and biotechnology.

Although Ghana has only four SEZs, they account for a considerable share of exports. In 2019, they attracted Foreign Direct Investment (FDI) worth $90 million, and the 144 companies in the zones were responsible for $1.94 billion of exports, representing 12 per cent of total exports from the country (UNCTAD, 2021). Since its creation in 1995, the Tema SEZ has pursued a policy of promoting multiple sectors of activity even if they do not have particular synergies: plastics processing, textiles/clothing, call centres/data centres, foam manufacturing, ICT, packaging, food processing machinery manufacturing, DVD manufacturing, credit cards, etc.

Finally, one of the most ambitious projects is certainly the Sikasso-Korhogo-Bobo Dioulasso SEZ. The geographical area of the SEZ is included in a triangle made up of the towns of Sikasso in Mali, Bobo-Dioulasso in Burkina Faso and Korhogo in Côte d'Ivoire.

This project aims to exploit the agricultural and mining potential of cross-border areas. It aims, in a logic of integration, to implement joint socio-economic

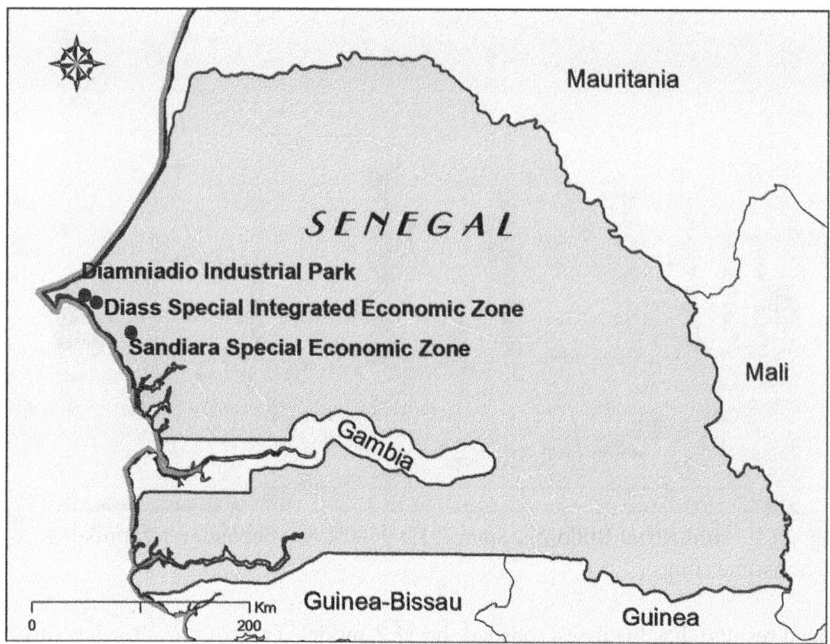

Fig. 20.2. SEZs location in Senegal. *Source*: Own elaboration.

development projects (infrastructure, industrial units, etc.). However, it is still slow in coming to fruition, given the numerous constraints.

Constraints on SEZ Expansion

While SEZs are multiplying on the continent, their results remain mixed for the moment. In West Africa, success stories are slow to emerge, with a few exceptions in Ghana and Nigeria. According to Farole (2011), the economic and institutional environment is one of the main constraints. For example, the ambitious Sikasso-Korhogo-Bobo-Dioulasso Special Economic Zone project has been slow to materialise since its launch in 2018. The lack of institutional arrangements and the late identification of joint projects to be implemented are the major obstacles to the start of the SEZ. This is compounded by the political instability faced by these countries. Furthermore, there is little complementarity between the activities present in the SEZs, which does not allow for the generation of economies of scale. Indeed, in most cases, SEZs are characterised by low sectorial specialisation. This sectorial dispersion is detrimental to complementarity effects. Moreover, the activities are mainly in low-value-added sectors requiring a low-skilled workforce. Finally, the relationship is often conflicting between national policy in favour of SEZs and the interests of local populations who consider themselves victims of the expropriation of their land. In Senegal, there has been an upsurge in land-related conflicts, particularly in the municipality of Diass, where the new airport has a land base of 4,500 hectares, the 10,000-hectare Special Industrial Economic Zone, and the Port of Ndayane, among others (Fig. 20.3). Therefore, the

Fig. 20.3. Blaise Diagne Airport in Senegal. *Source*: ID 185379194 © Anze Furlan | Dreamstime.com.

revival of land reforms and support policies for the impacted populations must be put in place, especially in the SEZs, in order to prevent conflicts and guarantee certain equity and good cohabitation.

Conclusions

SEZs are a development opportunity for West African countries. They offer an innovative model for the spatial organisation of economic activity which enables parts of the territory to have access to competitive infrastructures and services. However, it is important to find solutions to the many constraints that they face and that delay their emergence. Their development is not homogeneous, and even if there are examples of success in some countries, most SEZs do not meet the expectations placed on them.

References

Lorot, P., & Schwob, T. (1986). "Singapour, Taiwan, Hong Kong, Corée du Sud. Les nouveaux conquérants?", Hatier, París.

UNCTAD. (2021). *Handbook on special economic zones in Africa: Towards Economic Diversification across the Continent*. United Nations Conference on Trade and Development UNCTAD/DIAE/IA/2021/3. https://unctad.org/publication/handbook-special-economic-zones-africa

Farole, T. (2011). *Special Economic Zones in Africa: Comparing performance and learning from global experience*. The International Bank for Reconstruction and Development / The World Bank. https://documents1.worldbank.org/curated/pt/996871468008466349/pdf/600590PUB0ID181onomic09780821386385.pdf

Chapter 21

Technological and Institutional Innovations for Rural Development in Sri Lanka

Seetha I. Wickremasinghe

National Science Foundation, Colombo, Sri Lanka

Sri Lanka is an island in the Indian Ocean with a population of nearly 22 million, a literacy rate of 93% by 2020, and is classified as an agricultural country representing 70% of a rural community (Fig. 21.1). Since gaining Independence from the British in 1948, the significance of the country's agricultural sector has been gradually declining, yet it continues to play an important role in the Sri Lankan economy. By 2000, the gross domestic product (GDP) share of the agriculture sector had been 20% and it has fallen to about 6.9% in 2018. The share of agriculture in total employment had been 26% in 2020, while 31.5% of R&D expenditure is accounted for agriculture (Central Bank of Sri Lanka, 2021). Although the contribution of agriculture to GDP has significantly decreased over the years, it is an important determinant of GDP, directly accounting for about 1/5th of the national output, and employing more than 1/3rd of the labour force (36%).

It has been observed that many rural development projects were formulated as per the donor requirements and had been implemented either by the government or the private sector. In the process of project formulation and implementation, the grass-root level or end users (i.e. villagers or farmers) had not participated. As a result, many of these projects neither addressed the problems associated with the transfer of technologies to farmers nor assured any sustainability, after completion of the project. Thus, it is important to break the usual linear model (appearing below) that is in existence in public-sector R&D and maintain mutual dependencies among actors in the various networks.

Government → Ministry of Agriculture → Dept. of Agriculture → Res. Extension Officers → Farmers

Exploring Hope: Case Studies of Innovation, Change and Development in the Global South, 139–145

doi:10.1108/978-1-83549-736-420241025

Fig. 21.1. Rural Landscape with Fields and Female Worker Near Nuwara Eliya in the Highlands of Sri Lanka. *Source*: ID 266423431 © Meinzahn | Dreamstime.com.

The following case study shares the innovative experience of a research team where the technology transfer of tissue-cultured (TC) banana (Musa spp.) took place in rural development.

Case Study on TC Banana Production

The banana crop is widely cultivated, and still the most consumed fruit by people in Sri Lanka for its nutritional value and its comparatively low price. It gives a high income to farmers throughout the year. Around 60,000 ha of land is under banana cultivation, which is about 54% of the total land being used for fruit cultivation. About 13,000 ha is used to cultivate cooking banana (ash plantain) and the other 47,000 ha is used for dessert banana. Annual banana production is around 780,000 metric tons and the average yield is 13 Mt/ha. Of the total production of bananas grown, about 35–45% is wasted due to post-harvest losses, and only about 7% is exported. The post-harvest losses occur due to fruit fly disease, improper transportation, handling, packaging, etc.

Since the 1990s, the University of Colombo, Sri Lanka pioneered plant biotechnology viz., plant tissue culture technology in the country, especially in bananas (Musa spp.). The laboratory research on *in vitro* micropropagation of bananas was carried out, especially with the popular dessert banana varieties (AAB, Mysore), locally known as *Embul* and *Kolikuttu*. After establishing the *in vitro* banana propagation, the research team initiated a joint project with the Mahaweli Authority of Sri Lanka to introduce the TC banana planting material to Embilipitiya (about 225 km from the capital city of Colombo), the largest

Fig. 21.2. Map of Sri Lanka. *Source*: https://www.researchgate.net/figure/Location-map-city-of-Hambantota_fig2_45428829 Hambantota is a rural city where the Plant Production Unit (PPU) is located.

banana-growing area in the country. At the commencement of the project, the farmers in the area were interviewed to collect basic information regarding their livelihood patterns, monthly income, education level, and other information such as market accessibility, transport facilities, banking, etc. Many difficulties were faced at the beginning since farmers had no idea about technology other than seeing the small banana plantlets in vessels. They did not have any confidence in the feasibility of the TC planting material. However, two farmers initially agreed to work with the University to test the field performance of TC banana plantlets with close monitoring of the research team on agronomic aspects such as water availability, fertilizer requirements, susceptibility to pests, etc. When the banana plants started bearing fruits, which appeared large and healthy, it attracted the attention of the surrounding farmers since bunches could be sold at a higher price than conventional banana fruits, thereby bringing more money to the farmers involved in the project. Hence, the demand for TC banana plants immediately increased, and during this period, the officers of the Mahaweli Authority also worked closely with the research team and farmers to ensure water and land availability. A Plant Production Unit (PPU) was established in 1998 followed by an Agro-technology and Community Service Centre in 2002 at Weligatte in the Hambantota district (see Fig.21.2) to produce TC banana plantlets continuously. This Centre is well equipped viz., tissue culture laboratory,

Fig. 21.3. Pictures of TC banana project at Agrotechnology Community Service Center. *Source*: Courtesy of University of Colombo Institute for Agrotechnology and Rural Sciences (UCIARS), Hambantota, Sri Lanka

green house, computer lab (see Fig. 21.3), lecture halls, discussion rooms and so on, to facilitate the farmer education in TC banana plantlets production.

The project received financial support from the Council for Agricultural Research Policy (CARP), International Atomic Energy Agency (IAEA), Vienna, and World Vision Lanka (NGO). Considering the country's demand for TC banana planting material, the research team commenced an outreach programme covering many parts of the country. Later, the other actors were also involved in this outreach programme namely, the Irrigation Department (supplying water to farmers) and the Export Development Board (EDB) of Sri Lanka (exporting avenues). Observing the success of the project, the Ministry of Rural Development also joined along with the Southern Development Authority (SDA) and EDB, Sri Lanka. Later, the established technology was transferred to the banana cultivators in the Southern, North Central and Uva Provinces of the country.

During the first two years, the relevant agronomical aspects were addressed and delivered by the Centre, but at present, the farmers contact the Centre only when they need a piece of advice. By now, the Centre has worked with more than 4,000 farmers in almost all parts of the country including North and East, and the demand for TC plantlets has grown so high that the order needs to be placed at least 6 months ahead of planting. The relevant technology for TC bananas was transferred through a participatory approach to the farmers via direct interviews, group discussions, field demonstrations and workshops held in the rural districts of Sri Lanka using Information and Communication Technology (ICT).

The benefits of the project were: (a) increased farmer income, (b) acceptance of new technology by farmers, (c) rural youth attracted to farming, (d) increased interest of farmers for knowledge and education, (e) reduction of migration to urban areas seeking employment, (f) direct involvement of university academics in rural development, and (g) increased family harmony.

Furthermore, a questionnaire survey conducted at a later stage for benchmarking purposes revealed that the farmers involved in the project were happy since their monthly income had increased by 8–10 folds. Their purchasing power has been immensely improved, for example, the purchase of motorcycles, tractors, vans, TVs, mobile phones, kitchen appliances, as well as having renovated houses or new houses, etc.), thereby improving the living standards.

The project also proved that end-user collaboration with multi-disciplinary agencies was crucial to achieving sustainable development. During the process, a series of related innovative steps took place that uplifted the livelihood of rural communities while introducing farmers to systematic education. The project was followed by another survey in the Hambantota district to investigate the demand of the farming community for pursuing higher studies in agriculture technology while involved in the cultivation and it was revealed that more than 90% were interested. For this purpose, with the approval of the Government of Sri Lanka, the Agrotechnology & Community Service Centre was upgraded into the University of Colombo Institute for Agrotechnology & Rural Sciences (UCIARS) in 2008, which was an innovative approach to a paradigm shift in farmer education. As the first activity, a certificate course and a diploma course in Agrotechnology were launched via the open and distance learning (ODL) programme (Vidanapathirana et al., 2009), followed by a BSc course in Agrotechnology under the guidance of the University Grants Commission (UGC) in Sri Lanka. This approach was viewed as a new chapter in higher education because it provided an opportunity for the farmer community to pursue higher education while being involved in farming as their main source of income, towards a knowledge-based economy. However, due to the heterogeneous nature of the farmer community (i.e. 25–55 years range, academic background, not having computer skills, poor Internet connectivity, distance from home to institute, low interaction with others, etc.), it was a big challenge in the beginning, but an induction programme of 01 month on the use of the computer, Internet, email, etc. was offered to the farmers. Fig. 21.4 shows the project timelines over the years. Furthermore, the project shed light on the National Innovation System (NIS) concept (Lundwall, 1992) as to how various actors play different roles in the sustainability of research extension activities. With the

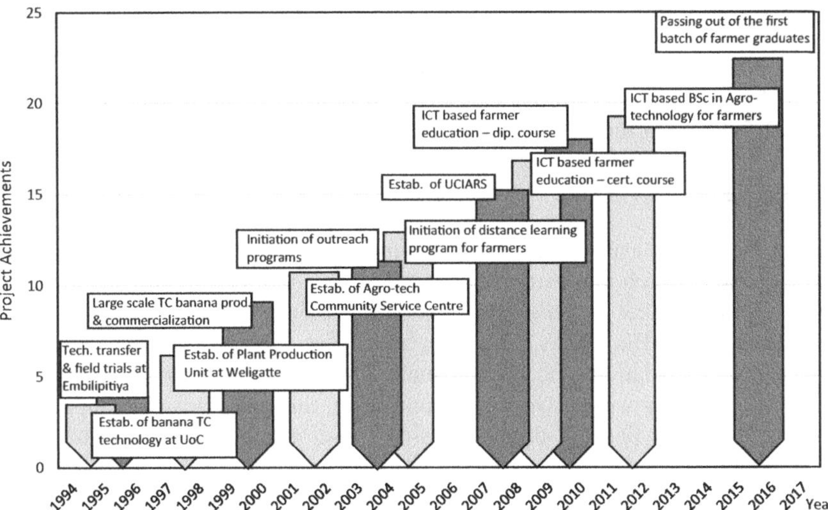

Fig. 21.4. Timelines of the TC banana project as against its achievements

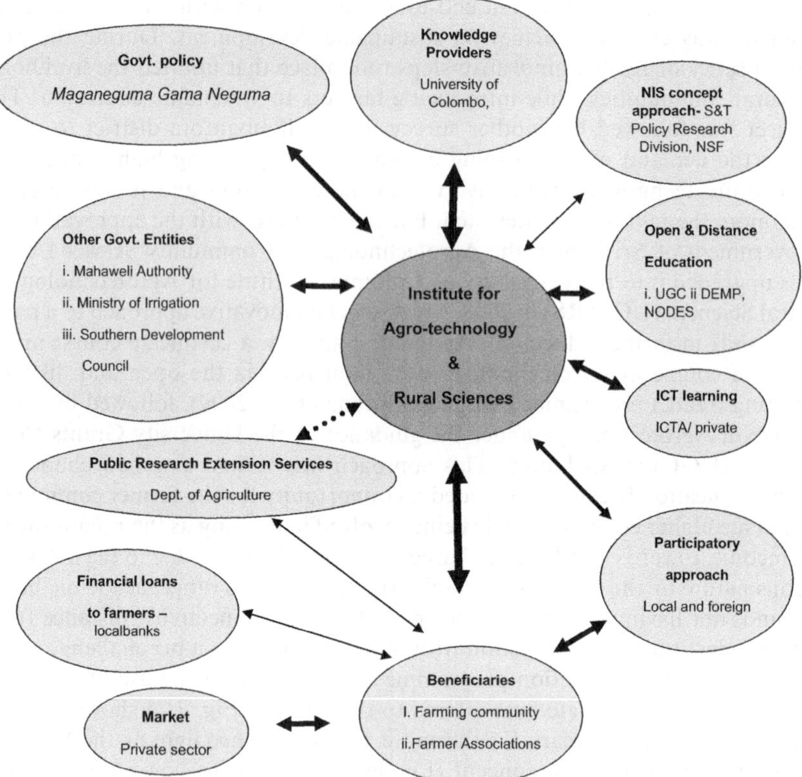

Fig. 21.5. IS Model Developed for TC Banana Innovation System Towards Rural Development (Thickness of the Arrows Indicates the Strength of the Link, While the Dotted Line Indicates the Lowest Link). Source: Own elaboration.

non-linear model of NIS, Sri Lanka has an enormous potential towards adopting it for rural agriculture development (Wickremasinghe & Krishna, 2007). Fig. 21.5 indicates the IS model developed for the TC banana case study.

Conclusions

As for the lessons learned, it must be mentioned that not only the public-sector agricultural research and extension services were essential, but also the involvement of many other stakeholders such as other government departments, the private sector, SMEs, banks, education authorities, NGOs, trade and markets, village-level associations, etc., were equally important in forming a strong network of a local innovation system. In conclusion, this case study also emphasises the necessity of a demand-driven grass-root level collaboration for sustainable rural development.

References

Central Bank of Sri Lanka. (2021). *Annual Report*, Colombo, Sri Lanka.

Lundwall, B. A. (1992). *National System of Innovation and Interactive Learning*. Pinter.

Vidanapathirana, N. P., Hirimburegama, K., Coomaraswamy, U. & Alluri, K. (2009). Role of the University of Colombo in building the capacity of villages through the L3 Farmers Project. *Proceedings of 17th Conference of Commonwealth Education Ministers Stakeholders Forum, Malaysia.*

Wickremasinghe, Seetha I., & Krishna, V. V. (2007). S&T policy and the Sri Lankan National System of Innovation: the role of public research systems. In T. Turpin & V. V. Krishna (Eds.), *Science, Technology Policy and the diffusion of Knowledge*. Edward Elgar Publishing.

Part 4

Ensuring Environmental Sustainability

Introduction

Aviram Sharma

Post-Growth Innovation Lab, University of Vigo, Spain

Environmentalism was studied and understood as a Western phenomenon for a long period, using multiple frameworks, such as wilderness thinking, post-materialism, eco-modernisation, eco-socialism and ecoefficiency theories (Grove, 1992; Inglehart, 1982), until scholars started analysing environmentalism in the global south using alternative theoretical and analytical perspectives (Guha & Alier, 2013). In the global south, environmentalism of the poor, indigenous environmentalism, Ecofeminism and community-led traditional environmentalism emerged as major frameworks for deciphering environmentalism during the initial phases (Guha & Alier, 2013; Sharma, 2021). Later, scholars from related disciplines explained varieties of other forms of environmentalism predominant in Asia, Africa and South America, such as Buddhist ecology, Hindu and Jain environmentalism and many others (such as *sumak kawsay, ubuntu*) having specific religious and cultural attributes (Eschenhagen, 2021; Jain, 2019). Rather than comparing and analysing environmentalism in the South and North as always founded on contradictory principles, we attempt to break this binary framing of environmental discourse. We argue that environmentalism emerging in the global south has complex characteristics (Death, 2016). The different sets of environmentalism have various shades. This section attempts to dismantle the polarised vision of environmentalism and the imagery of linear growth of eco-politics and eco-modernism debates in different spatial localities. In the process, this section charts the multiple stories of hopes emanating from the global south. These stories not only champion the struggles and efforts of common folks and stories from below but also identify and elaborate the environmental subjectivities, efforts and interventions planned by formal actors and mid and top-level socio-political actors and institutions in societies and countries from Asia, Africa and South America.

In the first chapter, under this section, Rivero Villar and colleagues explained how traditional governance can help address water poverty in major urban centres. Using the case from Oaxaca (in Mexico), they explained how traditional indigenous societies have actively collaborated to fix water poverty in their neighbourhoods, facing huge environmental burdens (water scarcity). Given the significant indigenous population in the city, learning from the specific historical and

Exploring Hope: Case Studies of Innovation, Change and Development in the Global South, 149–152

Published under exclusive licence by Emerald Publishing Limited
doi:10.1108/978-1-83549-736-420241026

cultural background was paramount. Drawing from ethnic rule-making practices, indigenous groups employed traditional governance mechanisms to alleviate water poverty. In Oaxaca, a direct democratic system based on indigenous practices of governance developed along with the formal representative democratic system. In the traditional system, members are directly elected in assemblies based on their community work and public services. The elected members from indigenous societies actively collaborate with the state actors and ensure collaborative and effective developmental interventions at the grassroots level to alleviate water poverty. Recognising these specific institutional pathways is crucial for addressing peculiar developmental challenges societies face in resource-constrained settings. Imposing institutional arrangements that historically emerged in other parts of the world often has little bearing on the local contexts in the global south and further exacerbates the inequalities.

Grasslands are one of the most sensitive and fragile ecosystems prone to destruction and deterioration due to their unhindered productive use for grazing and agriculture, which is quite true for the natural grasslands in South America known as Pampas Biome. Pablo Grilli has elaborated on the efforts of the Grasslands Alliance in Argentine is conserving and promoting the productive use of the vast swathes of grazing land by local grazers in collaboration with other actors. This regional alliance has not only helped negotiate the conservation or productive use debate but also showed new pathways for creating a lasting alliance between conservationists and small-scale grazers. The alliance has developed effective grassland management systems and practices. This initiative has helped maintain and conserve avian biodiversity and generate sustainable livelihoods. The alliance was created with the help of an international conservation NGO which aims to help conserve birds, their habitat and global biodiversity. The alliance used market-based mechanisms and promoted collaboration with small-scale grazers and producers to develop a collaborative, productive and conservation-centric agenda. This is an exciting case of collaboration of global and local actors and harmonisation of their aims, agenda and day-to-day practice to protect the livelihood of small farms in rural areas and nature in a non-extractive manner.

In the next chapter, Asaah Sumaila Mohammed explained how the extractive industries in Ghana (in this case, gold mines) had negated and failed to meet the needs and expectations of local communities. He explained the case from the perspective of energy justice. The local communities were overburdened with environmental and socio-economic ills due to the loss of livelihoods and destruction of the local environment. At the same time, the benefits emanating from mining were primarily harnessed by the big industry and other intermediaries. Using the lens of energy justice, the author explained distributional, procedural and recognition-based injustices met by marginalised local communities in Ghana. The extractive practices had colonial roots, and the big mining industries are deeply embedded in the global capitalist system, which promotes incessant wealth accumulation by few at the cost of the livelihood and dignity of local people and rampant destruction of nature. Such a grim situation has led to rampant environmental conflicts among the local communities and mining companies. The only way out, according to the author, is to recognise the injustices made to the local population and environment and find equitable benefit-sharing mechanisms and ways to democratise the regulatory decision-making processes and policies.

Sangay Dorji and Pema Latsho present an admirable initiative taken by one of the premier universities of Bhutan to improve the happiness and mental well-being of students and staff through institutional support. Rapid social, political and economic changes are bringing new challenges and opportunities for different sections of societies. Often many societal institutions and groups of people are not well-equipped to deal with such challenges. The increased reporting of mental health-related cases led to establishment of first-of-its-kind *Happiness and Wellbeing Centres* in 2019. This was a joint initiative of several European universities and the Royal University of Bhutan. Unlike a linear diffusion of policy innovation from North to South, in this case, the local actors infused their own ingenuity while institutionalising the plan. They reshaped the idea of counselling and wellbeing centres by integrating them with indigenous Bhutanese philosophy and cultural moorings. Several institutions and government agencies in Bhutan have shown keen interest in replicating and building on this idea. This is an excellent example of a hybrid model, where institutions of higher learning are vertically (across societies) and horizontally (within specific societies) collaborating and fulfilling the needs of their diverse stakeholders.

In the next chapter, Fazlullah Akhtar and colleagues present a scientific analysis of changing snow cover in Afghanistan. A war-torn country with a turbulent past still struggles to scientifically measure various endowed environmental resources due to the paucity of adequately trained human resources and devise appropriate management and governance schemes. Akhtar and colleagues present a scientifically robust analysis of changing snow cover patterns during the last two decades (between 2003 and 2018), which have a bearing on agriculture, water security and the daily life of millions of Afghanis. In general, the weak position of Afghanistan due to the geo-political instability in dealing with domestic and international transboundary water use hugely affects the local populace, national economy and environment. This study may help better plan the water resources use in the era of climate change at the local, national and regional levels if existing administrative and political institutions in the country would draw appropriate lessons.

In the final chapter, Aviram Sharma discusses the initiatives taken by the government of India to accelerate the energy transition and reach the goals of decarbonisation and a low-carbon future in a coordinated way. India and many other developing countries from Asia and Africa not only have to achieve environmental goals urgently to contribute towards their climate-change commitments but also have to balance their developmental priorities. These countries are still fighting a significant battle for addressing energy poverty for the most marginalised sections of their population. The efforts made by the Indian government at the local, regional and international levels in promoting the diffusion of renewables, especially solar energy, are worth appreciating. India played a crucial role in establishing the International Solar Alliance in collaboration with France to promote solar energy in other parts of the world, especially in the developing regions of Asia, Africa and South America. India, still an emerging economy, has taken commendable initiatives in addressing energy transitions and climate change goals both at the domestic and international front. In the process, India has championed not only south-south collaborations but also south-north collaborations. However, the pathways to energy transitions championed by India must address concerns related to energy injustices and climate injustice at multiple scales to make the transition just and resilient.

In a nutshell, the different chapters in this section explain the multiple varieties of environmentalism being experimented with and practised by a diverse set of actors in South America, Africa and Asia. Several shades of environmentalism reported here were rooted in indigenous traditions and philosophies prevalent in the Global South, yet, other initiatives are more mixed and hybrid in nature. In a few cases, actors and institutions in the South have worked in close collaboration with actors from the Global North. The collaborations, unlike the earlier years, were not only led by actors from the global north but were equally shaped, nurtured, initiated and led by the actors from the global south due to their diverse environmental sensitivity.

Unfortunately, the debates in academic and policy circles in the environmental domain still predominantly revolve around learning institutional and environmental innovations from the North. Global South is portrayed as a laggard who perennially tries to 'catch up'. In some other formulations, countries from the global south are conceived only as the cradle for communitarian and informal practices and innovations, catering to specific niches of local environmentalism. Unlike such polarised formulations, we explained the many shades of environmentalism growing in the Global South. We hope this exercise will contribute to documenting and advocating the study of diverse and complex forms of environmentalism in many under-studied regions and societies, including in the global south and north and the relationships and networks they create at multiple levels.

References

Death, C. (2016). Green states in Africa: Beyond the usual suspects. *Environmental Politics*, *25*(1), 116–135.

Eschenhagen, M. L. (2021). Nature and alternatives to development in Latin America: Contributions for a dialogue. In R. Bourqia & M. Sili (Eds.), *New paths of development: Perspectives from the Global South* (pp. 135–144). Springer.

Grove, R. H. (1992). Origins of western environmentalism. *Scientific American, 267*(1), 42–47.

Guha, R., & Alier, J. M. (2013). *Varieties of environmentalism: Essays North and South*. Routledge.

Inglehart, R. (1982). Changing values and the rise of environmentalism in western societies. Wissenschaftszentrum Berlin (Germany, F.R.). Internationales Inst. fuer Umwelt und Gesellschaft.

Jain, P. (2019). Modern Hindu dharma and environmentalism. In T. Brekke (Ed.), *The Oxford history of Hinduism: Modern Hinduism* (pp. 261–273). Ofxord Academic.

Sharma, A. (2021). The environment and development debate in India: The "Greening" of developmental discourse. In R. Bourqia & M. Sili (Eds.), *New paths of development: Perspectives from the Global South* (pp. 109–121). Springer.

Chapter 22

Building Urban Hope Recognising Traditional Governance: Overcoming Water Poverty in Oaxaca

Alejandro Rivero-Villar[a], *Antonio Vieyra*[b], *Yadira Méndez-Lemus*[b], *Cinthia Ruiz-López*[b] *and Alejandra Larrazábal*[b]

[a]*Centro de Investigación y Posgrado en Humanidades, Ciencia y Tecnología – Universidad Rosario Castellanos, Mexico*
[b]*Centro de Investigaciones en Geografía Ambiental – Universidad Nacional Autónoma de México (CIGA-UNAM), Mexico*

Urbanisation in the Global South is often portrayed as hopeless and chaotic (Davis, 2006; UN-Habitat, 2003). Cities in the Global South are full of contradictions: small pockets of development coexist with large areas of poverty that suffer the most from social and environmental threats exacerbated by the lack of urban services and infrastructures (Reckien et al., 2018). This uneven development is the result of poor governance, i.e. the inability of institutions and actors to enforce rules and provide services (Mitlin, 2008).

Despite this ominous diagnostic, popular settlements are incrementally improved by their own residents (Streule et al., 2020). This improvement happens longitudinally, often taking decades to achieve universal access to public services and infrastructures (Caldeira, 2016). Improvement of these areas depends on the ability of their inhabitants to work collectively in (an often contentious) collaboration with the state (Rivero-Villar, 2021). Thus, the possibility of achieving wellbeing in popular settlements rests on fixing governance in such areas (Horn, 2021). Governance can be improved by recognising often relegated sectors of society (Otsuki, 2016) as well as their governance practices (Holzinger et al., 2016); this can be a pertinent path to address urban problems (Aylett, 2010). In this chapter, we explore an example in which the recognition of traditional governance allowed addressing water poverty in the context of popular urbanisation.

Exploring Hope: Case Studies of Innovation, Change and Development in the Global South, 153–160

Published under exclusive licence by Emerald Publishing Limited
doi:10.1108/978-1-83549-736-420241027

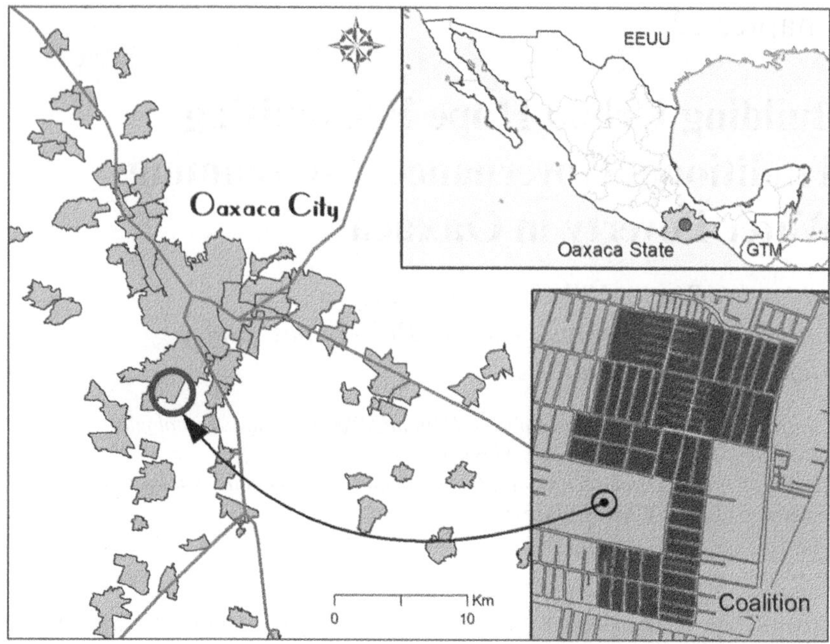

Fig. 22.1. Case Study Localisation. *Source*: Based on Esri, 2021; INEGI, 2020; SEPOMEX, 2017.

Evidence for this chapter was collected during exploratory fieldwork in the Metropolitan Area of Oaxaca (Oaxaca in short; Fig. 22.1) in March 2020, and a series of telephone interviews with neighbourhood leaders during 2020. Oaxaca is the capital city of Oaxaca State. Oaxaca State's ethnic diversity means that multiple indigenous groups coexist, speaking multiple languages, with different worldviews and governance practices (Anaya Muñoz, 2005).

Drone and satellite images and participatory mapping were used to locate neighbourhoods with limited access to the benefits of urbanisation (e.g. services and infrastructures), with exposure to environmental burdens (e.g. water scarcity), as well as active community organisations working to improve their wellbeing. In what follows, we explore the exemplar case of a coalition of five neighbourhoods (*Independencia, Ampliación Independencia, Granjas de Aguayo, La Paz* and *Oriental*) located in the municipality of Santa Cruz Xoxocotlán (Xoxo in short). This coalition, called *Colonias Unidas del Sur de Xoxo* (United Neighbourhoods of South Xoxo, hereafter the coalition), has actively cooperated to escape water poverty relying on traditional governance.

Governance

Governance refers to a form of governing undertaken by diverse stakeholders including the government, civil society and the private sector (Castán Broto, 2017; Romero Lankao et al., 2018). Governance encompasses multiple perspectives, power relations and knowledge systems that allow a more complete understanding of issues than a purely government-led decision making (Newig & Fritsch, 2009). This facilitates better-informed decision making and project implementation.

Urban problems can be solved through governance (Aust & du Plessis, 2018). Yet, in many cases, governance deficiencies are the root cause of urban problems, particularly when large sectors of society are excluded (e.g. when informal settlers are set aside from participating in governance structures) (Ziervogel et al., 2016). In multicultural settings, recognising traditional governance is particularly relevant for solving spatial issues (Graham, 1998; Membele et al., 2022). Traditional governance refers to ethnic procedural rules aiming at regulating collective decision making, such as leadership selection and service provision (Holzinger et al., 2016). Traditional governance is case-specific. Thus, the construction of effective governance networks and institutional frameworks depends on recognising historical and cultural trajectories that are contextual to certain places and moments (Grindle, 2004).

Oaxaca Governance

In Oaxaca State, two governance systems coexist: a direct democratic system based on indigenous practices: *usos y costumbres* (usages and customs, *usos* hereafter) and a representative democracy (political party system). Political parties are the system that predominantly mestizo (and mainly urban) municipalities use (Anaya Muñoz, 2005). In this system, government officials are elected through formal elections in which candidates are backed by political parties (Recondo, 2018). *Usos* is a traditional governance system in which government officials are not professional politicians (Recondo, 2018). *Usos* is used in the majority of Oaxaca's municipalities (417 out of 570) (Anaya Muñoz, 2005; IEE, 2020), and in some popular settlements.

Usos rests upon two main institutions: assemblies and *cargo* system. Assemblies are spaces for the deliberation and decision making of important public matters, including public spending, public works and the election of community representatives. In *usos* municipalities, the allocation of resources is decided collectively in community assemblies. In a sense, *usos* municipalities' public spending is a participatory budget (Diaz Cayeros et al., 2013).

Government officials are elected during periodical assemblies in which multiple candidates are proposed and elected through the deliberation of their peers. Eligible candidates are members of the community with a strong record of community service gained through their participation in the *cargo* system (Eisenstadt, 2007). *Cargo* system is a traditional public service, in which all adult members of the community are expected to engage (Eisenstadt, 2011). During their public careers, members of the community engage in community activities of increasing responsibility, from the organisation of community celebrations, to governing tasks (Anaya Muñoz, 2005). Municipalities governed through *usos* show a faster rate of improvement in accessing public services and infrastructures than municipalities governed through political party systems (Magaloni et al., 2019).

The Case of the Coalition

Usos is mostly used in rural settings. Nevertheless, popular settlements are located in urban peripheries where rural–urban migrants settle and bring with them their own governance traditions. In peri-urban areas of Oaxaca, as in other parts of Mexico with a strong indigenous presence, *usos* and political party systems coexist (Magaloni et al., 2019). In recently urbanised areas, settlers rely on *usos* to organise the improvement of their neighbourhoods in response to institutional tardiness or neglect. This is the case of the coalition.

In Xoxo, despite the municipality being formally governed through the political party system, neighbourhoods are ruled by *usos*. *Usos* are adapted to the urban context, and the cargo system is simplified to address specific urban needs. The governance structure of the cargo system at the neighbourhood level encompasses one steering committee (neighbourhood president, secretary, and treasurer) and multiple task-specific committees according to neighbourhood priorities (e.g. water supply and management) (Fig. 22.2). Each committee has its own chair-person, secretary and treasurer. Neighbourhood presidents are elected in neighbourhood assemblies every three years, mirroring municipal office terms. Neighbourhood presidents formally represent the interests of their neighbourhoods before municipal authorities. Municipal authorities recognise the authority of neighbourhood representatives and annually allocate public funds to address neighbourhood needs that are decided in a two-tier system of assemblies. First, at the neighbourhood level, the need of public works is discussed; projects are selected and prioritised. Second, a municipal assembly of neighbourhood

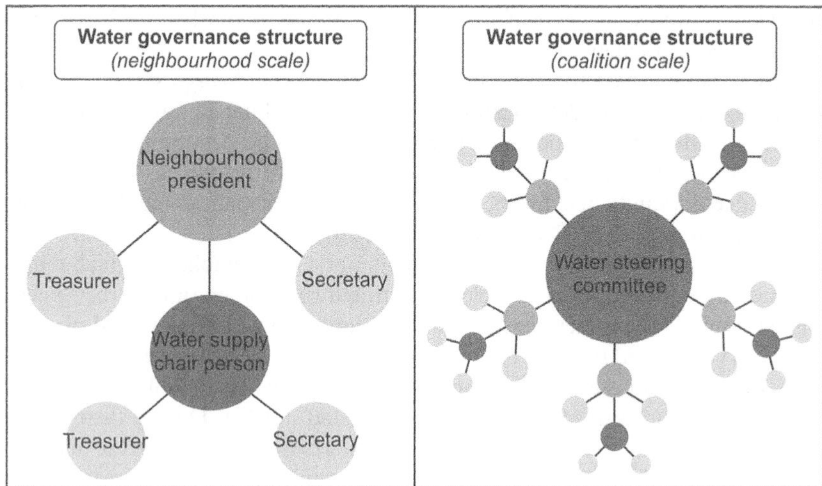

Fig. 22.2. Water Governance Structure. *Source*: Own elaboration.

representatives, along with municipal government officials, is held annually in which the public works are selected, and the budget allocated.

Xoxo's severe water scarcity is exacerbated by the lack of infrastructure and municipal inefficacy. To overcome these challenges, the coalition has been organised since the 1980s. Water is managed by a dedicated committee that is annually elected in assembly. Each neighbourhood elects its own water committee, and neighbourhood presidents form a water steering committee. Results of community engagement are the construction of a water distribution system including: water extraction permissions, deep wells, an elevated water tank, water supply pipes, house connections and an independent water supply utility company (Fig. 22.3). Costs of operation of the system (payments of staff and electricity bills) are equally divided among users. To secure affordable water prices, infrastructure improvements are not considered in water bills. Instead, the municipal budget allocated to each neighbourhood is used to maintain and improve the water supply.

The coalition has enabled neighbourhood presidents to negotiate the allocation of municipal resources beyond what is annually allocated to each neighbourhood. This has allowed them to fund the exploration of new sites for wells, acquire land for a new well and drill the well. Acquiring and installing the rest of the equipment for the operation of the new well, as well as connecting it to existing infrastructure is pending, but neighbourhood presidents expect to finish the works negotiating the allocation of further municipal budget, or joining their individually allocated budgets if each of the neighbourhoods' assemblies decides so.

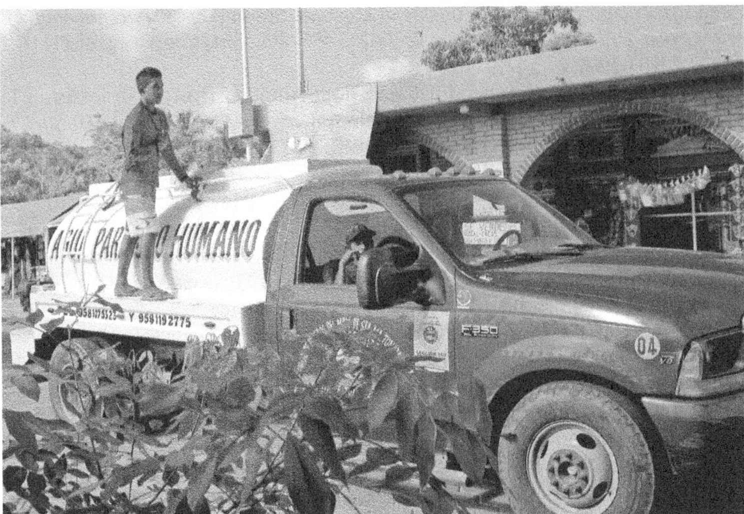

Fig. 22.3. Fresh Water Transportation in Mexico. *Source:* ID 37612355 © Ulita | Dreamstime.com.

Conclusions

The coalition is a case that shows how the recognition of traditional governance by the state is useful in boosting cooperation for development. Traditional governance recognises coalition residents as powerful decision-makers, able to steer development in a democratic way to address their most pressing issues. The institutions that allow the neighbourhood alliance to exist are specific to Oaxaca. Nevertheless, the coexistence of traditional and non-traditional governance is far from being exclusive to Oaxaca, and is present across most of the Global South (Holzinger et al., 2016). This case shows that it is possible to find hope for the improvement of popular settlements in the Global South by building governance practices relying on the recognition of traditional governance to enable development, instead of imposing institutional pathways that belong elsewhere.

References

Anaya Muñoz, A. (2005). Democratic equality and indigenous electoral institutions in Oaxaca, Mexico: Addressing the perils of a politics of recognition. *Critical Review of International Social and Political Philosophy*, *8*(3), 327–347. https://doi.org/10.1080/13698230500187201

Aust, H. P., & du Plessis, A. (2018). Good urban governance as a global aspiration: On the potential and limits of Sustainable Development Goal 11. In D. French & L. J. Kotzé (Eds.), *Sustainable development goals: Law, theory and implementation* (pp. 201–221). Edward Elgar Publishing.

Aylett, A. (2010). Conflict, collaboration and climate change: Participatory democracy and urban environmental struggles in Durban, South Africa. *International Journal of Urban and Regional Research*, *34*(3), 478–495. https://doi.org/10.1111/j.1468-2427.2010.00964.x

Caldeira, T. P. R. (2016). Peripheral urbanization: Autoconstruction, transversal logics, and politics in cities of the Global South. *Environment and Planning D: Society and Space*, *35*(1), 3–20. https://doi.org/10.1177/0263775816658479

Castán Broto, V. (2017). Urban governance and the politics of climate change. *World Development*, *93*, 1–15. https://doi.org/10.1016/j.worlddev.2016.12.031

Davis, M. (2006). *Planet of slums*. Verso.

Diaz Cayeros, A., Magaloni, B., & Ruiz Euler, A. (2013). Traditional governance, citizen engagement, and local public goods: Evidence from Mexico. *World Development*, *53*, 80–93. https://doi.org/10.1016/j.worlddev.2013.01.008

Eisenstadt, T. A. (2007). Usos y Costumbres and postelectoral conflicts in Oaxaca, Mexico, 1995–2004: An empirical and normative assessment. *Latin American Research Review*, *42*(1), 52–77.

Eisenstadt, T. A. (2011). *Politics, identity, and Mexico's indigenous rights movements*. Cambridge University Press.

Esri (Cartographer). (2021). *World Countries* (Generalized). Environmental Systems Research Institute. https://hub.arcgis.com/datasets/esri::world-countries-generalized/about

Graham, K. A. (1998). Urban aboriginal governance in Canada: Paradigms and prospects. *Zeitschrift Fur Kanada Studien*, *18*, 77–89.

Grindle, M. S. (2004). Good enough governance: poverty reduction and reform in developing countries. *Governance*, *17*(4), 525–548. https://doi.org/10.1111/j.0952-1895.2004.00256.x

Holzinger, K., Kern, F. G., & Kromrey, D. (2016). The dualism of contemporary traditional governance and the State: Institutional setups and political consequences. *Political Research Quarterly*, *69*(3), 469–481. https://doi.org/10.1177/1065912916648013

Horn, P. (2021). Enabling participatory planning to be scaled in exclusionary urban political environments: Lessons from the Mukuru Special Planning Area in Nairobi. *Environment and Urbanization*, *33*(2), 519–538. https://doi.org/10.1177/09562478211011088

IEE. (2020). *Sistemas Normativos Indígenas: catálogo de municipios sujetos al régimen de Sistemas Normativos Indígenas 2018*. Instituto estatal Electoral. https://www.ieepco.org.mx/sistemas-normativos/municipios-sujetos-al-regimen-de-sistemas-normativos-indigenas-2018

INEGI (Cartographer). (2020). *Marco Geoestadístico*. Instituto Nacional de Estadística y Geografía. https://www.inegi.org.mx/app/biblioteca/ficha.html?upc=889463807469

Magaloni, B., Díaz Cayeros, A., & Ruiz Euler, A. (2019). Public good provision and traditional governance in Indigenous Communities in Oaxaca, Mexico. *Comparative Political Studies*, *52*(12), 1841–1880. https://doi.org/10.1177/0010414019857094

Membele, G. M., Naidu, M., & Mutanga, O. (2022). Using local and indigenous knowledge in selecting indicators for mapping flood vulnerability in informal settlement contexts. *International Journal of Disaster Risk Reduction*, *71*, 102836. https://doi.org/10.1016/j.ijdrr.2022.102836

Mitlin, D. (2008). With and beyond the state – Co-production as a route to political influence, power and transformation for grassroots organizations. *Environment and Urbanization*, *20*(2), 339–360. https://doi.org/10.1177/0956247808096117

Newig, J., & Fritsch, O. (2009). Environmental governance: Participatory, multi-level – and effective? *Environmental Policy and Governance*, *19*(3), 197–214. https://doi.org/10.1002/eet.509

Otsuki, K. (2016). Infrastructure in informal settlements: Co-production of public services for inclusive governance. *Local Environment*, *1*(12), 1557–1572. https://doi.org/10.1080/13549839.2016.1149456

Reckien, D., Lwasa, S., Satterthwaite, D., McEvoy, D., Creutzig, F., Montgomery, M., ... Bautista, E. (2018). Equity, environmental justice, and urban climate change. In C. Rosenzweig, W. Solecki, P. Romero Lankao, S. Mehrotra, S. Dhakal, & S. Ali Ibrahim (Eds.), *Climate change and cities: Second assessment report of the urban climate change research network* (pp. 173–224). Cambridge University Press.

Recondo, D. (2018). "Usos y costumbres", y elecciones en Oaxaca. *Los dilemas de la democracia representativa, en una sociedad multicultural* (pt. 1), *2018*(36), 9. https://doi.org/10.22134/trace.36.1999.627

Rivero-Villar, A. (2021). Longitudinal resilience building in self-help settlements: Achieving transformations to unlock adaptations. *Geoforum*, *122*, 152–163. https://doi.org/10.1016/j.geoforum.2021.04.005

Romero-Lankao, P., Frantzeskaki, N., & Griffith, C. (2018). Sustainability transformation emerging from better governance. In T. Elmqvist, X. Bai, N. Frantzeskaki, C. Griffith, D. Maddox, T. McPhearson, S. Parnell, P. Romero-Lankao, D. Simon, & M. Watkins (Eds.), *Urban planet* (1st ed., pp. 263–280). Cambridge University Press. https://doi.org/10.1017/9781316647554.015

SEPOMEX (Cartographer). (2017). Códigos Postales, coordenadas y colonias. Servicio Postal Mexicano. https://datos.gob.mx/busca/dataset/codigos-postales-coordenadas-y-colonias

Streule, M., Karaman, O., Sawyer, L., & Schmid, C. (2020). Popular urbanization: Conceptualizing urbanization processes beyond informality. *International Journal of Urban and Regional Research*, *44*(4), 652–672. https://doi.org/10.1111/1468-2427.12872

UN-Habitat. (2003). *Global report on human settlements 2003: The challenge of slums*. United Nations. Earthscan.

Ziervogel, G., Waddell, J., Smit, W., & Taylor, A. (2016). Flooding in Cape Town's informal settlements: barriers to collaborative urban risk governance. *South African Geographical Journal = Suid-Afrikaanse Geografiese Tydskrif, 98*(1), 1–20. https://doi.org/10.1080/03736245.2014.924867

Chapter 23

The Grassland Alliance in Argentina and the Challenge of Conserving Nature in a Productive Landscape

Pablo Grilli

Programa Pastizales de Aves Argentinas, Universidad Nacional Arturo Jauretche, Argentina

Since the Industrial Revolution, our societies have taken the use of natural resources to the extreme. As a consequence, ecosystems have been profoundly degraded, with associated effects such as global climate change, pollution and biodiversity loss. The development of the most important civilisations in history was linked to the use of natural grasslands. Due to the potential of their soils, they were systematically replaced to use the land for the production of cereals and other crops. Those grasslands that remained standing became grazing land for different forms of livestock as the main source of animal protein. It is therefore not surprising that grasslands are one of the ecosystems most affected by human activity globally, mainly due to the production of raw materials.

In the Southern Cone of South America, a continuum of natural grasslands known as the Pampas Biome has developed: a territory of more than 1,000,000 km^2 covering the extreme south of Paraguay, the state of Rio Grande do Sul in Brazil, almost all of Uruguay and a large part of central-eastern Argentina (Fig. 23.1). The European colonial expansion of the Pampas Biome had the same effects that had already affected the grasslands of the rest of the world: the soils with the best agricultural aptitude were replaced by crops, while the rest was used for grazing (mainly cattle).

Argentina has two-thirds of the grasslands of the Pampas Biome. The productive capacity of its grasslands meant that they historically ended up in private hands, and it was unfeasible for the state to allocate considerable and functional extensions to the creation of protected natural areas. In more recent times, and thanks to new technologies for the production of pine, eucalyptus, soya, wheat, sorghum, sunflower and maize, the agricultural frontier advanced even further

Exploring Hope: Case Studies of Innovation, Change and Development in the Global South, 161–164

doi:10.1108/978-1-83549-736-420241028

Fig. 23.1. Grassland of the Pampas Biome Showing the Heterogeneity That Makes Possible a Great Diversity of Wild Species, Many of Them Threatened. *Source*: The author.

over the grasslands, pushing livestock into marginal regions, where cattle ranching and its transformative effects were concentrated. The result of this process was the loss of 80% of the total grasslands and the recognition of only a little more than 2% of its territory as a protected natural area (far below the 17% recommended by Aichi Biodiversity Target 11).

The country is the fifth largest beef producer in the world. The process that had to take place in order to do so profoundly affected the different forms of life unique to the grasslands. And it was the birds that showed this best: at least 2 species are now considered extinct in the wild, while 10 others experienced local extinctions. However, some of Argentina's most endangered grassland birds have managed to take refuge in cattle ranches. This was possible because livestock farming can be carried out in a wide variety of ways. While at one extreme there are conventional forms, based on the cultivation of exotic forage species and the use – and abuse – of inputs such as fertilisers, herbicides and insecticides, at the other extreme there are forms of production that rely on the use of native plants and the plant structure they generate, and on the correct 'reading' of natural environments, thus being able to dispense with most inputs and making use of what is known as process technology.

La Alianza del Pastizal (the Grassland Alliance)

The Grassland Alliance is an initiative coordinated by Bird Life International and led by its partner organisations in Brazil (*SAVE Brazil*), Paraguay (*Guyra Paraguay*), Uruguay (*Aves Uruguay*) and Argentina (*Aves Argentinas*). It was formed in 2006 with the aim of responding to a growing concern about the conservation status of grassland birds in these four countries, linking livestock producers with specialists in biodiversity conservation.

The first task of the Grassland Alliance in Argentina was to recognise the sites with the most threatened bird populations in the Pampas Biome. These were defined as Pilot Sites, where efforts were directed towards linking the owners of those fields that functioned as true biodiversity refuges. Originally, just over 20 farms were involved in the initiative, but they were fundamental, as they functioned as demonstration units where the interaction between producers and conservationists began to outline a prosperous working scenario.

The search for incentives for those producers who acted as 'guardians' of birds threatened with extinction was quickly established as a priority. Intensive work was done on the design of a seal of origin that would identify the meat produced in these fields, and that would function as part of a certification system for the production process behind it. A process capable of making the economic-productive demands of the establishment or company compatible with the conservation needs of the endangered birds.

The measures implemented on farms to conserve biodiversity include: (1) small strategic and temporary closures, to prevent the farm from entering and damaging the vegetation by grazing and trampling, (2) the management of internal watersheds, preventing the wetlands from drying out and controlling water surplus, (3) using the capacity of livestock to maintain vegetation structure, promoting heterogeneity in height and density of grasslands, (4) the construction of biodiversity connectors, especially at fields margins, (5) appropriate fire management, avoiding bird breeding periods, and (6) the implementation of nest protection strategies, consisting in the installation of nest protection nets and semi-permanent surveillance of breeding colonies to reduce predation, such as those applied to the Pampas Meadowlark (*Leistes defilippii*) and the Saffron-cowled Blackbird (*Xanthopsar flavus*), the two most endangered grassland bird species, which need every possible effort for their conservation (Fig. 23.2).

Fig. 23.2. A Male Pampas Meadowlark Guards the Territory Where It Is Going to Breed. This Is One of the Most Endangered Species in the Grasslands of the Pampas Biome. *Source*: The author.

Applying process technologies reduces production costs, which represents an advantage for producers and, at the same time, generates more stable livestock systems over time. At the same time, the Grassland Alliance has succeeded in increasing the price of meat from its farms on the domestic market, and in opening up export channels. A final stimulus came from the monetisation of greenhouse gas capture through carbon credits, given that livestock systems supported by well-managed natural grasslands are considered very efficient in capturing atmospheric carbon and retaining it in the soil.

What Next

Much remains to be done. This concept of nature-friendly production should be expanded beyond the Pampas Biome to include other forms of livestock and production (agricultural, forestry, mining, hydrocarbon, etc.). Generating scientific knowledge is a priority in this context and, although the guiding principles of the forms of work being applied are known, there is still a lot of research to be done. It is also necessary to train professionals and technicians specialised in this area, who can apply all the knowledge gathered along the way. In addition to meat and carbon sequestration, several other products and services come from well-managed farms (milk, honey, firewood, leather, seeds, timber, tourism and recreation, air and water purification, etc.) and should receive the same recognition as they do. Being made up of a growing collective of producers, advisors, environmentalists, technicians and scientists, the Grassland Alliance has enormous potential to impact public policy, something that has not yet been achieved in a profound way. However, during these 15 years of history, some achievements have been made, such as the elaboration and enactment of provincial laws for the conservation and sustainable use of natural grasslands, the intervention in the design of livestock plans and the signing of an agreement with the Argentine Rural Society, a leading organisation in livestock production at the national level, with which different lines of joint work have been drawn up.

Conclusions

The Grassland Alliance shows that the motivation and will of different social actors is the initial spark capable of lighting any torch. The fire must then be kept burning, going through different periods and facing its challenges, so that it is able to illuminate the paths to be travelled. All of us in the Grassland Alliance know that we can do better. We know this because what we did in the past has left us in this worrying present. That will and motivation of the initial spark makes it possible to overcome gaps, recognising that a producer and a conservationist – once at odds with each other – want the same thing: a better world for themselves, but above all for their children. The Grassland Alliance is an example of a meeting of interests, maintaining the necessary differences and visions, but with a clear horizon, where conservation and production are possible, and production and conservation are necessary.

Chapter 24

Sources of Environmental Conflicts from Energy Justice and Equity Perspective: Evidence from Gold Mining Sectors in Ghana

Asaah Sumaila Mohammed

Department of Environmental Science, CK Tedam University of Technology and Applied Science, Navrongo, Ghana

The literature generally agrees that people living in extractive areas around the world are dissatisfied with the benefits they receive from resource extraction (Amponsah Tawiah & Dartey Baah, 2011; Ayelazuno, 2014; Mohammed et al., 2019; Obi, 2014). Local populations have frequently expected that resource extraction would not displace them from their traditional livelihood activities. However, extractive companies have largely failed to meet this expectation, resulting in the formation of various interest groups at various levels to negotiate on behalf of extractive-affected communities and indigenous populations in extractive areas. Conflicts and civil wars have resulted from negotiations between local populations and extractive companies in many extractive countries, particularly in Africa (Bond, 2014; Global Witness, 2007; O'Faircheallaigh, 2013). Obi (2014) associated the recurring conflicts in the Nigeria's Niger Delta region with the presence of oil and gas production in the region.

The occurrence of these conflicts has been linked to a variety of factors. This chapter has broadly classified them into thematic areas based on perspectives on energy justice and equity. According to McCauley et al. (2013), energy justice includes both the physically unequal distribution of benefits and ills, as well as the unequal distribution of the responsibilities that accompany them. The inequity in distribution that results draws my attention to the nature and location of Ghana's unjust effects of gold mining production. As a result, the implementation of recognition justice could shed light on under-recognised groups in society, as well as farmers and others in Ghana who rely on the environment for a living.

Exploring Hope: Case Studies of Innovation, Change and Development in the Global South, 165–170

Published under exclusive licence by Emerald Publishing Limited
doi:10.1108/978-1-83549-736-420241029

Fig. 24.1. Abra a Pit Gold Mine, Africa. *Source*: ID 40250064 © Demerzel21 | Dreamstime.com.

Energy justice and equity also request to recognise of different points of view based on social, cultural, ethnic, racial, and gender differences (McCauley et al., 2013). Finally, energy justice necessitates the use of fair procedures that involve all stakeholders in an equitable manner (Walker & Day, 2012). It also necessitates participation by the government and corporations, impartiality, and complete disclosure of information, as well as the use of appropriate and sympathetic engagement tools (McCauley et al., 2013; McDermott et al., 2013).

Based on my previous research and experience working in the areas of extractive sector governance in Ghana, I apply the energy justice and equity perspectives to human-centred research on energy politics and benefit sharing, with a focus on the distributional, procedural, and recognition aspects of energy justice and equity. The following thematic sections categorise the causes of environmental conflicts in Ghana's mining sector and discuss them objectively based on empirical evidence from various mining areas in Ghana (Figs. 24.1 and 24.2).

Inequitable Distribution of Benefits from Mining

Several conflicts in Ghana's mining sector are generally caused by an imbalance between the benefits of resource extraction and the benefits to local populations whose livelihoods and social conditions are impacted by extraction. Local populations' rights have frequently been violated, resulting in issues such as environmental impact, inadequate compensation, unequal benefit sharing, and limited employment and development (Hilson, 2002; Mohammed et al., 2019). Farmlands were the most lost to agriculture in our previous study in the Obuasi and Takwa areas. Emphasising the magnitude of the land problem, an interview with Environmental Protection Agency (EPA) officers revealed that the entire Tarkwa

Fig. 24.2. Abra a Pit Gold Mine, Africa. *Source*: ID 40376595 © Demerzel21 | Dreamstime.com.

Township is part of the concession of the AngloGold Tarkwa Mine. All lands, including those used for human livelihoods, are indirectly owned by the company, which means that anyone farming on any land could be asked to leave at any time (Mohammed et al., 2019). Compensation paid to landowners and/or farmers whose lands are taken by mining companies is deemed insufficient. Our research discovered that mining companies pay compensations in violation of the Minerals and Mining (Amendment) Act 900 of 2015, Sections 72, 73, and 74, which govern how compensations are supposed to be paid. Responses from interviewees regarding compensation revealed that people whose lands/farms are taken for mining are paid on unsatisfactory terms.

Multinational Mining Companies (MNMCs) have been heavily criticised by both local and international pressure groups for engaging in unwholesome health, safety, and environmental practices in many mining areas in Ghana, particularly in Obuasi, Prestia, and Takwa, to name a few. As a result, host-community protests have erupted into a full-fledged assault on mining companies and their employees, resulting in violations of facilities and infrastructure (Ayelazuno, 2014; Doso Jnr et al., 2015; Hilson, 2002).

Another observation made was that conflicts between local communities and extractive companies were caused by inadequate environmental impact assessments (EIAs) and compensation. Residents in the Ahafo mining areas operated by Newmont Ghana Limited have raised several complaints about the company's levels of noise and air pollution. Communities frequently accuse the Ghana Environmental Protection Agency of failing to conduct effective environmental impact studies and regulations on the impact of mining in their area, particularly on agricultural livelihoods. According to some studies, EIA procedures in many extractive companies do not adequately address social impacts or the impacts on indigenous minorities' traditional livelihood activities resulting in ineffective Corporate Social Responsibility (CSR) Initiatives (Global Witness, 2007; Hilson, 2002; Idemudia et al., 2022; Mohammed et al., 2022).

According to my cursory estimation and confirmed by other studies, local communities bear the majority of the environmental and other social costs of mining, while extractive companies receive the majority of the profits and rents (Amponsah Tawiah & Dartey Baah, 2011; Ayelazuno, 2014; Doso Jnr et al., 2015; Hilson, 2002). Mining in Ghana, according to Ayeelazuno (2011), is a continuous primitive accumulation process as part of global capitalist development dating back to the pre-colonial era through free trade. My several years of research and practice as an advocate for responsible mining in the Ahafo, Obuasi, and Takwa mining areas confirm that basic social and economic infrastructure such as good roads, potable water, functional health facilities, and so on are grossly inadequate, resulting in preventable deaths and diseases (Mohammed et al., 2019). According to Maconachie and Hilson (2013), extraction communities are frequently among Africa's poorest and most economically depressed. He emphasised that the youth are particularly vulnerable. In response to these disadvantages, the youth frequently protest, usually violently, resulting in civil wars.

Under-Recognition of Community Rights and Injustice in Stakeholder Participation

Mining has been one of the most dangerous threats to socio-cultural rights in Ghana's mining communities, changing the social pattern and nearly the entire way of life of the people. Mining, for example, has resulted in the destruction of sacred sites such as cemeteries and shrines. In an interview with a chief in Obuasi, he revealed that there have been several instances where cemeteries have been completely relocated due to the discovery of gold in the area. He lamented that such actions were a violation of their cultural rights in the pursuit of gold.

Land ownership rights and control are the main factors contributing to many conflicts between mining firms and local communities in several parts of Ghana (Cuba et al., 2014). Poor land laws and regulatory structures in extractive regions lead to ongoing unrest and opposition to the operations of extractive businesses. According to several studies conducted in Ghana, there is an unequal business relationship between the country's miners and the farmers, who are usually denied access to their source of income (Cuba et al., 2014; Mohammed et al., 2019). Local populations typically lose significant land resources to extractive businesses, depriving them of their means of subsistence (Amponsah Tawiah & Dartey Baah, 2011; Ayelazuno, 2014; Doso Jnr et al., 2015). In many of these extractive nations, anomalies and contradictions in federal legislation are made worse by weak procedures for enforcing the law already in place. This has an impact on land entitlements and further impedes traditional economic operations and compensations in Ghana mining communities.

Poor participation in decision-making during the planning of social investment programs by extractive businesses is another issue contributing to disputes in the extractive zones. Local communities rarely take part in the design of social investment initiatives started by extractive companies in many extractive regions (Mohammed et al., 2022). As a result, corporations impose social investment programs on local communities whose interests conflict with their own. In certain instances, the companies build these projects to appease specific groups and individuals inside the communities, which results in an unequal distribution of benefits and, as a result, agitations and confrontations.

Conclusions

The chapter's evidence points to the unequal distribution of mining benefits, the inadequate recognition of the rights of the local communities, and procedural flaws in the engagement of key players, particularly local actors, as the main drivers of disputes in the mining sector in Ghana. I come to the conclusion that mining firms and government organisations in Ghana have neglected these reasons for years. Institutional and policy reforms are required to reflect on and address the injustice in the mining sector. The rights of communities to livelihood and a share of mining proceeds must be enshrined and adequately legislated in Ghana's mineral and mining laws.

References

Amponsah Tawiah, K., & Dartey Baah, K. (2011). The mining industry in Ghana: A blessing or a curse. *International Journal of Business and Social Science*, *2*(12), 62–69.

Ayelazuno, J. (2011). Continuous primitive accumulation in Ghana: the real-life stories of dispossessed peasants in three mining communities. *Review of African Political Economy*, *38*(130), 537–550.

Ayelazuno, J. A. (2014). The 'new extractivism' in Ghana: A critical review of its development prospects. *The Extractive Industries and Society*, *1*(2), 292–302.

Bond, C. J. (2014). Positive peace and sustainability in the mining context: Beyond the triple bottom line. *Journal of Cleaner Production*, *84*, 164–173. https://doi.org/10.1016/j.jclepro.2014.01.033

Cuba, N., Bebbington, A., Rogan, J., & Millones, M. (2014). Extractive industries, livelihoods and natural resource competition: Mapping overlapping claims in Peru and Ghana. *Applied Geography*, *54*, 250–261. http://dx.doi.org/10.1016/j.apgeog.2014.05.003

Doso Jnr, S., Cieem, G., Ayensu Ntim, A., Twumasi Ankrah, B., & Barimah, P. T. (2015). Effects of loss of agricultural land due to large-scale gold mining on agriculture in Ghana: The case of the Western Region. *British Journal of Research*, *2*(6), 196–221.

Global Witness. (2007). *Oil and Mining in Violent Places: Why voluntary codes for companies don't guarantee human rights*. Eldis. https://www.eldis.org/document/A33773

Hilson, G. (2002). The environmental impact of small-scale gold mining in Ghana: Identifying problems and possible solutions. *Geographical Journal*, *168*(1), 57–72. https://doi.org/10.1111/1475-4959.00038

Idemudia, U., Tuokuu, F. X. D., Essah, M., & Graham, E. (2022). Corporate social responsibility and community development in Africa: Issues and prospects. In U. Idemudia, F. X. D. Tuokuu, & T. A. Liedong (Eds.), *Business and sustainable development in Africa: Medicine or placebo?* (Chapter 4, pp. 80–97). Routledge.

Maconachie, R., & Hilson, G. (2013). Editorial introduction: The extractive industries, community development and livelihood change in developing countries. *Community Development Journal*, *48*(3), 347–359. https://doi.org/10.1093/cdj/bst018

McCauley, D. A., Heffron, R. J., Stephan, H., & Jenkins, K. (2013). Advancing energy justice: The triumvirate of tenets. *International Energy Law Review*, *32*(3), 107–110.

McDermott, M., Mahanty, S., & Schreckenberg, K. (2013). Examining equity: A multidimensional framework for assessing equity in payments for ecosystem services. *Environmental Science & Policy*, *33*, 416–427. https://doi.org/10.1016/j.envsci.2012.10.006

Mohammed, A. S., Ackah, I., Tuokuu, F. X., & Abane, S. (2022). Assessing the corporate social responsibility interventions in the Ghanaian oil and gas industry: Perspectives from local actors. *The Extractive Industries and Society*, *12*, Article 101145. https://doi.org/10.1016/j.exis.2022.101145

Mohammed, A. S., Osumanu, I. K., & Antwi, S. H. (2019). Extractivism and community development in Ghana: Local actors' perspectives from gold mining in Tarkwa and Obuasi. *International Journal of Development and Sustainability*, *8*(5), 311–328.

Obi, C. (2014). Oil and conflict in Nigeria's Niger Delta region: Between the barrel and the trigger. *The Extractive Industries and Society*, *1*(2), 147–153. https://doi.org/10.1016/j.exis.2014.03.001

O'Faircheallaigh, C. (2013). Extractive industries and Indigenous peoples: A changing dynamic? *Journal of Rural Studies*, *30*, 20–30. https://doi.org/10.1016/j.jrurstud.2012.11.003

Walker, G., & Day, R. (2012). Fuel poverty as injustice: Integrating distribution, recognition and procedure in the struggle for affordable warmth. *Energy policy*, *49*, 69–75.

Chapter 25

Happiness and Wellbeing Centre at Royal University of Bhutan: A Unique Approach

Sangay Dorji and Pema Latsho

Paro College of Education, Royal University of Bhutan, Bhutan

The colleges of the Royal University of Bhutan (RUB) have always aspired to enrich the quality of students' outcomes and behaviour while in college and upon graduation. However, creating an enabling environment for students' development through a good student support system, both in terms of services and facilities is one of the major challenges faced by the university today (Fig. 25.1). Amongst the various objectives set for enhancement of student support system, the university could never actualise the goal of establishment of counselling service centre at all the colleges. The concern about the establishment of an effective student counselling service centre is indicated in almost all the University's Annual Reports since 2008. One of the major constraints highlighted is the lack of proper resources, mainly expertise in the field of counselling, and trained counsellors. Today, the general consensus amongst the students and staff at the RUB is a belief that having an effective counselling services centre can contribute positively to mitigating many of the personal and academic issues faced by the students at the RUB. This belief is substantiated by a couple of studies, reports compiled by some external consultants and the existing literature (Brailsford, 2011; Gündogdu, 2010; Schuh et al., 2010; Schwartz et al., 2012).

At the national level, the practice of counselling is a relatively new concept in Bhutan. Also, there are very few trained professionals in the country. The establishment of guidance and counselling at the school level has been one of the primary priorities of the government's developmental activities since 1993. However, at the tertiary education institute, the establishment of guidance and counselling centres was never considered as a requirement until recent times. Therefore, the *Happiness and Wellbeing Centres* were established in 2019 to address the emerging wellbeing, academic, and career challenges at RUB colleges. The centres are supporting Paro Colleges in fulfilling the overall vision to become *An internationally recognized university steeped in GNH values*. The centres were established

Exploring Hope: Case Studies of Innovation, Change and Development in the Global South, 171–175

Published under exclusive licence by Emerald Publishing Limited
doi:10.1108/978-1-83549-736-420241030

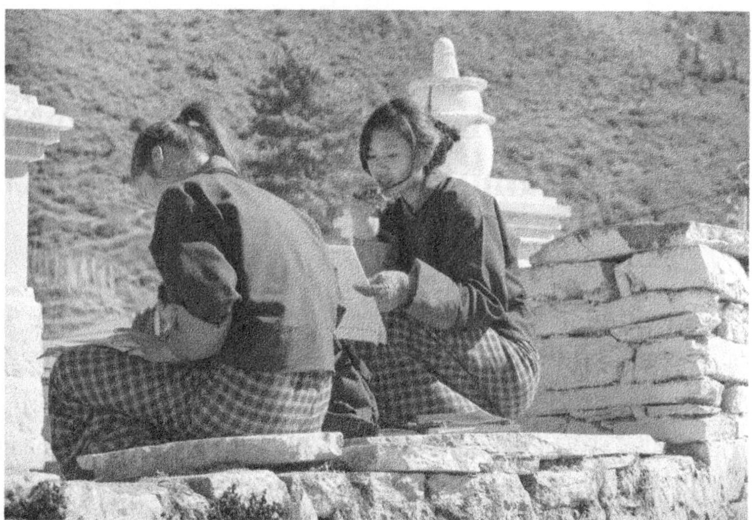

Fig. 25.1 Two Girls Studying in Front of the Entrance to the Rinpung Dzong in Paro, Bhutan. *Source*: ID 43116598 © Nicola Messana | Dreamstime.com.

with financial assistance from the European Union, Erasmus Plus Programme through a project developed and coordinated by Paro College of Education in partnership with three Universities from the European Union: VUB, Brussels, ISMAI, Portugal, and UoB, UK.

Furthermore, the need for mental health support has become even more pertinent post-COVID pandemic, hence the Happiness and Wellbeing Centres are serving as a safe place for the students at the RUB to seek refuge during difficult times and they provide opportunities for the interested students to build skills, enhance insight, and grow resilience, which will all go a long way in preparing them for life. The Happiness and Wellbeing Centres are leading in counselling & wellbeing education, training, and research programmes.

Also, the centres are assisting individual colleges in enhancing teaching-learning by providing academic support, reprographics services, internet facilities, books, and space for group discussion. Finally, the enhancement of mental health support through digital platforms was very useful during the pandemic.

Innovative Elements of the Centres

The Naming and the Design of the Counselling Centres

Taking into account the stereotype and reservation around the term 'counselling', the centre was named as 'Happiness and Wellbeing Centre'. This unique model of the counselling centre was developed according to the changing labour market needs, and to suit the mindset of students of the RUB aligned with cultural dynamics (Hoshmand, 2006). The services under the centre are informed by five thematic areas: working with life challenges, leadership of self, communication, social and emotional intelligence, and being Bhutanese. Unlike conventional counselling centres, this model of the centre was oriented towards empowering the individuals and development of self.

The Operation Framework

The centres are guided by an operation framework consisting of 14 chapters (233 pages book). The framework is an integrated model of contemporary theories and principles in the field of counselling, psychology, and wellbeing, infused with the Bhutanese philosophy of Gross National Happiness (Ura et al., 2012). The framework is guiding day-to-day operation of the centres. The framework contains knowledge, skills, and experiences regarding the practice of counselling, wellbeing & happiness in the form of detailed descriptions of contemporary psychological theories, counselling concepts, principles, and practices. Additionally, the framework includes chapters on indigenous Bhutanese philosophy, knowledge and practices based on the philosophy of Gross National Happiness.

The Digital Platform

Considering factors like accessibility, affordability, and authenticity, virtual support is exercised more frequently with young people, and this platform has different features devoted to several services related to wellbeing, mental health, and counselling. For instance, students can make an appointment with the counsellor under the theme 'working with life challenges' from their individual portal in the platform (Popoola, 2012). Likewise, students can drop their concerns/inquiries in the forum to seek support from the other peers and staff members both at their own campuses or other campuses of RUB.

Inclusive Approach

The Happiness and Wellbeing Centres acknowledge the diversity of the student population and strive to create an environment in which all students feel welcome, irrespective of social class, religion, ethnic background, functional impairments, etc. In case of a student undergoing difficulty, the centres' staff might learn from students which barriers they face that impede them from using all their capacities to learn in college. This could range from difficult access to classrooms for students using a wheelchair to learning material that is not adapted to students with visual impairments, etc. The centres support in understanding what the exact barriers are in consultation with the students and then look for solutions. This will often mean that the centres will contact teaching and other college staff to see how classes can be made more inclusive by adopting relevant accommodations.

Stakeholders

The centres are materialising Gross National Happiness, the national aspiration of Bhutan. These centres do not just provide an opportunity to enhance wellbeing, insight, and skills of PCE students, but it also provides an opportunity for the Bhutanese Agencies (NGOs and government) working in the field of human services, counselling, wellbeing, and young people to collaborate through a concerted and integrated approach and work towards addressing the issues concerning youth and general population in a sustainable way. The centres signed a Memorandum of Agreement (MoA) with nine stakeholders through four rounds of consultative meetings. The MoA highlighted key areas of collaboration between these Agencies and the centres in the area of mental health, counselling, and wellbeing. As a result of this MoA, the centres are offering a certificate-level course in 'career guidance and education counselling' to individuals working at educational consultancy and placement firms in Bhutan, in spring 2022.

Impact of the Centres and Way Forward

The project directly benefitted 9,446 students and 1,272 staff of the RUB through service support provided by the Happiness and Wellbeing Centres. The following extract from the Beneficiary Assessment Study captures some of the key impact of the centres:

> 'The COVID-19 pandemic, which began in 2020, did have a negative impact both on the HWCs themselves, and on mental health in general, which was unavoidable and widely experienced globally. Despite this, the HWCs did have a positive impact for students. The positive impacts that were found as a result of our evaluation focus group data are as follows:

- Increased awareness of mental health and positive attitudes towards counselling
- Positive change in interactions between staff and students
- Positive impact on student behaviour
- Providing a welcoming place for students
- Reduced number of disciplinary issues
- Reduced academic stress'

The Ministry of Education in Bhutan already communicated its interest in replicating the centres at different schools in Bhutan. A scholar from the Royal Education Council of Bhutan pursuing his PhD Studies at the University of New Brunswick, Canada is already working on replicating the Happiness and Wellbeing Centres at the UNB campus, under the Department of Education. The development of the centres in terms of theoretical framework, information, and necessary support is provided by RUB. Likewise, the enhancement plan of the 'Happiness and Wellbeing Centres' is highlighted as one of the key priorities of the overall strategic plan of the University, from 2018 to 2030. Major activities of the strategic plan in line with the sustainability of the centres can be found under the 'Development Theme III: Promote GNH-Inspired Environment'.

References

Brailsford, I. (2011). 'The ha'porth of tar to save the ship': Student counselling and vulnerable university students, 1965–1980. *History of Education*, *40*(3), 357–370. https://doi.org/10.1080/0046760X.2010.529833

Gündogdu, M. H. (2010). Life orientations among university students. *Egitim ve Bilim*, *35*(157), 192.

Hoshmand, L. T. (2006). *Culture, psychotherapy, and counseling: Critical and integrative perspectives*. Sage Publications.

Popoola, B. I. (Ed.). (2012). *Online guidance and counseling: Toward effectively applying technology: Toward effectively applying technology*. IGI Global. Information Science Reference.

Schuh, J. H., Jones, S. R., & Harper, S. R. (Eds.). (2010). *Student services: A handbook for the profession*. John Wiley & Sons.

Schwartz, V., Nissel, C., Eisenberg, D., Kay, J., & Brown, J. T. (2012). Increasing counseling center utilization: Yeshiva university's experience. *Journal of College Student Psychotherapy*, *26*(1), 50–60. https://doi.org/10.1080/87568225.2012.633047

Ura, K., Alkire, S., Zangmo, T., & Wangdi, K. (2012). *A short guide to gross national happiness index*. The Centre for Bhutan Studies.

Chapter 26

The Changing Face of Snow Cover in Afghanistan: Opportunities for Development Interventions

Fazlullah Akhtar, Abdul Haseeb Azizi, Christian Borgemeister, Bernhard Tischbein and Usman Khalid Awan

Center for Development Research (ZEF), Bonn, Germany

The global temperature increased by 1.1°C since 1880 (NASA Earth Observatory, 2022). Depending on the region and the relevant ecosystem, the varying temperature extremes and alterations of precipitation in different regions lead to a variety of changes. The climate changes are driven by various factors, basically natural, but modified by humans through certain interventions. The anticipated increase in global temperature will change snow and ice between liquid and solid states. Flash floods are caused by abrupt snowmelt and a change in the temporal dynamics of soil microbial functioning, which are primarily caused by temperature rise. These floods have severe consequences for people, other living organisms as well as the infrastructure. With the changing climate, it is also anticipated that water availability may change in terms of magnitude and temporal pattern which may include wetter springs and drier summers or otherwise wetter summers and drier winters (Akhtar et al., 2022).

Globally, the annual economic losses brought on by disasters, mainly driven – or at least enhanced – by climate change, have been estimated to be around $520 billion (Hallegatte et al., 2017). In order to mitigate these losses, the prerequisite is to manage water at all scales, e.g. at the field, farm, sub-basin and basin levels for which the soft and hard infrastructure is missing, especially, at the regional level in countries like Afghanistan (Fig. 26.1). Therefore, there is a dire need to develop new tools and techniques as well as support water managers and users in enhancing their technical capacity to effectively utilise these new tools. At present, it is challenging to engineer a solution to the nation's growing water

Exploring Hope: Case Studies of Innovation, Change and Development in the Global South, 177–182

Published under exclusive licence by Emerald Publishing Limited
doi:10.1108/978-1-83549-736-420241031

Fig. 26.1. Afghanistan Landscape. *Source*: ID 22260681 © Scaramax | Dreamstime.com.

shortage and the impacts of climate change on its land and water resources (Akhtar & Shah, 2020). In order to *gain some time* for water management to plan or at least frame water allocation for next spring/summer season, it is crucial to assess the country's overall snow cover (SC) for being the major source of water availability in the country. The SC estimation provides at least an approximate outlook on water availability in the following spring/summer season which represents the peak demand period. Since there is limited infrastructure available for the physical monitoring of SC and other meteorological parameters, therefore, given the country's current fragile situation, remote sensing-based assessments provide doable recommendations for shaping policies and investment plans for shaping sustainable land and water management. Thus, in this study, we are using an improved product of Moderate Resolution Imaging Spectroradiometer (MODIS) (i.e. MOYDGL06) to study variation in the SC across Afghanistan's river basins throughout the four distinct seasons from 2003 to 2018 (Muhammad & Thapa, 2020).

Estimation of the Variation in the SC in Afghanistan

Afghanistan is located at the crossroads of Central and South Asia. The total area of the country is 652,860 km^2. The country is divided into five river basins known as Panj-Amu, Kabul, Northern, Harirod-Murghab and Helmand having irrigated areas of 4.5%, 7.0%, 8.6%, 3.9% and 5.4%, respectively (FAO, 2016). The snowmelt from the Hindukush and Himalayan mountain ranges provides more than 80% of Afghanistan's water resources (Ahmad & Wasiq, 2004) and most of the precipitation falls within the months of November–February. The climate is classified as continental with hot summers and cold winters. The mean annual temperature across the country is 13.4°C while the mean annual precipitation is around 338 mm (World Bank, 2022).

In this study, variation in the SC was estimated while using a combined and improved snow-cover product (i.e. MOYDGL06). This product has a spatial resolution of 500 m and an 8-day temporal resolution. The MOYDGL06 combined and improved maximum SC product is made of combining both Terra (MOD10A2.006) and Aqua (MYD10A2.006) sensors which are available for the period 2002–2018 (Muhammad & Thapa, 2020). To lower the uncertainty in the estimation of SC, both products have been combined which is useful in lowering the overestimation because the corresponding pixel in both data sets is taken to be snow unless it is specifically marked as not having any snow (Muhammad & Thapa, 2020).

Spatial Changes in the SC

The spatial analysis shows that the Panj-Amu, Kabul, Harirod-Murghab, Northern and Helmand River basins respectively received 38.6%, 20.6%, 14.3%, 12.0% and 5.8% mean annual SC. The mean maximum SC was observed at the Panj-Amu River Basin which drains into the transboundary Amu Darya River Basin and accounts for 10% of its total runoff. The minimum SC was experienced by the Helmand River Basin which accounts for 5.76% of the total area of the basin (Table 26.1). The maximum SC during the study period was respectively 97.0%, 77.9%, 95.9%, 99.0% and 40.3%.

Temporal Changes in the SC

Analysis of the SC during 2003–2018 showed that 2018 had the lowest SC accounting for 10.6% while 2012 experienced the highest SC which accounts for approximately 16.1% of the total area of the country. Since 2014, the SC has been steadily descending until the end of the study period (i.e. 2018) and is likely to have further decreased after 2018 too (Fig. 26.2).

The seasonal analysis of the SC shows that the Winter season has been the highest recipient of the SC while in Summer, most of the snowmelt contributes to the streamflow except the permanent snow accumulated in the high elevations until they are supplemented again by the snowfall in autumn season (Fig. 26.3).

Table 26.2 shows that in the winter season the Panj-Amu, Kabul, Harirod-Murghab, Northern and Helmand River basins experienced a mean SC of 63.5%,

Table 26.1. Annual (Mean, Minimum and Maximum) SC Analysis of Different River Basins in Afghanistan During 2003–2018.

No	River Basin	Annual SCA (%)		
		Mean SC	Max SC	Min SC
1	Panj-Amu River Basin	38.6	97.0	5.7
2	Kabul River Basin	20.6	77.9	0.5
3	Harirod-Murghab River Basin	14.3	95.9	0.0
4	Northern River Basin	12.0	99.0	0.0
5	Helmand River Basin	5.8	40.3	0.0

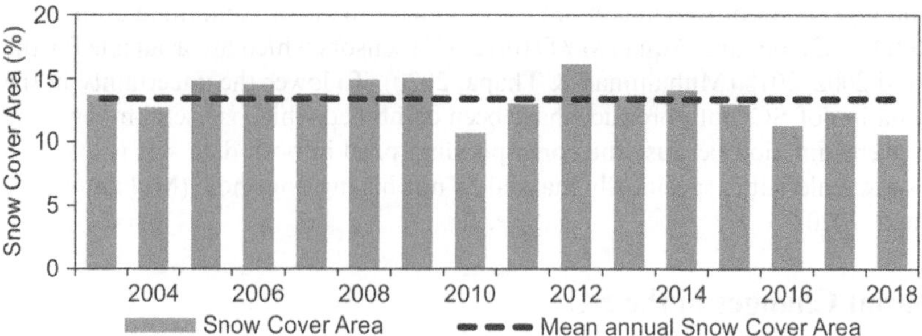

Fig. 26.2. Temporal Variation of SC Across Afghanistan. *Source*: Own elaboration.

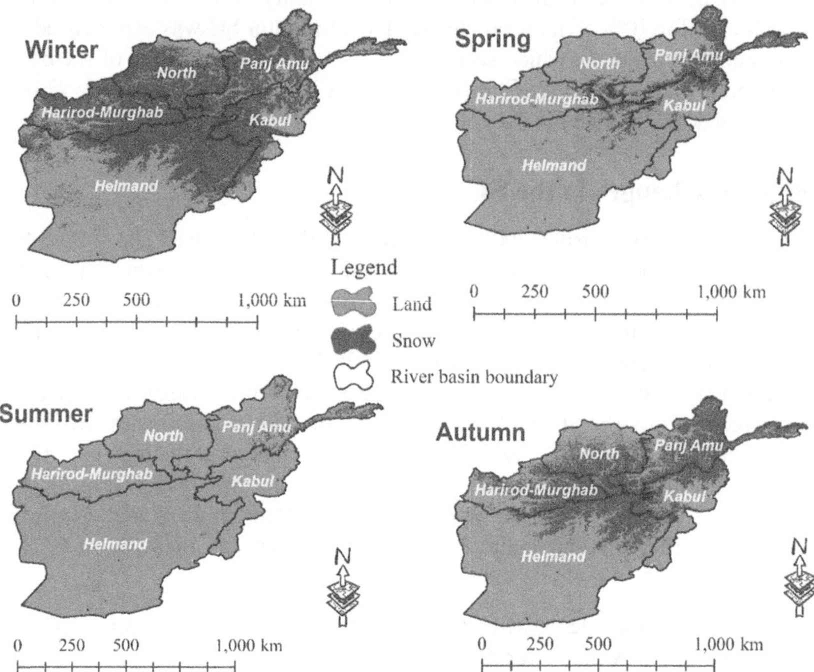

Fig. 26.3. Seasonal SC Extent of Different River Basins in Afghanistan. *Source*: Own elaboration.

45.3%, 38.5%, 29.5% and 16.1%, respectively, during the study period. Similarly, the mean SC in the Spring season was 34.8%, 13.9%, 2.41%, 3.09% and 1.24%, respectively. The permanent snow, that stays over the hot summer too, appears to be present only Panj-Amu and Kabul river basins.

Fig. 26.4 shows the SC anomalies over the study period (2003–2018) and a steady decrease in the mean annual SC from 2010 onwards becomes visible.

Table 26.2. Seasonal SC Analysis (%) of Different River Basins in Afghanistan During 2003–2018.

No	River Basin	Seasonal SCA (%)			
		Winter	Spring	Summer	Autumn
1	Panj-Amu River Basin	63.5	34.8	11.1	45.0
2	Kabul River Basin	45.3	13.9	2.27	20.1
3	Harirod-Murghab River Basin	38.5	2.41	0.0	14.7
4	Northern River Basin	29.5	3.09	0.0	14.0
5	Helmand River Basin	16.1	1.24	0.0	5.0

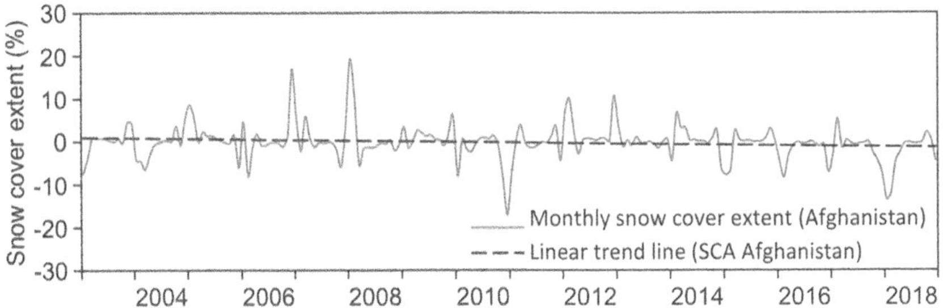

Fig. 26.4. Analysis of SC Anomalies Across Afghanistan. *Source*: Own elaboration.

Since SC is the main source of supply for irrigation, groundwater recharge, municipal use, industrial withdrawal and environmental flow, reduction in its quantity both in space and time will have lasting adverse impacts on local livelihood and the country's economic growth.

Conclusions

This study revealed that Panj-Amu River basin and Kabul River basin experienced the maximum SC throughout the study period. Except Northern River basin, the rest of the river basins are of transboundary nature and therefore are shared with neighbouring countries in terms of catchment area and inflow contribution. Despite contributing at least 10% of the annual runoff of the Amu Darya River basin, Afghanistan has not been involved in any discussion on transboundary sharing and management of the waters of the Amu Darya River basin, which otherwise highlights the unsustainability of water resource management and investment plans as well as anticipated future conflicts in Central Asian downstream countries. Since agriculture sector, accounting for a large portion of Afghanistan's GDP, is inefficient in meeting the local population's food demand. Therefore, around 6% area of Afghanistan is rainfed agriculture and 47% of rangeland (FAO, 2016), the existing snowmelt could be utilised for bringing parts of these lands (under irrigation accompanied by water management interventions improving the storage features of the basin to be introduced at all spatial scales).

The presence of maximum SC during autumn and winter highlights the need to raise storages and reservoirs for runoff which can be used during the peak demand period; this will on one side contribute to irrigation expansions and intensification, increasing agricultural productivity, stabilising groundwater recharge and on the other side will reduce adverse impacts of climate change by enhanced adaptation strategies. This study provides hope for the decision makers to optimise their water management plans in accordance with the assessments derived from these products because it shows an alternative for SC monitoring under vulnerable conditions where physical interventions are timely risky. Additionally, this study contributes to the development of new avenues for local, regional and transboundary cooperation on water resources by offering a solid knowledge base for interventions aimed at enhancing livelihoods and food security.

References

Ahmad, M., & Wasiq, M. (2004). *Water resource development in Northern Afghanistan and its implications for Amu Darya Basin*. World Bank Publications.

Akhtar, F., Borgemeister, C., Tischbein, B., & Awan, U. K. (2022). Metrics assessment and streamflow modeling under changing climate in a data-scarce heterogeneous region: A case study of the Kabul River Basin. *Water*, *14*(11), 1697. https://doi.org/10.3390/w14111697

Akhtar, F., & Shah, U. (2020). Emerging water scarcity issues and challenges in Afghanistan. In A. Ranjan (Ed.), *Water issues in Himalayan South Asia* (pp. 1–28). Palgrave Macmillan. https://doi.org/10.1007/978-981-32-9614-5_1

FAO. (2016). *The Islamic Republic of Afghanistan: Land Cover Atlas*. Food and Agriculture Organization of the United Nations. https://books.google.de/books?id=QtyJvgAACAAJ

Hallegatte, S., Vogt-Schilb, A., Bangalore, M., & Rozenberg, J. (2017). *Unbreakable: Building the resilience of the poor in the face of natural disasters*. World Bank Publications.

Muhammad, S., & Thapa, A. (2020). An improved Terra–Aqua MODIS snow cover and Randolph Glacier Inventory 6.0 combined product (MOYDGL06*) for high-mountain Asia between 2002 and 2018. *Earth System Science Data*, *12*(1), 345–356. https://doi.org/10.5194/essd-12-345-2020

NASA Earth Observatory. (2022). World of change: Global temperatures. NASA. https://earthobservatory.nasa.gov/world-of-change/global-temperatures

World Bank. (2022, September 11). *World Bank Climate Change Knowledge Portal*. World Bank. Retrieved September 11, 2022, from https://climateknowledgeportal.worldbank.org/country/afghanistan/climate-data-historical

Chapter 27

Energy Transition in the Global South: Combating Energy Poverty and Climate Change

Aviram Sharma

Post-Growth Innovation Lab, University of Vigo, Spain

After decades of policy and political push, the geography of renewable energy deployment has remained quite uneven (Sharma & Pandey, 2021). The renewable energy uptake and energy transition landscape are quite complex in the global south. Depending on geographical, historical, socio-political, and varied economic factors, developing countries in the global south have taken diverse pathways to meet their energy requirements from conventional and modern renewable energy sources. In recent years, energy transition received renewed interest due to climate emergencies and turbulences in the international energy market. Efforts are made to achieve complete decarbonisation of the economy and a 100% transition to renewable-based sources. Even transnational institutions, like, the United Nations have recognised access to sustainable energy as a major Sustainable Development Goal (SDG). The UN SDG 7 aims to ensure access to affordable, reliable, sustainable, and modern energy for all. However, despite all these efforts, around 770 million people do not have access to electricity, primarily in Africa and Asia (Fig. 27.1).

Countries in the global south do not only have to devise urgent measures to adopt renewables to mitigate climate change but at the same time, they need to ensure that large sections of marginalised and vulnerable populations living without proper access to modern energy receive an adequate supply of energy to realise their socio-economic goals. In this background, this chapter engages with the efforts made by the Indian government to promote sustainable access to modern and renewable energy (with a focus on solar) to achieve energy transition and full decarbonisation in India and other countries in the global south.

Exploring Hope: Case Studies of Innovation, Change and Development in the Global South, 183–188

Published under exclusive licence by Emerald Publishing Limited
doi:10.1108/978-1-83549-736-420241032

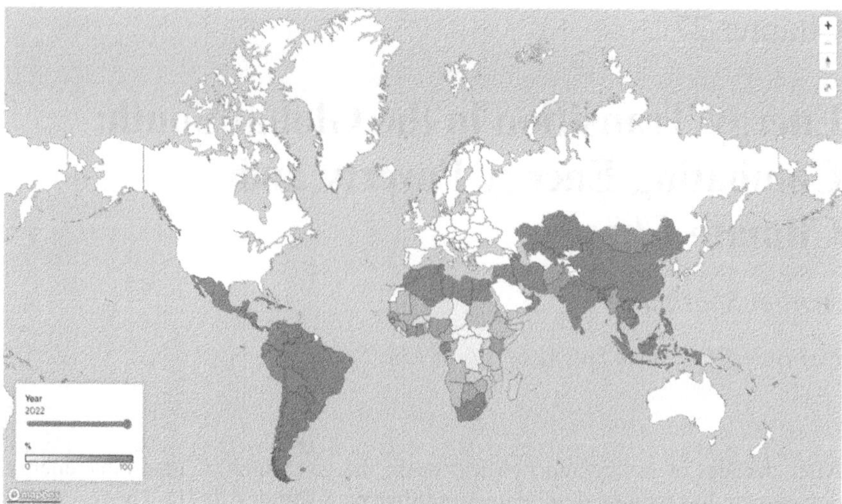

Fig. 27.1. Countries Having Significant Populations Without Access to Modern Energy Sources. *Source*: IEA (2022).

Energy Transition: Combating Energy Poverty and Climate Change

India is among the top five countries in the world with a sizable population that does not have access to modern energy sources (IEA, 2022). A large section of the Indian population did not have access to modern energy sources even after several decades after independence and energy poverty remained a perennial policy concern (Sharma, 2020). In the last two decades, huge efforts have been made to increase access to electricity (IEA/NITI Aayog, 2021). The number of people without access to electricity has reduced and the government claimed that 100% of villages are electrified (Sharma, 2020). The overall energy consumption increased several folds during this period and India became the third largest energy-consuming nation in the world (Fig. 27.2). The Indian government pledged to decarbonise its economy and wishes to cut its emissions to net zero by 2070 to fight climate change.

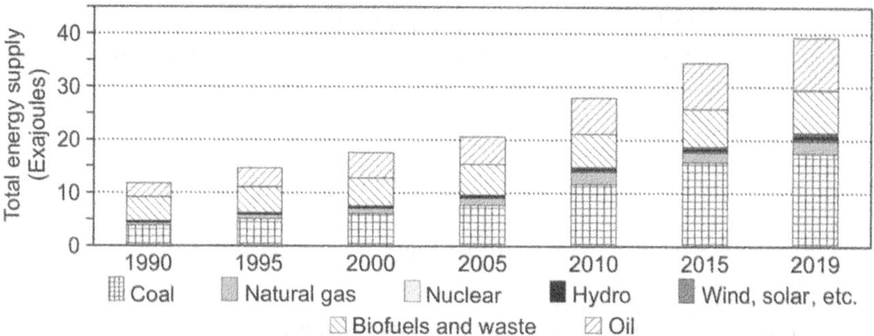

Fig. 27.2. Total Energy Supply in India by Source from 1990 to 2019. *Source*: Own elaboration based on IEA/NITI Aayog (2021).

Till now, the majority of the energy requirement is fulfilled by coal, oil, and biofuel. However, the rate of deployment of modern renewable energy significantly increased over the last decade. In 1990, only 437 TJ was supplied by solar and wind, which increased to 7,547 by 2000, 83,449 by 2010, and 480,115 by 2019 (IEA/NITI Aayog, 2021). The overall contribution of solar and wind in the total energy mix is still low, however, the Indian government plans to significantly increase renewable contributions over the coming decades, and especially enhance the deployment of solar.

Solar for All: Intertwining of Local, Regional, and International Cooperation

The Indian government has pushed different policies, plans, and interventions (such as National Solar Mission, National Green Energy Corridor, Synchronous Grid, Solar Park Scheme, Canal Bank & Canal Top Scheme, Grid Connected Solar Rooftop Scheme, and many others) to support the decarbonisation move (IEA/NITI Aayog, 2021; Ministry of New and Renewable Energy, 2022). India wishes to achieve 175 GW of renewables by 2022 and 500 GW by 2030. According to some projections, India's solar and wind contribution will reach 344 GW in 2030 and it will surpass the coal capacity of 269 GW by that time (IEA/NITI Aayog, 2021). In the coming decade, the contribution of coal will reach a peak and will start to decline, whereas, solar and other renewables contributions will increase during this period (IEA/NITI Aayog, 2021).

As a result of the varied policy push, solar uptake has significantly increased during the last several years in India and in other partner countries (Fig. 27.3). India has become the fifth largest country in terms of solar power deployment and solar power has increased from 6.8 GW in 2016 to 40 GW by 2021 (Ministry of New and Renewable Energy, 2022); the government wanted to achieve 100 GW (40 GW from decentralised solar rooftops, 40 GW from utility-scale solar parks [Fig. 27.3] and 20 GW from ultra-mega solar parks) by 2022. The objectives have not yet been completely achieved, however, there is considerable progress in a few states of India. At the same time, there are large-scale variations among different states. Karnataka, Rajasthan, and Gujarat are the leaders, whereas, West Bengal, Jharkhand, and Bihar are the laggards among the big states (IEA/NITI Aayog, 2021). Overall, one can argue that significant efforts were made to increase solar deployment at multiple levels during the last decade.

Unlike, the early efforts to push renewables, India is not only focusing on domestic policies but also playing a crucial role in pushing renewables at the regional and global levels (Jha, 2021). India played a major role in establishing the International Solar Alliance (ISA) with the support of France in 2015 during the United Nations Climate Change Conference of the Parties (COP-21) in Paris for the promotion of solar energy. So far around 90 countries have signed and ratified the ISA Framework Agreement, primarily from the global south (ISA, 2022). The alliance pushed the agenda of making solar energy available 24×7 at an affordable cost to all (ISA, 2022). India is acting as a steward who is guiding other developing countries in the Global South to deploy solar energy to meet developmental and environmental goals. The alliance is promoting the scaling

Fig. 27.3. Aerial View of a Solar Farm or Solar Power Plant Near Raichur, India. *Source*: ID 158721953 © Lakshmiprasad S | Dreamstime.com.

Fig. 27.4. Tapovan Solar Park in Deoghar, Jharkhand, India. *Source*: The author.

up of solar applications for agricultural use, affordable finance, the scaling of rooftop and solar mini-grids, the establishment of solar parks, encouraging solar-based e-mobility and storage, solarising heating and cooling systems, solar PV battery and waste management, and solar for green hydrogen (ISA, 2022). Overall, the alliance wishes to achieve an integrated, green, and global grid to meet energy transition and SDGs.

Through ISA, India is playing a major role in promoting solar in many other developing countries and regions through advocacy and analysis (ease of doing solar), capacity building (STAR-C program), and facilitating implementation programs (facilitating access to funds through Sustainable Renewable Risk Mitigation Initiative) in partner countries (ISA, 2021). Different projects are getting conceptualised and implemented in member countries (Fig. 27.4). For instance, 1,113 MW Solar Mini-Grids and 2260 MWp Solar Parks proposals are received from countries like Sri Lanka, Togo, Zambia, Congo, Peru, and many others (ISA, 2021). The ISA wishes to achieve the goal of investment of 1,000 billion USD by

2030 to finance solar projects in member countries (ISA, 2021). Many of these projects are at an initial stage of deployment, yet, these are crucial initiatives of the result of collaboration among developing countries to combat climate change and achieve SDGs.

Conclusions

The efforts made by India to promote solar at the domestic and international levels is a story of hope in a world facing huge uncertainties and risks in the wake of climate emergency and a global pandemic. The initial results are promising. However, any story of hope should be read with caution. There are roadblocks and hurdles that need to be dealt with if the objective is to achieve just energy transition while combatting energy poverty and climate emergencies.

Several studies elaborated that while promoting solar, one needs to take care of environmental injustices, energy justice, and climate justice-related concerns, otherwise, a techno-managerial approach will end up further exacerbating the existing inequalities and will create new vulnerabilities for marginalised sections and vulnerable and fragile ecosystems (Pandey & Sharma, 2021; Sharma, 2020; Yenneti et al., 2016). Moreover, often the decision-making processes for pushing solar-based projects are not participatory and democratic (Pandey & Sharma, 2021; Sharma, 2020); this will create hurdles in the long-term and effective adoption and sustainability of such interventions. Climate emergency and energy poverty cannot merely be tackled by techno-economic tools but will require socio-political commitments and allegiance to the idea of just energy transition. Hopefully, the south-south collaboration will help deepen the commitment to just energy transition.

References

IEA. (2022, August). *SDG7: Data and projections*. International Energy Agency. https://www.iea.org/reports/sdg7-data-and-projections/access-to-electricity

IEA/NITI Aayog. (2021). *Renewables integration in India*. International Energy Agency – NITI Aayog. https://www.iea.org/reports/renewables-integration-in-india

ISA. (2021). *ISA Annual Report 2021*. International Solar Alliance. https://isolaralliance.org/uploads/docs/43b561adfba59177e3d8a6317cdfb6.pdf

ISA. (2022, October). *Mission and vision*. International Solar Alliance. https://isolaralliance.org/about/mission-vision

Jha, V. (2021). 'Soft Law in a Hard Shell': India, international rulemaking and the international solar alliance. *Transnational Environmental Law*, *10*(3), 517–541. https://doi.org/10.1017/S2047102520000400

Ministry of New and Renewable Energy. (2022, October). *Solar energy*. Government of India. https://mnre.gov.in/solar/current-status/

Pandey, P., & Sharma, A. (2021). Knowledge politics, vulnerability and recognition-based justice: Public participation in renewable energy transitions in India. *Energy Research & Social Science*, *71*, Article 101824. https://doi.org/10.1016/j.erss.2020.101824

Sharma, A. (2020). 'We do not want fake energy': The social shaping of a solar micro-grid in rural India. *Science, Technology and Society*, *25*(2), 308–324. https://doi.org/10.1177/0971721820903006

Sharma, A., & Pandey, P. (2021). Innovations, policies, and implications for promoting a sustainable solar photovoltaic industry from a management perspective. In Jingzheng Ren; Zhipeng Kan *Photovoltaic sustainability and management* (pp. 7–1). AIP Publishing LLC.

Yenneti, K., Day, R., & Golubchikov, O. (2016). Spatial justice and the land politics of renewables: Dispossessing vulnerable communities through solar energy mega-projects. *Geoforum*, *76*, 90–99. https://doi.org/10.1016/j.geoforum.2016.09.004

Part 5

Inclusive and Caring Worlds

Introduction

Andrés Kozel

Laboratorio de Investigación en Ciencias Humanas (LICH), Universidad Nacional de San Martín (UNSAM) – Consejo Nacional de Investigaciones Científicas y Técnicas (CONICET), Argentina

The eight contributions that follow should be seen in the context of a far-reaching twofold process, whose contours and vanishing points remain difficult to pinpoint, given that we are still immersed in it. On the one hand, the process that has led us, as a result of a long series of experiences of demands and struggles, to move from the predominance of homogenising horizons and eventually suffocating edges, to others governed by a better appreciation of diversities, where affirmative gestures and, ideally, the taking of the floor and mutual listening are valued. On the other hand, the process that has led us to become more aware of the interconnections and reciprocal dependencies, not only between human beings, but between all beings and the cosmos.

Both processes have led to the resignification of the categories of inclusion and solidarity. Thus, the new forms of inclusion would no longer have to do so much with blurring differences in order to integrate them into a 'better' and 'stabilised' whole, but rather with recovering them and trying to bring them to their respective 'fullness', conceived as specific and open. For their part, new forms of solidarity would no longer have to do only with commiseration, but would be articulated with notions such as autonomy, agency, empowerment, reciprocal empowerment and more.

The category 'dignity' is useful to condense several decisive facets of these transformations. Indeed, much of the claims associated with inclusion and solidarity have been, and continue to be, made in its name. Dignity can be seen as the core of a semantic field of enormous significance across the global South, and not only in the global South. Something similar could be said about a couple of related notions. This is the case of 'human development' (UNDP, 1990) and 'interculturality' (UNESCO, 2005). In meditating on the significance of this set of notions, the aspiration to consider people and societies not only from an economic point of view becomes central. The intellectual history of these efforts could not leave out of consideration the contributions of the Indian economist Amartya Sen (Calderón, 2014; Sen, 1992, 2000) and, with the necessary mediations, of

Exploring Hope: Case Studies of Innovation, Change and Development in the Global South, 191–194

doi:10.1108/978-1-83549-736-420241033

the Modelo Mundial Latinoamericano, a key work from the point of view of highlighting the importance of moving towards a more equitable distribution of income and also for its contribution to the construction of the concept of 'Basic Needs' (Herrera, 2004).

The background to the above-mentioned double process can be traced practically ad libitum. It is impossible not to mention here the name of Mahatma Gandhi (1869–1948), probably the figure of the global South with the greatest projections. But beyond this huge name, it is not excessive to argue that the end of the Second World War was a significant watershed in relation to what we have been arguing, and that, within it, some relevant milestones can still be identified with some precision. Indeed, after the end of the war, the process of decolonisation in Asia and Africa gained decisive momentum, while at the same time, there was an enormous advance in anti-racism at the global level, largely thanks to the series of declarations made by the United Nations (UNESCO, 1969). This did not mean, of course, that racism disappeared from the face of the earth, but it did mean that its explicit enunciation in academic and even political orbits was seriously hindered from then on (Wieviorka, 1992).

The long captivity of Nelson Mandela (1918–2013, imprisoned for a quarter of a century), the end of apartheid and the Nobel Prize awarded to him in 1993 can be taken as a precious allegory of the road travelled in this direction, as well as of the many difficulties that had to be faced and that remain to be faced in this difficult journey. The allusion to the South African leader is of course emblematic, and by no means exhausts a list of processes and names that cannot be offered here, and which should include, in a preponderant place, the Afro-American movement, with its different strands and effects that are felt to this day, and not only in the United States.

It is possible to detect, in the 1970s and 1980s, significant changes in the way of relating to the indigenous question in Latin America (Masferrer Kan, 2023). The aforementioned movement deepened on the occasion of the commemoration of the V Centenary of the so-called 'Encounter of two worlds', marked by a very different tone from that of the IV Centenary (1892). The debates that were generated in the run-up to 1992 were very intense and, in a way, gave way to milestones of high significance and global visibility: the Nobel Peace Prize awarded to Rigoberta Menchú in 1992; the Zapatista uprising in Mexico, the election of Evo Morales as president of Bolivia, to name but a few. It is essential to take these processes into account in order to understand the meaning of initiatives such as the recovery of ancestral languages at risk of disappearing or the creation of indigenous universities, understood as spaces from which it is possible to take up and refocus alternative visions of the world to the predominant modes of inter-relationship. In this fifth part, there are two contributions devoted to these crucial questions ('Custody of native languages' and 'Indigenous universities').

A key aspect of the double process to which we have been referring has to do with the history of feminisms and, in particular, with the growing visibility of the unjust realities experienced by women, including the multiple forms of violence they endure. It is not possible in this short space to draw up a satisfactory periodisation, nor is it possible to delineate an appropriate typology of contemporary feminisms. The nuances are so many and so significant that they seem to force us to use the plural – feminisms – and to think of situated feminisms. Also, of course, to deploy an attitude of prudence and respect towards the differences between traditions, cultures and civilisations, an aspect that becomes extremely delicate when thinking about the different realities that make up the global South. The category of 'intersectionality', coined by Kimberlé Crenshaw (1991) and taken up by many scholars, is a key term in these debates. Effectively, it refers to the 'simultaneity of oppressions', including, but not limited to, those of gender and race. Moreover, within the feminisms of the global South, critical positions of 'Western', also called 'hegemonic', feminism can be detected. Contributions such as those of Oyèwùmí (2017) are of the utmost relevance. In academic terms, comparative studies have begun to emerge and, given the importance of the issue, are likely to acquire even greater weight and density in the years to come. At the political level, the articulations between the different positions are not simple, and there is ample space for the exploration of alternatives. In this fifth part, there are two contributions that analyse two different experiences of women's empowerment: in one, women organise in networks and collectives to take care of themselves and resist structural violence; in the other, they organise to produce and market goods at a local fair, supported by a network of community organisations and guided by a vocation of *horizontality*.

Resilience is a category that has been gaining ground in recent decades. It has also had its critics, as it can be used to 'celebrate' the capacity to withstand unjust situations, and can even be linked to a certain 'glorification' of individual heroism. Towards the end of his intellectual itinerary, Sergio Bagú (1911–2002), a classic author of Latin American social theory, wrote an extraordinary work in which he set out to recover hopeful experiences. He did so without alluding to the word 'resilience', but rather to the 'creative potential of the anonymous human', and offered several examples (Bagú, 1997). Three of the contributions in this fifth part draw attention to experiences related to the pathos of Bagu's work. One highlights solidarity in the face of a natural catastrophe: the earthquake that devastated Mexico City in 2017. The others narrate experiences that took place in Africa, in the context of the recent COVID-19 pandemic, and which can be thought of in the same way. As Bagú would say, these experiences having taken place is, in itself, something hopeful. Bagú warned that, despite their extreme relevance, these kinds of processes have been scarcely elaborated by social theory: there is an open challenge there. Moreover, these processes are often difficult to translate into institutional frameworks or public policies: this is another open challenge, in this case for planning disciplines.

It is also interesting to note that the experiences recovered here are also revealing that the vindication of ancestral legacies and community values, as well as the activation of solidarity in more or less 'extreme' situations, are not only not opposed to the new technologies, but can be strengthened by them.

The role of music and its relationship to hope merits reflection here. There are numerous allusions to music in this work on hope. Music appears in this part, of course, in the chapter that narrates the stimulating experience of children's and youth orchestras in Latin America. It also appears in the chapter on solidarity in the face of the earthquake (in the hashtag that serves as the title: #CantayNoLlores). And in the chapter on women organising to resist structural violence. And, also, in a chapter corresponding to another section, referring to the forms of political participation of young people.

What Can Be Said About It?

Almost all of the aspects associated with the dual process that we review here, along with others that we do not get to touch on – such as the unfortunate disconnections between the South and the North's enjoyment of its rich fabrics, at times lapsing into standardised exoticisation – can be illustrated by dozens of musicians' names. I would like to mention Sona Jobarteh, a member of one of West Africa's leading griot families and the first female kora player. Virtually all the songs on her album Fasiya are about consolation and hope. It is difficult to conceive of more inclusive and caring worlds without music: music helps us to imagine those worlds and to walk towards them. There is – there cannot be – hope without music.

References

Bagú, S. (1997). *Catástrofe política y teoría social*. Siglo Veintiuno/UNAM.

Calderón, F. (2014). Rethinking human development. In M. Castells & P. Himanen (Eds.), *Reconceptualizing development in the Global Information Age*. OUP.

Crenshaw, K. (1991). Mapping the margins: Intersectionality, identity politics, and violence against women of color. *Stanford Law Review*, *43*(6) (July).

Herrera, A. M. (2004). *Catástrofe o Nueva Sociedad? Modelo mundial latinoamericano*. IDRC-CRID/IIED.

Masferrer Kan, E. (2023). Etnodesarrollo. In A. Kozel, D. Rawicz, & E. Devés (Eds.), *Problemáticas étnicas y sociales desde el pensamiento latinoamericano*. Ariadna.

Oyèwùmí, O. (2017). *La invención de las mujeres. Una perspectiva africana sobre los discursos occidentales del género*. En la frontera.

Sen, A. (1992). *Inequality Reexamined*. Claredon Press.

Sen, A. (2000). *Desarrollo y libertad*. Planeta.

UNDP. (1990). *Human development report*. United Nations Development Programme. https://hdr.undp.org/content/human-development-report-1990

UNESCO. (1969). *Four statements on the race question*. United Nations Educational, Scientific and Cultural Organization. https://unesdoc.unesco.org/ark:/48223/pf0000122962

UNESCO. (2005). *Convention on the protection and promotion of the diversity of cultural expressions*. United Nations Educational, Scientific and Cultural Organization. https://unesdoc.unesco.org/ark:/48223/pf0000142919

Wieviorka, M. (1992). *El espacio del racismo*. Paidós.

Chapter 28

Custody of Native Languages: The Experience of the Nivaclé Communities of Formosa

Nelida Sotelo

Centro de Estudios sobre la Acción y el Desarrollo Territorial (ADETER), Departamento de Geografía y Turismo, UNS, Argentina

In the North of Argentina, especially in the so-called *Gran Chaco Americano*, numerous indigenous peoples, including the *Wichí*, *Qom*, *Pilagá* and *Nivaclé*, have lived together since ancient times. Most of these indigenous peoples sustained themselves through hunting, fishing and gathering activities, living together peacefully and sharing the same *Mataco-Mataguayan* linguistic family. Many of these indigenous peoples, especially the Nivacle, moved around the Pilcomayo River, which today forms the border between the Republic of Paraguay and Argentina. The consolidation of the two countries and the definitive establishment of borders between them at the end of the 19th century forced this community to live in communities on either side of the border, losing their territorial mobility and their nomadic lifestyle. At the same historical moment, different military campaigns took place in Argentina with the aim of occupying and organising these vast territories, which resulted in the subjugation and reduction of the different indigenous communities. This process of territorial organisation was finally consolidated with the creation of the Province of Formosa in 1957, a province defined by new, arbitrary boundaries that ignored the historical territorial formation of all the peoples who have inhabited these territories for centuries.

The history of the *Nivaclé* people is a clear example of subjugation to new forms of political and territorial organisation, and of displacement and violation of territorial, identity and cultural rights. Indeed, as a nomadic people who moved around the borders of the Pilcomayo River, which divides Argentina and Paraguay, they were always considered to be a cross-border people. This had a very serious consequence because in Argentina they were considered as foreigners, and therefore historically they were denied recognition as a native community

Exploring Hope: Case Studies of Innovation, Change and Development in the Global South, 195–197

Published under exclusive licence by Emerald Publishing Limited
doi:10.1108/978-1-83549-736-420241034

of the country and therefore were not granted citizenship, consequently, they do not have citizenship papers, and their native language is not recognised in the education system. Fig. 28.1 shows this situation, from a model of territorial organisation in which aboriginal peoples moved throughout the territory, to a political and territorial model that conditions the functioning of these communities.

Today, there are still communities in Argentina in the provinces of Salta and Formosa, and several other communities in Paraguay. But in Argentina, the *Nivaclé* population does not live in communities made up only of this ethnic group, but also in other communities and territories of the *Wichi* and *Pilagás* peoples, where the children are educated in Spanish and in the languages of the other ethnic groups, *Wichi* and *Pilagás*, through native language teachers. It is in this context that the *Nivaclé* language is being lost as it is no longer taught in schools, leaving only family transmission.

The *Nivaclé* people are currently claiming their basic rights to citizenship, territories, lifestyles, language and identity. In this context, the recognition and learning of the language is fundamental, since the recognition of the language implies the recognition of their own identity and culture. Faced with the risk of language loss, the six *Nivaclé* communities living in Argentina have come together to organise a project to teach the Nivaclé language to children, young people and adults. Community leader Eulogio Corvalán, in consensus with the oldest members of the *Nivaclé* people, took on the responsibility of keeping the language alive. To this end, educational material and a booklet with words and elements of the *Nivaclé*'s daily life have been prepared. With all this teaching material, the community leader and language teacher travels twice a month to the various communities spread over a radius of 300 km, organising workshops with children

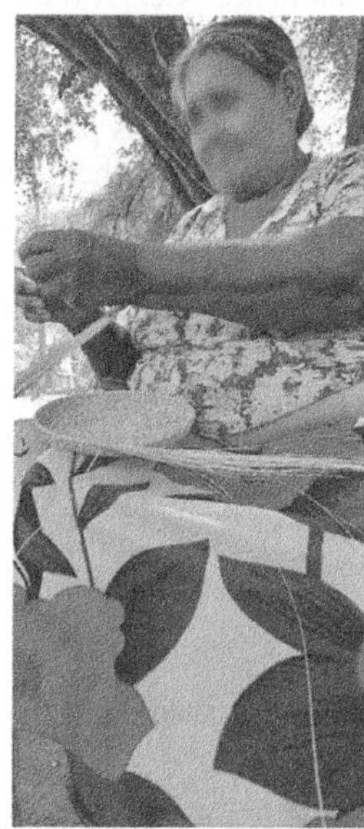

Fig. 28.1. The Nivaclé Community. *Source*: The author.

and young people to teach their language. This is an itinerant teaching project that arises from the struggle of a people to be recognised and to preserve their language and culture. This effort has been carried out entirely by the Nivacle people, without any official support, it is the families themselves who provide the training places, as the provincial government does not allow this activity to be carried out in public schools, the members of the communities themselves provide their homes and temples and the economic resources required to carry out this initiative.

> I have been travelling for 6 years and there is a lot of enthusiasm from my people, they receive me with great expectation, they are interested in the children maintaining the language, we made a lot of effort on our own, because we did not receive support from any state organisation.

This is how Eulogio relates his experience as a teacher, highlighting the demands of his people.

This effort has enabled more than a hundred children and young people to start using their own language more frequently, thus reinforcing their own identity. This has also had an important political impact, as the strengthening of identity and culture has made it possible to make these people visible and to leverage the demand for political recognition. Now in the Province of Formosa, the existence of three aboriginal peoples (*Wichi*, *Pilagá* and QOM) is not only talked about as it has been historically, but now the existence of the Nivaclé people is also recognised, even though it is not officially recognised in Argentinean and Formosa Province law.

Conclusions

This experience of guardianship the language and the efforts to teach and disseminate it opens the door to the recognition of the identity and rights of a forgotten and marginalised people. The teaching of the language is ultimately the hope of the *Nivaclé* people to be recognised and accepted, leaving behind decades of invisibility and ignorance on the part of the governments. For the future, the Nivacle people want to persist in the dissemination of their language and identity, deepening this itinerant education, a reflection of their ancient nomadic habits that characterised these ancestral communities in the heart of South America.

Chapter 29

Children's Orchestras: Living to Play, Playing to Live

Federico Escribal

Departamento de Folklore, Universidad Nacional de las Artes – Facultad de Artes, Universidad Nacional de La Plata, Argentina

Although the contemporary tradition of creating and sustaining children's and youth orchestras is often traced to Venezuela, where they achieved early development and extraordinary institutional insertion, giving rise to a network of training activities that have come to be known as *El Sistema* (Sánchez, 2014; Verhagen et al., 2016), their origins can be genuinely traced further south.

Specifically, in Chile, associated with the figure of Jorge Peña Hen and the collective he led, and with the political persecution of the 1970s as a backdrop. In 1964, Peña Hen founded the first Children's Symphony Orchestra in Latin America in La Serena (Concha Molinari, 2012). A militant of the Socialist Party, Peña Hen was assassinated in the so-called Caravan of Death. However, his action had spread to other cities and had germinated in other promoters. Some teachers who participated in the experience – such as Hernán Jerez and Sergio Miranda – went into exile in Venezuela, where they disseminated a model based on the collective reading of the orchestra's scores and group instrumental classes from the beginning of the training.

Beyond the above, *El Sistema* has its own founding myth, which naturally refers to Venezuela. The anecdote places José Antonio Abreu, the spiritual father of the process, as a witness to an act of arson based on frustration: faced with an adverse result in a competition for a place in a professional orchestra at the hands of a foreigner, a Venezuelan musician burnt his bassoon in his presence. This unfortunate event would have been the final straw in his determination to set his idea in motion: the creation of a Youth Orchestra with its own personality and an eclectic repertoire, bringing together students from various music schools in Caracas. The year was 1974. The founding story tells how Abreu gathered 11 young people to play music in a garage. Nearly half a century later, *El Sistema*

Exploring Hope: Case Studies of Innovation, Change and Development in the Global South, 199–203

Published under exclusive licence by Emerald Publishing Limited
doi:10.1108/978-1-83549-736-420241035

serves more than 300,000 young people, mostly from socio-economically disadvantaged backgrounds, through approximately 140 orchestras.

His initial diagnosis drew attention to the fact that 80% of the Venezuelan Symphony Orchestra's musicians were of foreign origin; also, to the high level of desertion in institutionalised musical education in the country. Only one year after its creation, its orchestra had a relevant participation in the International Festival of Youth Symphony Orchestras in Aberdeen (Scotland), with a staff that included musicians with previous orchestral training. Five years later, the national state recognised the power of the tool by creating the Foundation for the National System of Youth and Children's Orchestras of Venezuela (FESNOJIV). From this institutional framework, the national academies per instrument were born, seeking to standardise both curricular and pedagogical aspects.

If the 1980s marked a moment of consolidation of the programme in this process, the following decade marked its international visibility: in 1993, UNESCO recognised the model with the International Music Prize, while the Berlin Philharmonic sponsored seven high-level seminars given by Venezuelan instrumentalists. In 1995, UNESCO created its own programme, inspired by the Venezuelan experience: the World System of Children's and Youth Orchestras and Choirs for Peace in the World. Three years later, the Organisation of American States recognised and promoted *El Sistema* as a model of community education. In 2012, within the International Society for Music Education – a prestigious community of peers in the quest to build knowledge around the relationship between music and social justice – a Special Interest Group was created, the first to work specifically on a concrete music education policy model, looking at the experience of *El Sistema*.

In 1994, Venezuela took a transcendental step with the creation of the National Children's Symphony Orchestra: after two decades of decentralised orchestral training, a space of confluence was born, aimed at raising the technical level of children's performance to the highest level. Subsequently transformed into the Simón Bolívar Venezuelan Youth Orchestra, this formation consolidated a group of musicians who would go on to transcend internationally, among whom maestro Gustavo Dudamel is possibly the leading exponent. Trained in *El Sistema*, having begun his violin studies at the age of four, he went on to become conductor of the Los Angeles Philharmonic Orchestra and even won four Grammy Awards (2012, 2020, 2021 and 2022), which is why he has been described as Abreu's 'heir' in the leadership of the movement (Swed, 2007). It should be noted that Dudamel's trajectory does not express the archetypal path of social inclusion of the hegemonic narratives around the Venezuelan model: he is not a subject of the popular sectors, devoid of his own imaginary around the professional practice of music, but, on the contrary, the son of a trombonist and a vocal teacher.

The musical tradition within the family also links him to maestro Abreu, a charismatic leader, the son of European immigrants who acted as promoters of collective musical practice in the Venezuelan city of Trujillo (Sánchez, 2007). The recipient of the Right Livelihood Award, popularly known as the Alternative Nobel Prize, from the Swedish Parliament in 2001, the profusion of international recognition is an indication of the impact that the so-called Venezuelan model has had in recent decades. In 2006, in the framework of the GlobArt Teacher Award, the Venezuelan filmmaker Alberto Arvelo Mendoza presented *Tocar y luchar*, a documentary of just over an hour in which the main figures of *El Sistema* presented their experiences, which is recommended for viewing.

It is not excessive to say that Abreu has been *El Sistema*, and vice versa. However, with the beginning of the 21st century, a generation trained in *El Sistema* began to assume relevant roles within it, beyond Dudamel. In 2012, construction began on the Centro de Formación Docente del Sistema Nacional de Orquestas y Coros Juveniles e Infantiles de Venezuela, again with funding from the Interamerican Development Bank (IDB). The System is already a national and international emblem in terms of artistic, musical and humanist training. An analysis of the values at stake in the framework of *El Sistema* registers a high degree of affiliation of the participants, with a strong of commitment to the micro-society that constitutes it, although somewhat less focused on political issues. The archetypical subject formed within it appears as someone who values his or her freedom to act and think, focused on the acquisition of excellence through teamwork and discipline, also committed to the training of the youngest (Burgos García, 2015).

A process with this level of impact and visibility is also expected to reap detractors. While there are analyses that positively ponder the intra-institutional mechanics of *El Sistema* – considering it a school that learns through the flexibility of its organisational structures and the feedback of experience (Carvajal & Melgarejo, 2009) – there are academics who question, among other aspects, the lack of a consistent and carefully elaborated pedagogical method. The level of global visibility of the Venezuelan experience, together with its impact on the proliferation of processes inspired by its model in other countries, has generated a growing public, journalistic and academic interest in the democratisation of access to musical training and production, as well as in the way in which it promotes processes of social inclusion, and the degree to which it actually does so. Some detractors question certain caudillo-like traits attributed to its organisational culture, which determine, in their perspective, tendencies towards institutional disorganisation, leading to negative impacts (Aharonian, 2004; Baker & Frega, 2016).

Another criticism focuses on a certain idealisation bias based on an alleged overestimation of the socially transformative capacity, which is assessed as conscious (Pedroza, 2015); however, a certain salvationist bias can be observed at the discursive level on the part of the system's referents, it is clear that this is a limitation that is not exclusive to the Venezuelan experience. A majority of the singular critiques of *El Sistema* may be overly polarised by the way in which chavismo as a political process supported and strengthened the policy and, consequently, extend critiques of left-wing populism from the North Atlantic academy to the analysis of music education policy (Silva Ferrer, 2018). The reality is that the history of *El Sistema* is longer than the aforementioned political process; even some of its referents have made public critical remarks at certain moments that are indicative of degrees of autonomy.

Other criticisms, which could be more interesting, start from a consideration of the degree of popular participation and massiveness of the arts education promoted by *El Sistema* and focus on particular issues such as, for example, the ecological dimension of its purchasing policy from a de-colonial perspective in a geopolitical key (Di Niscia, 2019).

Another critical academic observation about *El Sistema* that we would like to draw attention to is the absolute centrality of the philharmonic model and the European repertoires of academic music. Although *El Sistema* has a programme of Venezuelan popular music called *Alma Llanera*, this was only created in 2011, several years after the Children's Orchestras model had been comprehensively rethought from a popular music approach in other parts of the continent. This speaks, in our opinion, of the maturation of a regional cultural policy. In this sense, the experience of the Andrés Chazarreta Social Programme in Argentina – and of any other programme that prioritises its own repertoires, instruments and formats, complementing music and traditions from the rest of the world – is uniquely powerful (Avenburg, 2018; Escribal, 2020). Cultural policies aimed at reproducing Western canons of legitimacy in other geo-cultural situations have not led to real processes of development; while decolonisation is gaining centrality as a goal of contemporary cultural policies (Paquette, 2016).

The international projection of the Venezuelan experience has been extremely fertile at the regional level, which is even pondered by musicians trained in *El Sistema* who have managed to transcend internationally and occasionally share the observations on the shortcomings of the original model previously mentioned (Scripp, 2016).

The debate about the origins and, in particular, the invisibility of the Chilean antecedent, becomes abstract insofar as it is clear that the effector of the internationalisation of the experience is undoubtedly the Venezuelan experience. It is estimated that at least 54 countries have adopted or adapted music education policies for children based primarily on the *El Sistema* experience (CAF, 2017). Describing the details of each modulation is an unapproachable undertaking for an article of this nature; each national environment determines particular equalisations between cultural diversities, territorial tensions and cultural policies.

Beyond the limitations that can be observed, the Children's and Youth Orchestras have been the main strategy at the regional level to address social inclusion through arts education. In this way, the challenges observed since the beginning of this century have been taken into account by UNESCO, an organisation that understands arts education as a tool for the comprehensive transformation of education systems in response to the challenges presented by a global context of accelerating social and political transformations derived from the economic and labour impact of digitalisation. In its two central documents in relation to Arts Education, the Lisbon Roadmap, in 2006, and the Seoul Charter, in 2010, suggest the use of the arts as a transversal pedagogical tool for the teaching of all disciplines, including those designated as 'hard sciences', on the understanding that the systemic presence of art and artists in the classroom favours the cognitive development of students in contexts of constant change.

References

Aharonian, C. (2004, November 26). A propósito del Sistema Nacional de Orquestas Infantiles y Juveniles. Música y políticas educacionales. *Red Voltaire*. https://www.voltairenet.org/article122990.html

Avenburg, K. (2018). Disputas en el orden simbólico: orquestas infantiles y juveniles en Argentina. *Runa*, *39*(1), 95–116.

Baker, G. J., & Frega, A. L. (2016). Los reportes del BID sobre El Sistema: Nuevas perspectivas sobre la historia y la historiografía del Sistema Nacional de Orquestas Juveniles e Infantiles de Venezuela. *Epistemus. Revista De Estudios En Música, Cognición Y Cultura*, *4*(2), 54–83. https://doi.org/10.21932/epistemus.4.2751.2

Burgos García, O. (2015). *La música y los valores humanos. Análisis del flujo de valores humanos dentro del Sistema Nacional de Orquestas Juveniles e Infantiles de Venezuela.* [Unpublished doctoral dissertation, Facultad de Ciencias de la Comunicación, Universidad de Málaga].

CAF. (2017, January 15). Música para crecer, una iniciativa de CAF. Juntos transformamos vidas. Caracas: Corporación Andina de Fomento. *Scioteca – Espacio de Conocimieto Abierto*. Banco de Desarrollo de América Latina. https://scioteca.caf.com/handle/123456789/1014

Carvajal, B., & Melgarejo, I. (2009). El sistema nacional de orquestas juveniles e infantiles de Venezuela. La escuela que aprende. *Estudios – Revista del Centro de Estudios Avanzados de la Universidad Nacional de Córdoba*, *21*, 39–52.

Concha Molinari, O. (2012). El legado de Jorge Peña Hen: las orquestas sinfónicas infantiles y juveniles en Chile y en América Latina. *Revista musical chilena*, *66*(218), 60–65. https://dx.doi.org/10.4067/S0716-27902012000200004

Di Niscia, A. L. (2019). Develando el Lado Oscuro de las Maderas Tonales: Un Estudio de Caso sobre la Demanda de Instrumentos Musicales para El Sistema de Orquestas Venezolano. *Action, Criticism, and Theory for Music Education*, *18*(3), 226–258.

Escribal, F. (2020). Orquestas infantiles and children's musical education in Argentina. *Oxford Research Encyclopedia of Latin American History* [online article]. https://doi.org/10.1093/acrefore/9780199366439.013.960

Paquette, J. (2016). Theories of professional identity: Bringing cultural policy in perspective. In J. Paquette (Ed.), *Cultural policy, work and identity* (pp. 1–23). Routledge. https://doi.org/10.4324/9781315575346

Pedroza, L. (2015). Of orchestras, mythos, and the idealization of symphonic practice: The Orquesta Sinfónica de Venezuela in the (Collateral) History of El Sistema. *Latin American Music Review*, *36*(1), 68–93. https://doi.org/10.7560/LAMR36103

Sánchez, F. (2007). El Sistema Nacional para las Orquestas Juveniles e Infantiles. La nueva educación musical de Venezuela. *Revista da ABEM, Porto Alegre*, *18*, 63–69.

Sánchez, F. (2014). El Sistema Nacional para las Orquestas Juveniles e Infantiles. La nueva educación musical de Venezuela. *Revista da ABEM*, *18*, 63–69.

Scripp, L. (2016). *The need to testify: A Venezuelan Musician's Critique of El Sistema and his Call for Reform*. [Unpublished Case Study Interview Report]. http://www.researchgate.net/publication/285598399

Silva Ferrer, M. (2018). *El cuerpo dócil de la cultura: Poder, cultura y comunicación en la Venezuela de Chávez*. Vervuert Verlagsges.

Swed, M. (2007, April 8). Maestro will pass baton to up-and-comer in '09. *Los Angeles Times*. https://www.latimes.com/archives/la-xpm-2007-apr-08-me-phil8-story.html

Verhagen, F., Panigada, L., & Morales, R. (2016). El Sistema Nacional de Orquestas y Coros Juveniles e Infantiles de Venezuela: un modelo pedagógico de inclusión social a través de la excelencia musical. *Revista Internacional de Educación Musical*, (4), 35–46.

Chapter 30

Indigenous Universities, Houses of Wisdom

María Luisa Eschenhagen

Grupo de Investigación "Economía Ambiente y Alternativas al Desarrollo", Universidad Nacional de Colombia, Colombia

A hope and an alternative must emerge from the depths of being and dwelling.[1] If new proposals do not touch these core fibres in order to emerge from them, they will hardly be genuine alternatives. We live in a time of profound civilisational crisis, expressed increasingly explicitly through the environmental crisis, which questions precisely those ways of being and dwelling that the modern world has made possible with very particular ways of knowing it – on the unsustainability of modern ways of knowing, I recommend consulting the environmental philosopher Enrique Leff, who demonstrates throughout his work how ways of thinking intervene in the real and transform it.

A modern world has been built 500 years since colonisation, where in the Global South are those who have most explicitly suffered the impacts and effects such as the elimination, invisibilisation and marginalisation of their ways of seeing and knowing the world. Entire cultures have been victims of a historical process of cultural, linguistic, religious, territorial and identity dispossession, which has also been exercised to a large extent through educational mechanisms such as schools and universities. Their struggles of resistance and vindication have been and continue to be a constant throughout the length and breadth of Latin America. Therefore, there is now a need to recover, protect and reclaim one's own knowledge; and more specifically a need to decolonise universities.

It is within this context that indigenous universities are a very interesting proposal and alternative. However, it is essential to make a series of clarifications and

[1][Translator's note] The author writes: 'Una esperanza y una alternativa deben emerger desde lo más profundo del ser, del estar y del habitar'. In Spanish, there is a difference between the verbs *ser* and *estar*, which is hard to capture in translation. Throughout the text, the expression being refers to both *ser* and *estar*. It is more than a nuance, as it has philosophical implications.

Exploring Hope: Case Studies of Innovation, Change and Development in the Global South, 205–210

doi:10.1108/978-1-83549-736-420241036

delimitations in order to better identify the alternatives that effectively aim to go beyond conventional universities.

First, it is one thing to speak of universities for indigenous audiences, but which continue to offer conventional degrees, remaining within conventional assessment and accreditation regimes, with scholarships for indigenous people with a view to their *integration* into modern society, and which are usually promoted by institutions set up by governments or multilateral agencies. Another thing is to speak of universities that are the product of the self-organisation of the indigenous movements themselves, born of their initiatives, based on their knowledge, without simply replicating conventional careers, with clear objectives for the benefit of the communities themselves, and with their own principles and values. This is the case of the Kawsay Intercultural Indigenous University (Bolivia), when it proclaims: 'The bases or foundations of our pluri-world of pluriversity will be the principles and values of our original cultures: vitality, reciprocity, complementarity, cyclicity, parity, redistribution and equity' (Cerruto, 2009, p. 135).

Second, it is important to point out the difference between multicultural and intercultural proposals. While the former is more of a neoliberal proposal to reconcile differences, leaving the problems of social, political and economic inequality unaddressed, the latter seeks to challenge homogeneity and dominant cultural control through new counter-hegemonic practices that start from one's own cultural identity but open up to dialogue with the diversity of other ways of knowing and being in the world: they are decolonising projects (Bernabé Villodre, 2012; Castillo Guzmán & Guido Guevara, 2015; Cruz Rodríguez, 2013).

Within this panorama, it is possible to identify a boom of Indigenous Higher Education Institutions (IHE-Is) in Latin America since the beginning of the new millennium. More than a hundred IHE-Is have been created, either by state agencies, pre-existing conventional IHEs or recognised indigenous organisations. Some are officially recognised by governments (which implies their submission to accreditation regimes); others appear as independent, non-formal educational offerings (Mato, 2009). The right to education is enshrined in Article 27 of the International Labor Organization Convention No. 169, signed by 14 Latin American countries, which states:

> Governments shall recognise the right of these peoples to establish their own educational institutions and facilities, provided that such institutions meet the minimum standards established by the competent authority in consultation with these peoples. Appropriate resources shall be made available to them for this purpose. (OIT, 2014, p. 56)

Most IHE-Is have not been in existence for more than 20 years. They face a host of problems linked to financial stability, political interest in their continuity, lack of academic staff with decent contracts, difficult relations with government education administrations, inappropriate evaluation and accreditation regimes and criteria, discussions about accepted languages, difficulties in access to facilities for students. However, they continue to persist and resist. One strategy has been to create a Network of Indigenous Intercultural and Community Universities *Abya Yala*.

Among the universities that have roots in indigenous movements are the following:

- Bolivia: *Universidad Indígena Boliviana* Comunitaria Intercultural Productiva Aymara. '*Tupak Katari*', Universidad Indígena Tawantinsuyu
- Colombia: Universidad Autónoma Indígena Intercultural (UAIIN)
- Ecuador: Universidad Intercultural de Naciones y Pueblos Indígenas (UINPI) *Amawtay Wasi* (2004–2014); Instituto Superior Tecnológico Jatun Yachay Wasi
- México: Universidad Autónoma Comunal de Oaxaca; Instituto Superior Intercultural Ayuuk, Universidad indígena campesina en Red; Universidad de la Tierra (Oaxaca)

These universities are therefore characterised by promoting pedagogical and knowledge proposals that are closer to the communities, and seek to strengthen their own knowledge and interculturality. A number of graduate and undergraduate dissertations have delved into the proposals, including the works of Huanca Soto (2019) on the indigenous universities of *Abya Yala* (Ecuador), Vega Camacho (2018) on the Tawantinsuyu Indigenous University (Bolivia), and Hervas Parra (2015) on the Instituto Superior Tecnológico *Jatun Yachay Wasi* (Ecuador).

To get an idea of the contributions of these IHE-Is, it may be useful to review, on the one hand, their vision and mission proposals and, on the other, their educational offerings. UINPI declares as its foundations interculturality, plurinationality, dialogue and epistemic sovereignty, and the full exercise of cultural and linguistic rights. For the UAIIN, the guiding principles are taken from the diverse indigenous worldviews based on unity, land, culture and autonomy (Fig. 30.1). A central aspect of this is the presence of the university directly in the territories, through the itinerancy of the *training fabrics*, threads that are based on four principles: unity, land, culture and autonomy.

Fig. 30.1. La espiral y la Tulpa UAIIN – CRIC. *Source*: Rosana Sarria Bustamante (Authorisation Granted).

In terms of educational offerings, most IHE-Is are limited to the undergraduate level; only a few also offer master's or doctoral degrees. The Universidad de la Tierra in Oaxaca (Mexico) does not offer subjects, but learning networks around the themes of learning, eating, living and speaking, where the courses offered are defined with and from the community in order to ensure the relationship with the needs of the community. The UAIIN in Colombia is woven around four systems (not to say faculties) which are (i) its own system of governance (intercultural self-rights, good community living, and intercultural self-communication), (ii) indigenous educational system, including degrees in pedagogy for the revitalisation of native languages, in arts and ancestral knowledge pedagogy, and technology in pedagogy and applied linguistics for the revitalisation of the *Nasa* language (Fig. 30.2), (iii) territorial, economic and environmental authority system (revitalisation of Mother Earth) and (iv) self-administration and self-management systems in special public administration for indigenous ancestral territories. Other HEIs-Is offer conventional undergraduate degrees and more innovative proposals at postgraduate level; for example, in Bolivia: Industrial Food Engineering or Agronomic Engineering, and a doctorate in Higher Education and Interculturality. In terms of research and publications, important efforts are being made to promote their own paths, with spaces such as the journal *Sentires y Pensares Tejiendo Memorias*.

Fig. 30.2. The Passage of Time in the Sun and the Moon from the Worldview of the Nasa People, Sath Tama Kiwe Territory – Cauca. *Source*: Rosana Sarria Bustamante (Authorisation Granted).

Conclusions

As the Mexican specialist García Campos (2013) points out, even though many of the IHE-Is may still largely move within hegemonic rationalities, their mere emergence definitely generates fissures, ruptures and changes in the world of conventional universities, as they constantly challenge them and slowly manage to permeate them. Indigenous proposals clearly promote an approach based on land and life, and thus end up intersecting with environmental concerns, and above all with approaches associated with strong sustainability (Baronnet et al., 2018). They also require rethinking central foundations of modernity such as linear temporality, the idea of nature, the ontology of the body. There are also bridges between environmental education and interculturality (Corbetta, 2021; García Campos, 2013). Likewise, IHE-Is challenge conventional universities to rethink their own work by questioning what the good life would be in their own classrooms, as well as ways of constructing tools and methodologies to promote this good life (Eschenhagen, 2013). In synthesis, it can be affirmed that the IHE-Is – created, organised and proposed from the very bases of indigenous organisations and social movements – are creative spaces, proposing other possible worlds.

References

Baronnet, B., Mercon, J., & Alatorre, G. (Eds.). (2018). *Educación para la interculturalidad y la sustentabilidad: aportaciones reflexivas a la acción*. Elaleph.com. https://www.uv.mx/tecoaac/general/educacion-para-la-interculturalidad-y-la-sustentabilidad/

Bernabé Villodre, M. del M. (2012). Pluriculturalidad, multiculturalidad e interculturalidad, concocimientos necesarios para la labor docente. *Revista Educativa Hekademos*, *5*(11), 67–76. https://roderic.uv.es/handle/10550/47898

Castillo Guzmán, E., & Guido Guevara, S. P. (2015). La interculturalidad: ¿principio o fin de la utopía? *Revista Colombiana de Educación*, *69*, 17–43. http://www.scielo.org.co/pdf/rcde/n69/n69a02.pdf

Cerruto, A. L. (2009). La experiencia de la Universidad Indígena Intercultural Kawsay (UNIK). Bolivia. In D. Mato (Ed.), *Instituciones Interculturales de Educación Superior en América Latina. Procesos de construcción. Logros, Innovaciones y Desafíos* (pp. 123–154). IESALC-UNESCO. https://unesdoc.unesco.org/ark:/48223/pf0000185698

Corbetta, S. (2021). Educación Ambiental y Educación Intercultural: hacia una construcción de puentes desde un pensamiento ambiental y latinoamericano crítico. *Gestión y Ambiente*, *24*(1), 107–130. https://doi.org/10.15446/ga.v24nsupl1.91903

Cruz Rodríguez, E. (2013). Multiculturalismo e interculturalismo: una lectura comparada. *Cuadernos Interculturales*, *11*(20), 45–76. https://www.redalyc.org/pdf/552/55228138003.pdf

Eschenhagen, M. L. (2013). ¿El "Buen Vivir" en las universidades?: posibilidades y limitaciones teóricas. *Revista de Investigación Educativa, Integra Educativa*, *6*(3), 89–105. http://www.scielo.org.bo/scielo.php?pid=S1997-40432013000300005&script=sci_arttext

García Campos, H. M. (2013). La educación ambiental con enfoque intercultural. Asisbos latinoamericanos. *Biografía. Escritos Sobre La Biología y Sus Enseñanzas*, *6*(11), 161–168. https://doi.org/10.17227/20271034.vol.6num.11bio-grafia161.168

Hervas Parra, A. A. (2015). *Experiencia de educación superior intercultural en la provincia de Chimborazo. Caso del Centro Superior de Sabiduría Ancestraly Nueva Conciencia Jatun Yachay Wasi* [Undergraduate dissertation, Universidad Politécnica Salesiana]. UPS Repository. https://dspace.ups.edu.ec/handle/123456789/9900

Huanca Soto, R. R. (2019). *¿El entretejido de la pluriversidad?. Conocimientos en tensión y diálogo en universidades indígenas de Abya Yala: Amawtay Wasi (Ecuador),*

UAIIN-CRIC (Colombia) y Tupak Katari (Bolivia) [Doctoral dissertation, Universidad Andina Simón Bolívar]. UASB Repository. https://repositorio.uasb.edu.ec/handle/10644/6863

Mato, D. (Ed.). (2009). *Instituciones Interculturales de Educación Superior en América Latina. Procesos de construcción. Logros, Innovaciones y Desafíos*. IESALC-UNESCO. https://unesdoc.unesco.org/ark:/48223/pf0000185698

OIT. (2014). *Convenio Núm. 169 de la OIT sobre Pueblos Indígenas y Tribales. Declaración de las Naciones Unidas sobre los Derechos de los Pueblos Indígenas*. Organización Internacional del Trabajo, Oficina Regional para América Latina y el Caribe. https://www.ilo.org/wcmsp5/groups/public/---americas/---ro-lima/documents/publication/wcms_345065.pdf

Vega Camacho, V. H. (2018). *La Universidad indígena Tawantinsuyu "hacia una alternativa educativa en la educación superior* [Undergraduate dissertation, Universidad Mayor de San Andrés]. UMSA Repository. https://repositorio.umsa.bo/bitstream/handle/123456789/17695/242.pdf?sequence=1&isAllowed=y

Chapter 31

Mexican Women: Organisation and Resistance Against Structural Violence

Diana Tamara Martínez Ruiz[a] *and*
Deyani Alejandra Ávila Martínez[b]

[a]*National School of Higher Studies (ENES) Morelia, National Autonomous University of Mexico (UNAM), Mexico*
[b]*Coordination for Gender Equality, National Autonomous University of Mexico (UNAM), Mexico*

In Mexico, as in Latin America, we women have fought throughout history to fully exercise our citizenship and freedom, both in public and private spaces. For a long time, we have engaged in gaining access to spaces that are mainly occupied by men, struggling to have more feminised societies, as Camps (1998) proposes, this doesn't mean removing men out of such spaces, but to 'transform the dichotomy between public and private, both for public activity being more compatible with private life, and for political life to soften some of its forms and manifestations' (p. 19). It is in the search for new spaces, that we acknowledge how women in Mexico have accomplished to articulate, throughout the country, by organising in collectives or networks that enable confronting violence, crises and adversities, with the hope of living safer, more effective and sympathetic physical and symbolic spaces, for all women and for the society we inhabit.

The organisation of women in our country has a historical legacy of more than one hundred years, starting with *soldaderas*, who organised during the Mexican Revolution to provide food, firewood, clothing and care to revolutionary soldiers, who would have not survived without them. According to Poniatowska (2018), 'It is not that they were *bragadas* (brave) and strong, they were *chiquitas* (small-sized); they had the kind of hunger that doesn't end, they were hungry for change' (p. 45).

That hunger for change and quest for organisation had variations during the 20th century, and there were moments when it was clearer, like when suffragists

Exploring Hope: Case Studies of Innovation, Change and Development in the Global South, 211–216

Published under exclusive licence by Emerald Publishing Limited
doi:10.1108/978-1-83549-736-420241037

organised in the fifties, or when hundreds of women participated in the 1968 student movement; both moments left a huge precedent of the relevance of women's engagement in social and political transformations in Mexico. One of the most notorious cases of women's organisations in Mexico is the mothers looking for their sons and daughters, as is the group *Madres buscadoras de Sonora*, which undertake great and difficult journeys in the quest of their relatives.

To the present day, women in Mexico are organised to confront different kinds of violence, but we prioritise the attention to violence experimented specifically for being women, namely, gender violence. The initiative of women's organisations has been marked by the increase of violence in multiple ways. According to official data from the Secretary of Security and Citizen Protection, in 2020, 11 women were killed each day, on average, indicating an unprecedented clime of violence. As reported by the National Survey on the Dynamics of Household Relationships (ENDIREH, 2021), which provides information, on the national level, regarding the experience of physical, economic, sexual, psychological and patrimonial violence by women aged 15 or more in the familiar, school, work, community and relationship context. As Fig. 31.1 shows, violence against all age groups has increased, particularly, against young women.

We acknowledge that due to a measurable national increase of 4% in violence from 2016 to 2021, organisations and resistance networks have emerged as a response to this emergency. As a tribute to the organised participation of Mexican women, which we believe represents materialised hope, we present a feminist cartography, based on some women's organisations, which, from resistance, have achieved to move our country, to the point of shaking it up completely (Figs. 31.2 and 31.3). We evoque *Canción Sin Miedo* (Fearless song) by Vivir Quintana, a Mexican singer-songwriter who, since March 2020, has given voice to the pain of millions of Mexican women, and which lyrics have become a hymn for the contemporary Mexican feminist struggle.

We present a cartography of the Mexican case, as an image of other possible scenarios in Latin America, or any other part of the world, where the organisation

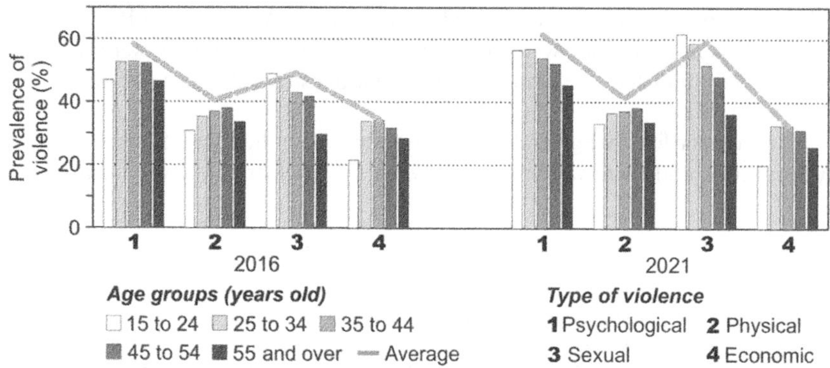

Fig. 31.1. Prevalence of Violence by Age Group and Type of Violence in Women. *Source*: Own elaboration based on ENDIREH (2021).

Fig. 31.2. MEXICO CITY, MEXICO – 03/08/2020: Several Feminist Protesters Participate in a Protest Against Gender Violence Against Women After.
Source: ID 175021140 © Leoncio Ruiz De La Garza | Dreamstime.com.

of women and collective participation takes different names, meanings and forms, materialising in the creation of collective entities that we want to show. Because naming is visibilisation, we acknowledge, at least, five forms of organisation:

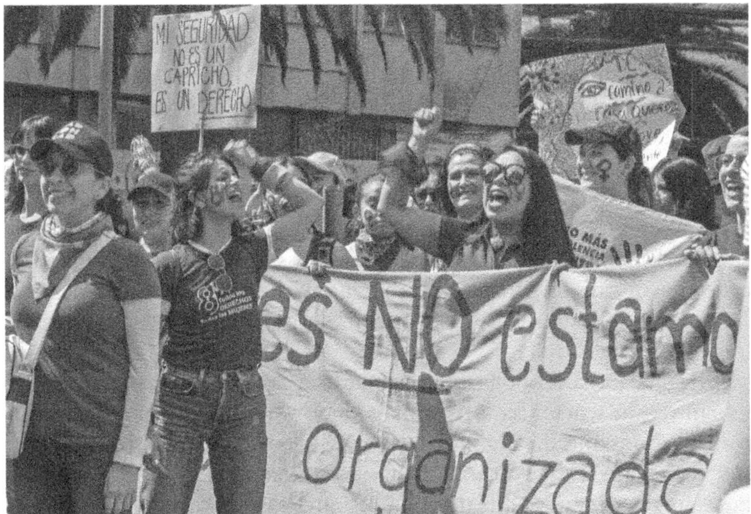

Fig. 31.3. Women's protest on International Women's Day.
Source: ID 175021140 © Leoncio Ruiz De La Garza | Dreamstime.com.

Collective: groups that use the feminine adjective in Spanish to highlight that it is a group of women: *La colectiva*.

Care networks: women's clusters that contribute to the integral health of other women, namely, their physical, mental and emotional wellbeing.

Okupas: it is written with a *k* to highlight the feminist *okupa* movement and the acquisition actions it promotes. The use of the *k* stands for political, visible and claimed occupation in opposition to that other that has always existed but has been invisibilised by power and by the wish to remain unnoticed (González & Araiza, 2016).

Civil associations: of all organisation forms, these are the most institutionalised, because they have to be notarised in order to be able to look for private and public funding that allows them to undertake projects that benefit women.

Institutional organisation: they execute comprehensive programs to eradicate gender violence and to advance towards substantive gender equality. As an example, we mention the action plan for equality of the National Autonomous University of Mexico (UNAM), conducted by the Coordination for Gender Equality (CIGU), dependency created in 2020.

Although these forms of organisation can diversify, depending, among other facts, on the year they were created, their objectives, location, political stances and the type of feminism pursued, we observe they all concur in putting all their efforts in protecting the lives of women; yes, in plural. The act of caring is the fundamental pillar of their efforts. These innovative forms of organisation and feminine resistance can be understood based on their actions and their work with women in different strategic lines:

Health: they are women's organisations that handle reproductive, sexual, psychological, and physical, as well as comprehensive health.

Violence: women's organisations that accompany violence cases such as femicides, forced-disappearances, institutional, sexual, vicarious, psychological, political, economic, work, school and obstetric violence, among others.

Citizenship and Political Participation: organisations that fight for the full exercise of women's political rights. They focus on strategies such as law reform proposals and advocacy to include women in the agenda.

Training: organisations that conduct socialisation of feminist postures by organising workshops, seminars and forums addressing the general population.

Education: women's organisations that analyse, using feminist pedagogies, the national education system, forming new generations and producing knowledge.

Human Rights: organisations that pursue the comprehensive exercise of the human rights, while accompanying women whose rights have been violated by institutions and the State. For example, the *Okupas* and NGOs.

Art and virtual activism: women's organisations that use any kind of art manifestation as their main political action resource, as well as virtual activists that spread feminist demands and information.

We observe that these forms of feminine organisation, action and resistance are formative assessments for the realignment of a different State-Nation sense, in a country such as Mexico, in desperate need for a radical change; they come from an empathic drive, geared to dissolve the ancient and piteous logic of thought and hierarchic way, known as patriarchy.

The primary source for our research is a list of women's organisations found in the Social Media; though, algorithms of the different platforms influence the outcome. Great urban capitals have more representation, but we are a country of outskirts. We created a list of 250 Mexican feminist organisations; 10 of them have national operations and are not represented on the map. From the rest of them, we found that 23 organizations are working in women's health; 26 fighting violence; 27 advocate for women's citizenship and political participation, 29 focus on training, 19 work in education, 7 advocate for human rights, and 109 distribute feminist information through art and virtual activism.

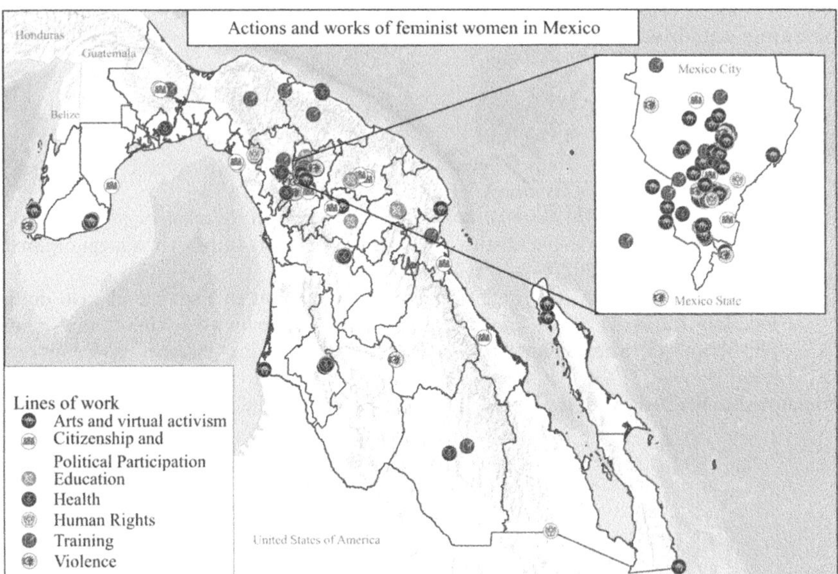

It was a challenge to interpret the complexity of diverse feminist movements in a Cartesian language, the same that has explained, for a long time, the organisation of the world, both symbolic and material. Language has transmitted the ways of western, hegemonic, colonial and androcentric conceptions while invisibilising all the other views and experiences.

Our proposal is to present data in an *upside down*, non-hegemonic, non-Eurocentric and non-androcentric map, inspired by the map *América Invertida*, created by Uruguayan artist Joaquin Torres García in 1943. On one hand, it symbolises how feminist movements and organisations are realities that can be geolocated, helping to change self-perception in space, while giving hope, in the light of the violent Mexican scenario, proving it is possible to exercise the dignified rage, taking action and head for new fertile fields to achieve comprehensive wellbeing; here, organising in *Colectivas* (in feminine and plural), materialises the hope of Mexican and Latin American women.

Conclusions

We conclude by acknowledging the hopeful force that organised women generate, thanks to the power of their union; even after recognising the force of one lone woman, it is during weak moments that all resources are needed, to fight all battles and achieve a better future. This is the strategic power of acting as a collective: to rely on the strength, love and help of other women, to create initiatives that are not isolated, but powerful enough to tear down patriarchal and Eurocentric structures, by using a new logic based on care, cooperation, love and empathy. Where hope it is possible when a common future is envisioned, one we women are pursuing: equality and a life free of violence.

References

Camps, V. (1998). *El siglo de las mujeres*. Ediciones Cátedra.

ENDIREH. (2021). *Encuesta Nacional sobre la Dinámica de las Relaciones en los Hogares*. Instituto Nacional de Estadística y Geografía INEGI. https://www.inegi.org.mx/programas/endireh/2021/

González, R., & Araiza, A. (2016). Feminismo y okupación en España. El caso de la Eskalera Karakola. *Sociológica (México)*, *31*(87). http://www.scielo.org.mx/scielo.php?script=sci_arttext&pid=S0187-01732016000100007&lng=es&nrm=iso&tlng=es#nota

Poniatowska, E. (2018). *Las indómitas*. Editorial Planeta.

Chapter 32

#CantayNoLlores: Forms of Solidarity During the 2017 Earthquake in Mexico City

Édgar Adrián Mora

Universidad Iberoamericana e Instituto de Educación Media Superior de la Ciudad de México, México

Around midday on 19 September 2017, an earthquake measuring 7.1 on the Richter scale shook the capital of Mexico. The earthquake left 369 people dead in several cities of the country; in Mexico City, 228 deaths were recorded. Something else was dramatically stricken: hundreds of thousands of homes and people were either lost or severely damaged. Local authorities estimated that the monetary cost of reconstruction would be 48 billion pesos (about 2.5 billion dollars at the current exchange rate). About 24,000 people were assisted in various shelters located in different parts of the city. At the end of the day, after a few days, about a thousand buildings were declared uninhabitable.

Numbers were grim, but they do not compare with those recorded 32 years before this incident: in 1985, Mexico City experienced the worst tragedy related to the seismic nature of the region. At that time the death toll was established at approximately 10,000 victims. However, that event contributed to several facts that allowed the tragedy of 2017 not to be repeated with the same dimensions. In general terms, we can mention the emergence and development of a culture of prevention that would allow citizens to know how to act in the event of similar events, as well as some regulation of the construction industry and changes in legislation that sought to protect the inhabitants from these natural phenomena.

One thing remained similar in both cases, i.e. the response of civil society to the emergency. The solidarity of citizens was reflected in multiple ways, especially in the days immediately following the flare-up of buildings, lives and spirits. The response of the authorities was insufficient in the face of the magnitude of the tragedy, but this was remedied by the immediate reaction of a civil society used to joining together in adversity, a society that immediately took it as a personal

Exploring Hope: Case Studies of Innovation, Change and Development in the Global South, 217–220

Published under exclusive licence by Emerald Publishing Limited
doi:10.1108/978-1-83549-736-420241038

and social endeavour to help, something almost everyone did according to their possibilities and talents. 'This is our city and nothing is going to take it away from us', said a rescue worker in a testimony recorded at the disaster area, amidst the rubble of one of the collapsed buildings where survivors were being sought. And this ownership of the city manifested itself in multiple ways.

The most evident was the massive arrival of volunteers for the removal of debris in search of survivors under the concrete and dust (Fig. 32.1). This activity was symbolised by a raised fist, a collective sign that demanded silence from the crowd surrounding the area, in order to hear noises, voices, screams, any evidence of life that could come from under the bricks and cement. The discipline manifested itself in a diversity of social classes, creeds and occupations that are not common to see gathered in the same place: students, doctors, soldiers, psychologists, engineers, professional rescuers, boy and girl scout associations, ordinary neighbours, senior citizens, etc. In the midst of those twisted rods, many personal stories were yet to be told: Don Roberto, an 89-year-old expert volunteer, who had spent 68 years of his life devoted to the Red Cross; Don Eduardo, a young man who travelled from the state of Michoacán to load debris, carrying it on his back in a wheelchair; Don Héctor, who, in Jojutla, Morelos, came to the aid of his neighbours, despite not having a leg. These stories have names although, mostly there were common, anonymous people who happened to save lives, risking their own. Like the story of an elderly woman who, in the 10 seconds that the shock lasted, entered a neighbourhood in Colonia Roma and rushed the inhabitants to safety. Like a ghost, survivors report that none of them knew for sure who she was or where she had gone after verifying that everyone had been evicted.

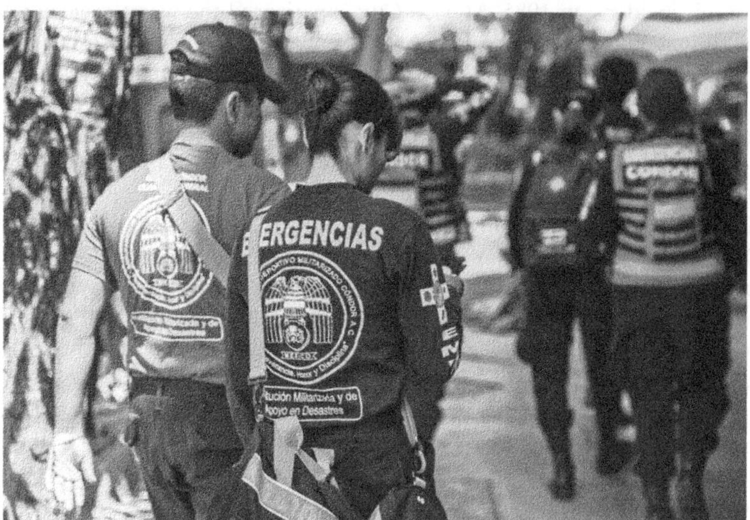

Fig. 32.1. MEXICO – SEPTEMBER 20: Team of Rescuers Walking on the Street the Day After the Earthquake. *Source*: DNI 117884483 © Carlos Araújo | Dreamstime.com.

Simultaneously came other anonymous people who brought food and fed volunteers, victims, rescuers, soldiers of the DNIII plan and relatives, who waited for any news that could come, standing in front of the collapsed buildings. For the Mexican people, food has always been a way to offer comfort, support and encouragement. That's why, a young man appeared with a huge pot of *tamales* that he handed out left and right. There was a lady carrying a basket of bread and a carafe of hot coffee offering her help to anyone who asked for it. A retired couple who donated indiscriminately and generously the luncheon meat sandwiches they pulled out of a giant plastic bag. A *taqueria* that moved the whole meat spin and everything necessary to feed a society that was tired, but not defeated.

Food did not only manifest itself on site. Suddenly, in addition to the collection and support centres organised by the government, there were gathering spots spontaneously organised in the most diverse scenarios: universities, high schools, schools, hospitals, markets, social centres, private homes, parks, cars and vans. Groceries accumulated quickly and excessively, which is remarkable in a city where large numbers of people live at or below the poverty line. At some point, the requests changed, they no longer required food supplies, but ways to transport them or instead, some other supplies, such as medicines, tools to remove debris, and facemasks for volunteers. Motorcycle clubs, movers, cab drivers, organised cyclists and individuals attended the petitions.

In the parks of the Condesa neighbourhood, the movement was visible. Young people were most active with megaphones directing traffic, giving instructions, shouting the names of the rescued ones, asking everyone to make way for ambulances, asking some of the volunteers who kept spontaneously arriving to mobilise to other parts of the city where help was also needed. In a park in Taxqueña, south of the city, donations of bottled water filled the surface of the cobblestones and showed the strength of society organising itself. In a school in the Jalalpa neighbourhood, among the ravines inhabited by the most marginalised population of the capital city, gigantic bags of clothes, tuna cans, bean bags and water bottles were deposited in the only high school in the area: it was to be given to people who really needed them. A brigade of organised students departed from that school. Travelling in an almost rickety car and on scooters, they went to the disaster area of Xochimilco, far from the media spotlight due to its remoteness and difficulty of access, to help the affected inhabitants.

The coordination of help efforts was almost instantaneous (Fig. 32.2). The Internet and the tools associated with digital communication, social networks and instant messaging, contributed largely to this matter. Through these media, the needs for donations of materials to support the rescue efforts, the victims and the volunteers were publicised. Hashtags such as #FuerzaMexico or #CantayNoLlores dominated the digital interaction trends. Messages multiplied to help lost children find their families, to locate the injured in hospitals and to publish lists of rescued people in sync with events. That urge led the large telecommunications companies to provide facilities for connecting telephones and devices in disaster areas. But the greatest support came from the homes of ordinary people who opened their doors to shelter those who had been left homeless; and who, at the same time, opened their Wi-Fi networks so that anyone who wanted to connect to

Fig. 32.2. MEXICO – SEPTEMBER 20: Young Adults Playing Performing with Violins on the Street to Gather Money for the Earthquake Victims. *Source*: ID 117883258 © Carlos Araujo | Dreamstime.com.

the internet could do so. Through social networks, help of various kinds was offered: psychologists who donated their time and knowledge to support people with stress, anxiety, fear, loss and grief; engineers who ruled free of charge the degree of structural damage that the buildings had in the days immediately after the tragedy; masseurs who moved to the landslide areas to momentarily relieve the muscles of people who moved debris, groceries, to their fellow men; veterinarians who came to heal pets who also witnessed how walls and roofs fell around them.

Animal shelters were filled with pets who in the confusion and haste of flight, or in terror of the moving ground, ran to the streets, away from their owners. The activists of this animal cause were overwhelmed by the number of new members of their shelters as houses, garages and gardens were improvised as shelters where dogs, cats, rabbits and other fauna waited for their human companions or for an opportunity to join new families. On the street, people brought bottled water, kibble, cans of food, plastic garbage bags, toys; some returning days later to adopt one of the furry survivors of the catastrophe.

The New York Times, in its Spanish edition, reported the dialogue of a child who, unable to carry the weight of a box of groceries, allowed his father to help him. 'I want to be supportive', the boy says to his father; 'You will be, because you are Mexican', the father replies. Before they arrive at the disaster area, they pass by a pole where other supporters have posted photos of lost people with the caption *Found* or *Rescued*. One of those photos could be an impossible one: that of the entire Mexican society that, organised in the face of adversity, preserved hope, raised its fist, kept silent and supported its fellow men and women.

Chapter 33

Local Products Fair: Women's Empowerment and Social Cohesion in Piribebuy, Paraguay

María José Aparicio Meza[a], *Carmiña Soto*[b] *and Amado Insfrán Ortíz*[a]

[a]*Carrera de Ingeniería en Ecología Humana, Universidad Nacional de Asunción, Paraguay*
[b]*Dirección General de Postgrado y Relaciones Internacionales, Universidad Nacional de Asunción, Paraguay*

Paraguay has followed a traditional or indicative planning model based on rural development, like other countries in the region, where the state plans, organises and executes management. The results have not always been what was expected, community empowerment and consequent development, and many rural villages remain in a state of poverty. The experience with the rural women's fair 'Productos de mi tierra Piribebuy' breaks with this traditional model and opts for a horizontal planning model, including rural families, local institutions, social organisations and the academy.

Piribebuy district is located in the centre-west of the eastern region of Paraguay, at the Cordillera Department. The city is located 20 km from Caacupé (departmental capital) and 73 km from Asunción (Fig. 33.1). The district has approximately 32,000 inhabitants according to projections, mostly young and rural (INE, 2021). The Permanent Household Survey (2017) indicates that 36.2% of the rural population was in poverty and 8.97% below the extreme poverty line. This situation is exacerbated in rural households headed by women, 55.3% of female-headed households live in poverty and 35% in indigence; in addition, 38.5% of rural women lack their own income (DGEEC, 2018).

Rural Piribebuy is characterised by the permanence of peasant family agriculture, on a smallholder scale. Like other territories in the country, it has insufficient labour opportunities for young people and market limitations for agricultural production. This is related to the gradual depopulation due to rural–urban migration

Exploring Hope: Case Studies of Innovation, Change and Development in the Global South, 221–227

Published under exclusive licence by Emerald Publishing Limited
doi:10.1108/978-1-83549-736-420241039

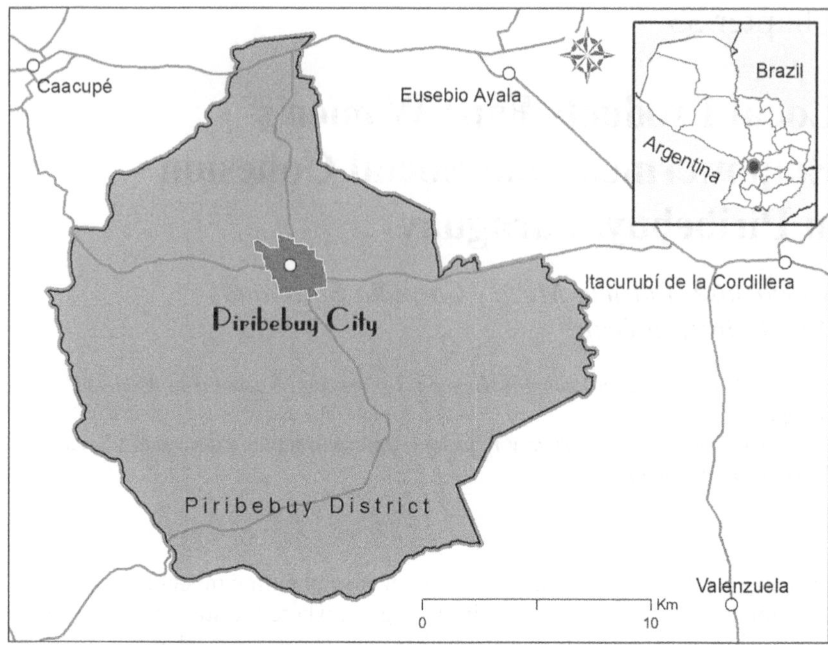

Fig. 33.1. Piribebuy, Departamento de Cordillera. *Source*: Own elaboration based on DGEEC (2002).

for work or studies, mainly to Asunción and its metropolitan area (AMA), Argentina, Spain and Canada (Cabral Antúnez, 2015). Finnis et al. (2012) indicate how agriculture in Piribebuy has changed in the face of an aging rural population.

For decades, commercialisation limitations of agricultural products have required the strengthening of the local organisation that brings together and channels community efforts, linking social agents. Piribebuy, also presented a certain social vulnerability, understood as 'the inability of a person or household to take advantage of opportunities, available in different socioeconomic areas, to improve their welfare situation or prevent its deterioration' (Donawa Torres, 2018, p. 17).

The district has an abundance of watercourses and hills. It has natural and cultural potential for tourism, which is perceived by 75% of the population (Vargas Román & Duarte, 2011). Although it is a municipality with slow growth, it receives a significant number of visitors and tourists in summer, even without adequate infrastructure to accommodate and provide recreational options (Cabral Antúnez, 2015). Meanwhile, local services and industries are still developing.

In this scenario and as a concrete response, the local products fair has emerged since 2012 with the participation of several local agents. The initiative was accompanied by the National University of Asunción, in particular by the Human Ecology Engineering Career (CIEH) of the Faculty of Agricultural Sciences (students and teachers especially of the subjects of Extensions I and II, Agroecology I and II). Central and municipal government institutions, a non-governmental organisation and an international organisation participated. The focus of action was represented by women, some of them heads of household in a situation of social vulnerability.

The background of the initiative can be traced back to 1994 when the CIEH and the municipality organised a fair with the intention of reactivating the city's municipal market (Vera, 2022, personal interview). Later in 2010, during the first CCTA Field Day, was noted the need for a space to link rural women producers with urban consumers (Insfrán Ortíz 2022, personal interview).

From the theoretical-conceptual aspect, the initiative was based on the scope of community development, the concept of which has been discussed by several authors for decades. In this case, it can be understood as:

> a method of intervention that incorporates all the agents that make up the community, establishing processes of participation and articulation between the population and the institutions (mainly municipal structures, although not only) that, enhancing a pedagogical process, and the participatory capacities of the actors and mediating structures (technicians, professionals and social entities).... (Camacho Gutiérrez, 2013, p. 209)

It seeks common objectives and improvement of community conditions and the possibility of evaluation. In addition, it has been supported for its management tool the social projects or community projects, understood as a set of actions carried out in an active and protagonist way by the members of a community, whose objective is to meet the needs and solve common or everyone's problems (Donawa Torres, 2018). The protagonist's participation of the community in its action with future projection, marks the fundamental difference between the rural development model and the community or horizontal development model implemented.

Empowerment, or the 'equitable delegation of authority and responsibility for carrying out activities aimed at achieving an objective' (Donawa Torres, 2018, p. 17), was the cornerstone that made it possible for the experience to continue to date. Above all, social empowerment is understood as the 'personal self-recognition as rights-bearing subjects, and the strengthening of the institutional fabric and the development of the organizations' capacity to influence the different spheres of life, the economy, politics, culture and institutions' (Crespo et al., 2007, p.7). Another key factor was the underpinning of social cohesion that allowed the district's inhabitants to perceive how the relationship between inclusion and exclusion mechanisms can occur, and how they operate (ECLAC, 2010). It is emphasised that subjectivity is a basic condition for understanding social cohesion where without people's opinions and knowledge of their culture, the analysis lacks legitimacy.

Likewise, the Human Ecology approach applied to rural development in Paraguay was the backbone of the whole experience (De Barros Barreto, 1991) from the academy intervention. The family (not only individuals) and the community are considered at the centrality of development (Aparicio Meza & Insfrán Ortiz, 2015; Ferreira & Vera, 2002).

The agricultural fair *Productos de mi Tierra, Piribebuy* is carried out in downtown, at Mariscal López square. The *Asociación de Feriantes de Productos de mi Tierra Piribebuy* plans, orders and presents the products. Until before the pandemic (2019), it involved 8 committees of women producers totalling 84 people, currently there are 5 committees: San Roque González de Santa Cruz, Vy'a raity, Ñepytyvõ rekávo, Teko Phyaju and Chococue Kyre'y. The fairs are the last days of each month. Occasionally it is carried out two or three times a month (two times in March or April for Easter and three in December for the end-of-the-year festivities) (Pereira, 2022, personal interview).

The initiative brings together social organisations, institutions and committees. The main actions have been: training about agroecological approach production (Fig. 33.2), administration and marketing and technical assistance from

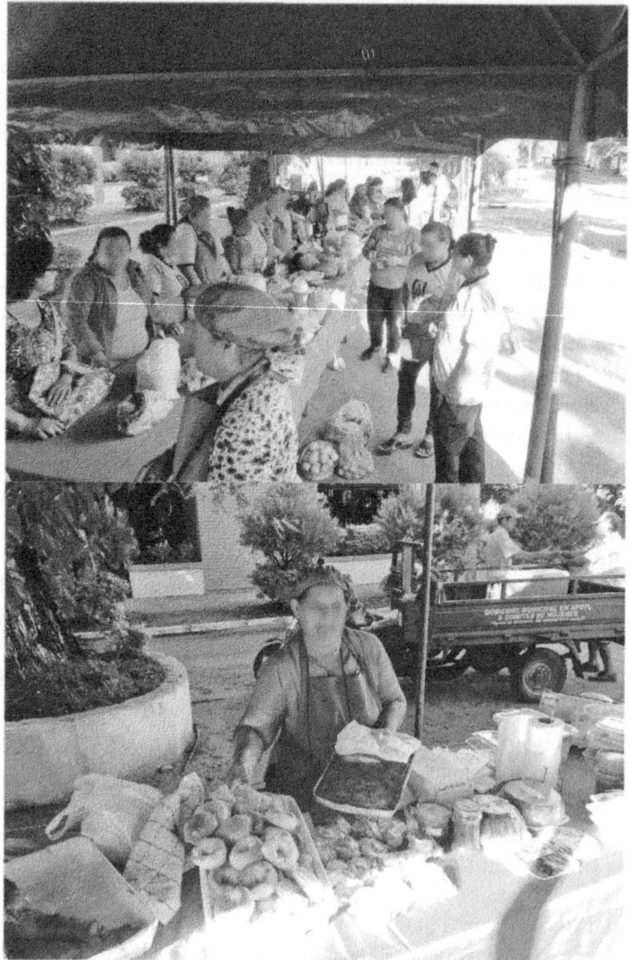

Fig. 33.2. Fair for Women Entrepreneurs. *Source*: The authors.

Universidad Nacional de Asunción (UNA) professors and students. The activities are planned and organised in monthly meetings; the women have support transportation, accompaniment and talks during the fair day. In addition, media and social network diffusion is done. Training is organised mainly by the CIEH-FCA through teachers and students by university extension projects (Vargas, 2022).

The main achievement of the experience is the empowerment and visibility of rural women, who reached an average monthly income of US$25. This allowed them to buy some food (not produced in their farms) and to gain economic independence from their partners, recognising women as effective producers by different social agents. The fair's organising committee was strengthened with the incorporation of the mayor's office, consolidating the initiative and improving the local economy. In addition, the local community is provided with fresh, chemical-free food at fair prices through short chains and relationships between producers and consumers (Vargas, 2022).

A factor that influenced the success of the initiative was the planning and co-management model. Without the typical perspectives of development planning, very much in vogue in the 20th century, called *top-down* and *bottom-up* (Diez et al., 2013). Instead, the horizontal planning model was adopted, with the preponderant role of the community and the dynamising role of the academy through students and teachers. The task aimed at stimulating joint work through consensus to manage actions of common interest, where the opinion of each community member and the culture were valued. This allowed social cohesion, a fundamental aspect of the sustainability of the initiatives. Another important factor for success was the homogeneity and identity of the territory. The inhabitants are mainly natives of Piribebuy (several generations) with traditional customs, which made possible the search for common productive and cultural elements capable of structuring the territory, according to Sumpsi (2006). This helps to advance towards a sense of belonging and strength of institutions (CEPAL, 2010). The intermediate cities as territory backbone also represented an opportunity for the commercial outlet of developed products (CEPAL, 2010). Piribebuy can today be considered a middle city surrounded by other important cities such as Caacupé, Paraguarí and Yaguarón. Finally, the quality and legitimacy of leadership was a community development key factor. The Human Ecology Engineering program, having been permanently represented in the community through its Center for Training and Appropriate Technology (CCTA) since 1994, and become an actor who collaborated in local capacities construction.

Conclusions

This experience in Piribebuy leaves some reflections: (1) Community development is a gradual and sustained process that requires the presence of committed and legitimised actors, (2) Successful cases, such as the one presented, can be scalable when there is clear vertical coordination or when local territorial development programs are articulated in subnational and national rural development policies and programs, and (3) Social cohesion, around collective interests, enables the success and sustainability of actions undertaken at the local level.

References

Aparicio Meza, M. J., & Insfrán Ortiz, A. (2015). Contribución a la revisión histórica de ecología humana y a su abordaje en Paraguay. *Ecologías Humanas*, *1*(1), 1–15.

Cabral Antúnez, N. D. (2015, September 24–27). *Zonificaciones urbanas y crecimiento urbano: una propuesta para la ciudad de Piribebuy* [Conference presentation]. Congreso Internacional de Geografía, 76° Semana de Geografía (GAEA), Salta, Argentina. https://www.gaea.org.ar/ACTAS-%20PDF%20web/Cabral%20Antunez%20Actas%202015.pdf

Camacho Gutiérrez, J. (2013). Desarrollo comunitario. Eunomía. *Revista en Cultura de la Legalidad*, *3*, 206–212.

CEPAL. (2010). *Cohesión Social en América Latina. Una revisión de conceptos, marcos de referencia e indicadores*. Comisión Económica para América Latina y el Caribe (CEPAL). https://www.cepal.org/es/publicaciones/2978-cohesion-social-america-latina-caribe-revision-conceptos-marcos-referencia

Comisión Económica para América Latina y el Caribe (CEPAL). (2010). *Cohesión Social en América Latina. Una revisión de conceptos, marcos de referencia e indicadores* (218p). Comisión Económica para América Latina y el Caribe (CEPAL).

Crespo, P., de Rhan, P., González, G., Iturralde, P., Jaramillo, B., Moncada, M., Pérez, A., & Soria, C. (2007). *Empoderamiento: conceptos y orientaciones. Serie Reflexiones y aprendizajes,* Secretaría Técnica ASOCAM – Intercooperation.

De Barros Barreto, N. (1991). Ecología Humana: una nueva opción para desarrollo rural. *Población y desarrollo*, *2*(4), 9–12.

DGEEC. (2002). *Atlas Censal de Paraguay: Cordillera*. Dirección General de Estadísticas, Encuestas y Censo, Instituto Nacional de Estadística. https://www.ine.gov.py/Publicaciones/Biblioteca/Atlas%20Censal%20del%20Paraguay/6%20Atlas%20Cordillera%20censo.pdf

DGEEC. (2018). *Principales Resultados Anuales de la Encuesta Permanente de Hogares Continua (EPHC) 2017 y 2018*. Dirección General de Estadística, Encuestas y Censos, Instituto Nacional de Estadística. https://www.ine.gov.py/resumen/MTA0/principales-resultados-anuales-de-la-encuesta-permanente-de-hogares-continua-ephc-2017-y-2018

Diez, J. I., Gutiérrez, R. R., & Pazzi, A. (2013). ¿De arriba hacia abajo o de abajo hacia arriba? Un análisis crítico de la planificación del desarrollo en América Latina. *Geopolíticas*, *4*(2), 199–235.

Dirección General de Estadística, Encuestas y Censos (DGEEC). (2018). *Principales Resultados. Encuesta Permanente de Hogares 2017*. DGEEC.

Dirección General de Estadísticas, Encuestas y Censos (DGEEC). (2002). *Atlas Censal de Paraguay: Cordillera*. s/p.

Donawa Torres, Z. A. (2018). Proyectos sociales, una herramienta para el empoderamiento de comunidades vulnerables. *Inventio*, *14*(32), 15–21.

Ferreira, E., & Vera, R. (2002). Ecología humana en Paraguay: enfoque académico y de Extensión. *Investigación agraria*, *4*(2), 31–42.

Finnis, E., Benítez, C., Candia Romero, E. F., & Aparicio Meza, M. J. (2012). Changes to -agricultural decision-making and food procurement strategies in rural Paraguay. *Latin American Research Review*, *47*(2), 180–190. http://www.jstor.org/stable/23321738

Instituto Nacional de Estadística (INE). (2021). *Cordillera. Proyecciones de la población por sexo y edad*, 2021. Revisado el 26 de julio 2022. https://www.ine.gov.py/Publicaciones/Proyeciones%20por%20Departamento%202021/03_Cordillera_2021.pdf

Pereira Barrientos, D. (2022). *Characteristics of the fair Productos de mi tierra Piribebuy*. Personal interview. San Lorenzo, Paraguay.

Sumpsi, J. M. (2006). *Experiencias Piloto de Desarrollo Local Rural en América Latina: Lecciones del Proyecto EXPIDER en Bolivia, Ecuador y Honduras*. Banco Interamericano de Desarrollo. https://publications.iadb.org/publications/spanish/document/Experiencias_piloto_de_desarrollo_local_rural_en_Am%C3%A9rica_Latina_Lecciones_del_proyecto_EXPIDER_en_Bolivia_Ecuador_y_Honduras.pdf

Vargas Román, J. C., & Duarte, R. A. (2011). Potencial para el turismo rural en la compañía Paso Jhú del distrito de Piribebuy, Departamento de Cordillera, Paraguay. *Investigación Agraria*, *13*(2), 113–117.

Vargas, L. F. (2022). Estrategias para el empoderamiento económico de mujeres rurales: productos de mi tierra Piribebuy, Paraguay. In M. E. Sili & M. C. Martin (Orgs.), *Innovación y recursos bioculturales en el mundo rural. Lecciones para el desarrollo sostenible* (pp. 225–227). Editorial Biblos.

Vera Caballero, R. M. (2022). *Background of the fairs promoted by Ecología Humana in Piribebuy*. Personal interview. San Lorenzo, Paraguay.

Chapter 34

Community Action Networks in Cape Town: Possibilities of Development Beyond COVID-19

Crain Soudien

Nelson Mandela University, Gqeberha (Port Elizabeth), South Africa

The background against which the discussion of development in South Africa takes form has stitched into it the deep divisions and inequalities which the country has inherited from its past. Colonialism and apartheid provided South Africans with the fundamentals for how they lived, how they were supported in terms of their health and education opportunities, and how they came to think of themselves as human subjects.

Despite its wide and deep reach, apartheid did not succeed in switching off the agency of black people. It did not extinguish their desire to improve their lives. They did so, as is well-known, in political terms (Lodge, 1983), less well-known is the activism that arose in other facets of everyday life. Historically, black people have a long history of community-based activism (Marais, 1998), including the movements for better housing in the 1940s in Johannesburg which have re-emerged in contemporary Durban in the Abahlali base *Mjondolo* movement (Stadler, 1979). There were over 5,000 civil society initiatives operating in the country when democracy came in 1994 (Habib & Taylor, 1999). Democracy, however, led to the demobilisation of many civil society structures. The new government took on many of the responsibilities that community organisations and non-governmental organisations (NGOs) had assumed during apartheid. NGOs came to play a different role in the post-apartheid period to that which they played earlier, but they remained important sites of social mobilisation. A prominent example of this work is the Treatment Action Campaign (TAC) for anti-retroviral treatment for AIDS sufferers in South Africa which was started in 1998 (Colvin & Robins, 2009).

The purpose of this contribution is to foreground the most recent iteration of this long history of activism – the work of the Community Action Networks

Exploring Hope: Case Studies of Innovation, Change and Development in the Global South, 229–235

Published under exclusive licence by Emerald Publishing Limited
doi:10.1108/978-1-83549-736-420241040

(CANs) which emerged during the current COVID-19 pandemic. A reason for looking at them, therefore, is to explore what they might teach us about engaging with power in the current political and economic circumstances in which we find ourselves here in South Africa and around the world.

In undertaking this exercise, I am influenced by the works of Howard Richards (2013) and Andersson and Richards (2015) and the concept they use of *unbounded organisation*. As Charman et al. (2020) explain, a great deal of the social innovation that is taking place in poor and oppressed environments is motivated by 'a sophisticated reading of cultural and social needs, (and so) providing goods and services in ways that are unique and appropriate to people's requirements, much township entrepreneurship is the outcome of the struggle for survival'.

The material I use in this contribution is drawn largely from sources in the public domain and from participation in a workshop with representatives of several CANs focused on their experience of working with established political and civil society structures in and around Cape Town.

The Emergence of the CAN Movement

CANs represent the latest iteration of civil society's struggle to come out of the socio-cultural and economic legacy of inequality in South Africa. Operating in the complexity of the post-apartheid period, formally democratic as it is, they responded not only to the exigencies of COVID-19 but helped to spawn a reinvigorated critical counter-dominance discourse. This development is important to highlight, because operating alongside the CANS were multiple other welfare agencies doing significant relief work. These, however, largely depended on volunteers. Different to these agencies, significant members of the CAN community came to the realisation that there was something wrong with the basic politics of South Africa, based on conceits of power which fed off and reproduced complex systems of oppression and exclusion and kept the poor in states of dependence. This analytic posture was developed as CAN members managed and worked their conditions of possibility, introducing them to the relationships between different kinds of power, the formal and the informal, the structural and the symbolic, high tech and low tech, the personal and the collective.

The CANs grew directly out of the emergency created by the conditions of COVID-19 (Figs. 34.1 and 34.2). Extraordinarily, they sprang up all over South Africa. In the big metropolitan areas of the country, they gathered themselves together in collectives. In Cape Town, they formed a movement called *Cape Town Together* (CTT), around the cities of East London and Gqeberha a structure called Eastern Cape Together and around Johannesburg another called Gauteng Together. By the end of March 2020, more than 70 had come into being in a number of Cape Town suburbs and townships (Silwana, 2020). Their establishment was the direct result of community organisers, social activists, and public health professionals deliberately coming together to ask how they could respond to the nationwide lockdown which the South African government had announced would take effect in a matter of days. Their primary purpose at the beginning

Fig. 34.1. April 2020 – Cape Town, South Africa: Empty Streets in the City of Cape Town During the Lockdown for COVID-19. *Source*: ID 177704591 © Timwege | Dreamstime.com.

Fig. 34.2. Grocery Store Check-Out Staff and Customers Wearing Face Masks During Flu Pandemic. *Source*: ID 206454982 © Michael Turner | Dreamstime.com.

of the life of this movement was to organise neighbourhoods and communities to keep themselves safe during the pandemic. Within days they had catalysed a network of 'self-organizing neighbourhood based groups responding to COVID-19 in their neighbourhoods, and connecting across the city drawing on collective energy and wisdom' structured around CTT (HSRC, 2020, p. 3).

The CANs' first order of business was to assist in keeping people safe during the pandemic. They were aware of community health workers being sent into communities to collect data on cases of infection and quickly came to realise that the issues and challenges were not simply and narrowly epidemiological.

To respond to the complex new conditions in which communities found themselves, the CANs made the decision to work in what they described as a 'bottom-up' way and to build an 'adaptive network (not a structured and bureaucratised organisation) that enables the dynamic, bottom-up ways of working to respond to hyper-local needs' (HSRC, 2020, p. 10). This *bottom-up* way involved mapping communities to locate, on the one hand, where the most urgent needs and vulnerabilities were, and, on the other, where possible resources within and outside communities were. Out of the initiative came mask-making and mask-distributing initiatives, feeding scheme groups and market-gardening networks. It also involved recruiting 'champions' in every street who could co-ordinate the effort to address the emergency. Communities' physical needs were paramount and involved the making and sharing of preventative aids such as masks and sanitising equipment, the provision of fresh water to communities in informal settlements, the establishment of community kitchens and food gardens. Equally important was helping people understand what was happening. This effort included managing COVID-19 awareness and education initiatives. They particularly and deliberately understood that consciousness raising meant dealing with people's fears and the potential for the outbreak of anti-social activities such as stigmatisation. Critical developments, to which I return below, were the emergence of neighbourhood-based models of care and the building of solidarity across a city riven with legacies of race and class divisions.

The Making of a CAN

An important factor in the making of the CANs, as Auerbach (2021) argues in her book *Archive of Kindness*, is the basic capacity human beings have to care for each other (Auerbach, 2020). In taking this approach, Auerbach is, moreover, implicitly helping to put in a larger temporal perspective the COVID-19 pandemic experience through which human beings have gone and the framing explanations they have for making sense of who they are and their relationships with one another, especially in periods of global stress. This is, of course, the debate about human beings' essential ontological urges – instinctual self-preservation or social solidarity.

To this activism, significantly, also came critical intellectuals. While intellectuals have long sat at the head of or near the leadership of the country's history of activism (Southall, 2016), they played roles in the formation of CANs which were fundamental for how they developed. There was present at the very early moments of the CANs a confluence of social activism and science that had marked and gained organisational traction in earlier struggles such as the struggle for anti-retroviral in the HIV/AIDs Treatment Action Committee (TAC) and the struggle for education for in the Equal Education movement (Heywood, 2009). They had learnt from the experience of working in TAC the importance of combining informed knowledge of the issues and problems with social activism.

Simply living in a marked location is not, of course, immediately an indication of groundedness. But it helps people to both know and want to understand the circumstances of those with whom they live. Material for the CANs, as a practical resource, was underlying memories of social activism. These memories lay close to the surface in the communities themselves and in key professional networks which came into the CANs. COVID-19 helped to re-energise this activism.

But the groundedness also benefitted from communities' and activists' familiarity with technological tools such as Facebook, Whatsapp, and other facilities. It significantly facilitated opportunities for communities to interact across geographical and social and professional divides. These tools made possible both regroundings and new groundings.

CAN Principles

Strikingly, the CANs in Cape Town, through their collective, CTT began their movement on the basis of what they described as 'scientifically accurate and medically sound' information (CTT, 2020, p. 1). Their booklet, *Community Action Starter pack*, was available within weeks of the establishment of the network. They insisted on decentralising the entire operation of CTT so that there wasn't a top-down command centre which would oversee and determine the movement. Every CAN was independent and could make decisions by itself. The objective was to flatten hierarchies. But everyone was connected. In CTT, every CAN had access to others to whom they could reach. Treatment Literacy, Heywood (2009, p. 17) had explained in describing how TAC worked, was central in its organisational apparatus. And so it was too for CTT.

CANs' Challenge: Politics Is Not a Kind Business

As the pandemic receded, predictably, activity levels in the CANs reduced significantly. However, this is the significance that this contribution seeks to make, structures were laid down or deepened in communities where existing initiatives had already been present, and critical learnings and insights were developed about working in relation to dominant forms of power in the city and the country.

Importantly, in the wake of the pandemic, the CTT and its leading members continued to work in the communities in which they were located. Important spin-offs included food gardens, the maintenance of food-supply networks for informal settlements, and notably, the establishment of community kitchens such as the Community Kitchen Muizenberg. The Gugulethu CAN has evolved into the Gugulethu-Seaboard CAN and continues to feed people after three years. It also has begun assisting the community in educational initiatives and in community campaigns against gender-based violence (see facebook.com/guguse-aboardCAN/). It has an arrangement with its friends in Sea Point in a project called Ladles of Love which supports feeding and organic gardening initiatives. The Muizenberg kitchen operates on CTT principles. It sells food sourced from the community gardens established by the CAN at affordable prices and the profits are used to cover the costs of making food for people in the nearby informal settlement community of Vrygrond.

Conclusions

The CAN movement, it is clear, is not in its reach and in the outcomes it produces a social revolution. CANs are not able to displace the formal state and the web of apparatuses and infrastructural capacities it has command over. But what they have achieved and what they are doing have implications for the development discussion. To be seen there is the institutionalisation of a practical alternative approach to managing how people might live, survive, and even grow.

What is emerging in the CAN experience, through members of the CANs themselves, as interlocutors, is the rejection of the neo-liberal orthodoxy of TINA – 'there-is-no-alternative' to the free market and its ideological imperatives of competition and hyper-individualism, and, most significantly, the making of new development theories of living in the present. Critical of this unboundedness is a willingness to open up the question of how the democratic project of people participating in their own development can be explored.

References

Andersson, G., & Richards, H. (2015). *Unbounded organizing in community*. Dignity Press.

Auerbach, J. (2020, April 15). Micro kindnesses are laying the foundation for a transformed South Africa. *Daily Maverick*. Retrieved June 12, 2022, from https://www.dailymaverick.co.za/article/2020-04-15-micro-kindnesses-are-laying-the-foundations-for-a-transformed-south-africa

Auerbach, J. (2021). *Archive of kindness*. BK Publishing (Pty) Ltd.

Charman, A., Petersen, L., & Govender, T. (2020). *Township economy: People, spaces and practices*. HSRC Press.

Colvin, C., & Robins, S. (2009). Social movements and AIDS in South Africa. In P. Rohleder, L. Swartz, S. C. Kalichman, & L. C. Simbayi (Eds.), *HIV/AIDS in South Africa 25 years on* (pp. 155–164). Springer.

Habib, A., & Taylor, R. (1999). South Africa: Anti-apartheid NGOs in transition. *Voluntas: International Journal of Voluntary and Nonprofit Organizations*, *10*(1), 73–82.

Heywood, M. (2009). South Africa's treatment action campaign: Combining law and social mobilization to realize the right to health. *Journal of Human Rights Practice*, *1*(1), 14–36. https://doi.org/10.1093/jhuman/hun006

HSRC. (2020). *Cape Town Together, Community Action Networks (CANs) & Sharing Resources and Learning*. Conference paper presented at the Human Sciences Research Council Seminar, Cape Town, 27 August.

Lodge, T. (1983). *Black politics in South Africa since 1945*. Longman.

Marais, H. (1998). *South Africa, limits to change: The political economy of transformation.* UCT Press.

Richards, H. (2013). Unbounded organisation and the future of socialism. *Education as Change*, *17*(2), 229–242.

Silwana, P. (2020, March 31). Crisis sees Cape Town Suburbs Reach Across the Great Social Divide. *Daily Maverick*. Retrieved June 12, 2022, from https://www.dailymaverick.co.za/article/2020-03-31-crisis-sees-cape-town-suburbs-reach-across-the-great-social-divide/

Southall, R. (2016). *The new Black middle class in South Africa*. Jacana Media.

Stadler, A. (1979). Birds in the Cornfield: Squatter Movements in Johannesburg, 1944–1947. *Journal of Southern African Studies, Special issue on Urban Social History*, *6*(1), 93–123.

Chapter 35

Virtual Mobilisations and Reinvention of the Social Link for the Survival of Vulnerable Populations Confined for the Fight Against COVID-19 in the Republic of Congo

Ossere Nganongo

Université Marien NGOUABI, Brazzaville, Republic of Congo

In the first quarter of 2020 the world is worried, shaken by the speed of spread of Covid-19 due to the SARS-CoV-2 virus (Fig. 35.1). In developed countries, with structured social protection systems, and in underdeveloped countries whose main social protection system is essentially that of mechanical solidarity (Durkheim, 1893), the option to curb the spread of this virus was that of containment by prohibiting the intra and extra muros movements of the populations, with strict control by police patrols circulating through the streets, fining and arresting those who are apprehended outside their homes. In addition to this repressive system, there are barricades, manned by law enforcement officers, on the main arteries of the cities.

On 30 March 2020, the Congolese government (Republic of Congo) declared a state of emergency which quickly resulted in general lockdown in all territories and a halt to the movement of people from town to country. This decision, which came after the discovery of a first case of a patient carrying the virus, immediately gave rise to general concern within the population, especially in this context where the official social system does not really protect lower-income social classes. Also, the fact that Congolese society is characterized by a predominance of the informal sector (60.3%), run by actors living day to day, raises the dual question of their survival in periods of containment and that of maintaining social links in this configuration of disruption of movements and contacts between populations.

Exploring Hope: Case Studies of Innovation, Change and Development in the Global South, 237–241

doi:10.1108/978-1-83549-736-420241041

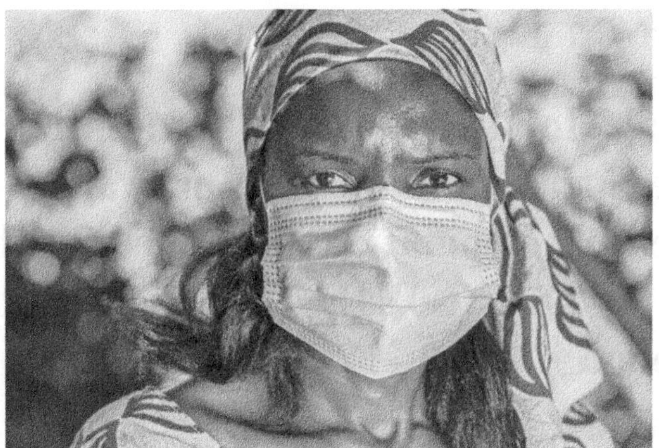

Fig. 35.1. African Woman Wearing Face Mask in Coronavirus COVID-19 Pandemic. *Source*: ID 218445238 © Darren Baker | Dreamstime.com.

This reflection was fuelled by the careful monitoring of social networks in the context of confinement. In the beginning, twenty (20) Facebook pages were chosen, but as observations were made, it was found that only eight (8) of them had interesting content, i.e. photos, videos and related comments, calling for the virtual mobilisation of Congolese people, living in situ and those in the diaspora, to collect the resources needed to help people in distress.

The Need to Revisit the Concepts of Solidarity, Social Ties, Social Protection and Virtual Mobilisation Due to the Effects of the Pandemic

From the outset, the pairing of the concepts of solidarity and social ties calls for an explanation. The analysis of Ladouceur (2008), based on the work of Serge Paugam, seems to have a relevance that meets the concerns of this analysis. He explains *Solidarisme et lien social* by the evolution of the social bond in modern societies, in particular, the importance of autonomy characterising the individual in the present age, which is only possible in the context of increasingly intense interdependencies with other members of society. Benoît Ladouceur shows the importance of the social protection system for all within an institutionalised framework that allows individuals to maintain social ties in their own way through informal mechanisms. However, countries such as the Congo, despite various political, military and economic crises, have not yet succeeded in setting up these social protection systems and, in so doing, have given free rein to the inventiveness of the population, which to a certain extent allows them to avoid the erosion of social cohesion.

In this case, what was observed would seem to resonate with the work of Rezende Ribeiro (2018), who showed that social networks configure and operate a politics of effects, which also prevents intolerance towards the other, with the particularity of another form of *catharsis* towards empathy. Moreover, the solidarities developed seem to correspond, as mentioned earlier, to Goffman's concept of a *total institution*, defining a place of life in which a large number of individuals quarantined or cut off from the outside world for a certain period of time live according to a *modus operandi* imposed by the authority. The rules of strict restriction refer to the disciplinary societies described by Foucault (1975) and whose reflection was, in a sense, continued by Gilles Deleuze who introduced the dimension of the control of individuals by the digital.

Social Networks to Compensate for Government Failures in Congo

The strict application of the state of emergency has greatly altered the social links between and within vulnerable population groups, particularly those dependent on others and those surviving from day to day. This is the case, for example, of students in Brazzaville who have obtained their baccalaureate in rural areas and who, faced with the problem of accommodation, find themselves staying with a relative and eating the only meal of the day at the home of another, obliged to travel many kilometres between the two. There is also the case of actors in the transport sector, who have found themselves without income during the period of confinement. In this sector, where work is informal, there are bus drivers, bus inspectors, taximen or drivers, to which should also be added the women and men involved in urban–rural trade, particularly those selling food products and those who buy manufactured products in town to sell in rural areas (Ngouma et al., 2018).

It is in this situation that mobilisation via social networks helps to recreate social ties through the effect generated by videos of individuals in distress. In this way, social networks help to connect segments of the population scattered around the world. The latter act in favour of com-patriots, sometimes beyond the tribal-ethnic considerations that could have re-fuelled the surge of solidarity of nationals of one ethnic group in favour of a com-patriot of another ethnic group (Fig. 35.2).

In this logic of actions originating in 2.0 mobilisations in favour of vulnerable people confined by COVID-19, analysis of social networks has made it possible to identify a foundation called Fondation Michel Mboungou pour l'Emergence au Congo-Brazzaville (n.d.), which was very active during the confinement with a *modus operandi* via videos. Indeed, during the containment period, the actors of the said foundation shared videos, broadcast on Facebook, highlighting the distress of populations left to their own devices. In a 24-minute video (James K. Page, 2020), we see the teams of this foundation visiting vulnerable families, pensioners, widows, elderly people, etc. for food donations (bags of rice) and protective masks. These products come from a food bank, visibly located in Pointe-Noire, the economic capital of Congo-Brazzaville. It appears from the speeches of the various actors that the foundation first identifies vulnerable people via social networks and then provides them with assistance to enable them to survive the confinement for a few days.

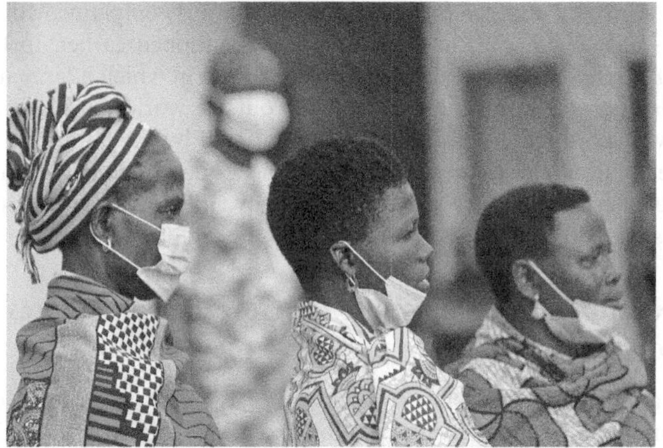

Fig. 35.2. Daily African Life. *Source*: ID 230093391 © Pascal Deloche | Dreamstime.com.

Virtual Mobilisations in Times of Confinement as a Gateway to Strengthening Sustainable Social Ties

In a society where the mobile telephone market has a penetration rate of 109%, and where the main mobile telephone operators (MTN and Airtel) have a total of 3.10 million Internet subscribers out of a population estimated at 5.41 million (ARCEP, 2021), it would be difficult not to find virtues in these forms of mobilisation. Thus, far from distending and dehumanising social or societal relations, cyberculture appears to be an opportunity to reinvent social ties in a society in which the very strong mechanical solidarities run the risk of being weakened by the predominance of new forms of communication. Virtual mobilisations thus make it possible to perpetuate the famous African solidarity by giving it new appearances. Above all, they can even help to transcend tribalism inward-looking attitudes if they are oriented towards inclusive solidarities.

Conclusions

In the end, it appears that when faced with an unexpected shock, society knows how to reinvent itself and invent new mechanisms that allow it to continue to be a society. In fact, African societies in general, and that of the Congo in particular, are those in which the notion of interaction has its full meaning. These are societies with permanent, close and deep contacts in which individualism, although gaining ground as a result of the social mutations favoured by the 'dynamics of the outside world' (Balandier, 2004), does not totally supersede the mechanical solidarities that are their main characteristic. This is how confinement, a total social fact (Tarot, 1996), despite the force conferred on it by the pernicious character of the COVID-19, through the fear it inspires, has not succeeded in preventing the maintenance of the social link. In fact, since physical contact between populations was limited, the virtuality made possible by cyberculture allowed the emergence and reinforcement of new forms of solidarity that eluded the public authorities, but contributed to the resilience of thousands of individuals who would not have been able to cope with the shock without the maintenance of this new form of social link.

References

ARCEP. (2021). *Observatoire du marché de l'internet mobile* (Rapport du 3ème trimestre 2021). Autorité de régulation des communications électroniques, des postes et de la distribution de la presse. https://www.arcep.fr/fileadmin/cru-1677573101/reprise/observatoire/3-2021/obs-marches-T3-2021_140122.pdf

Balandier, G. (2004). *Sens et puissance*. Presses Universitaires de France. https://doi.org/10.3917/puf.balan.2004.01

Fondation Michel Mboungou pour l'Emergence au Congo-Brazzaville. (n.d.). Home [Facebook page]. Facebook. http://www.facebook.com/Fondation-Michel-Mboungou-pour-lEmergence-au-Congo-Brazzaville-1933288166762812/

Foucault, M. (1975). *Surveiller et punir*. Gallimard, collection Tell.

James K. Page. (2020, May 2). Congo-Brazzaville: Comment faire face au coronavirus et au confinement [video attached]. Facebook. https://www.facebook.com/100000332854663/videos/3309994052354991/

Ladouceur, B. (2008). Serge Paugam, Le lien social. *Lectures* [Online]. https://doi.org/10.4000/lectures.653

Ngouma, D., Ndey Ngandzo, P. H., & Ngomeka, R., (2018). Ngo, une petite ville du Nord-Congo: cadre de vie et rôle régional. *Études caribéennes* [Online], 39–40. https://doi.org/10.4000/etudescaribeennes.12896

Rezende Ribeiro, R. (2018). Réseaux d'affects et d'intolérance: l'imaginaire politique et la catharsis dans le quotidien médiatisé. *Sociétés, 142*, 47–56. https://doi.org/10.3917/soc.142.0047

Tarot, C. (1996). Du fait social de Durkheim au fait social total de Mauss: un changement de paradigme? *Revue Européenne Des Sciences Sociales, 34*(105), 113–144. http://www.jstor.org/stable/40370965

Chapter 36

Crisis Management in Chinese Universities – Shanghai Universities' Response to COVID-19 Outbreak in 2022

Li Juan

Human Resources Department, Shanghai International Studies University, China

When COVID-19 broke out in Shanghai in the first half of 2022, Shanghai universities were struggling on two fronts: *actual administration*, where most students were in school, and collective *online courses* in closed spaces like dorms that lasted almost an entire semester. Drawing on the author's personal experience as a temporary building manager (TBM), this chapter focuses on the emergency management of universities in Shanghai and shows how all college members mobilised in the face of public crisis (Fig. 36.1).

Since 2020, with the global outbreak of the COVID-19 pandemic, online teaching has become the *new normal*. Foreign scholars have studied the emotional and psychological problems associated with online teaching (Restubog et al., 2020; Rutkowska et al., 2022). Coincidentally, Chinese universities were on winter break when the first wave of COVID-19 hit China in late December 2019, and most students had already returned to their hometowns. From March to May 2020, in line with China's epidemic prevention and control policy, universities implemented an online teaching model, teaching students from home. Fewer students stayed on campus, reducing pressure on school administrators. After that, universities resumed classes, students returned to campus and went on summer and winter breaks as usual. Chinese scholars have focused on the quality of online instruction (Li, 2020; Wang, 2022; Zheng, 2020).

When the 2022 pandemic broke out in Shanghai, the new semester had already begun and most students were back in school. According to a news report (Da Shu Cheng Zhang Ying, 2022), there are more than 60 universities in Shanghai, all of which have been closed since mid-March, with more than 700,000 students, about 75% of whom are from other places, who were confined to campus and could only study online in their dormitories. Both students and

Exploring Hope: Case Studies of Innovation, Change and Development in the Global South, 243–247

Published under exclusive licence by Emerald Publishing Limited
doi:10.1108/978-1-83549-736-420241042

Fig. 36.1. Diving in the Sea of Knowledge. *Source*: ID 74766722 © ZhangMing Wang | Dreamstime.com.

schools were under tremendous new pressure. Shanghai universities adopted the *Three Lines of Defence* strategy. The first line was a security centre composed of college leaders; the second line was a 3- to 5-member building emergency response team composed of general secretaries, faculty and student party members, student advisors, league officers, and support staff; the third line was an 8- to 10-member group of student volunteers. This study examines the three lines in detail and how universities act like one during emergencies (Fig. 36.2).

Fig. 36.2. A Square in Shanghai University. *Source*: DNI 168624313 © Evan Luo | Dreamstime.com.

The First Line of Defence

In China, the state higher education institutions practice the system of presidential responsibility under the leadership of the People's Committees of the Communist Party of China in higher education institutions. With the Party secretary and the president at the core and the vice presidents and heads of relevant offices as members, each Shanghai university established a special leadership team to take care of the control affairs of COVID-19.

In the age of the Internet, information can be obtained and disseminated quickly. If the official channels do not release timely and effective information during an emergency, rumours and misinformation will make the rounds and cause unnecessary panic. For example, the author's college, Shanghai International Studies University (SISU), was the first to send out pandemic prevention SMS messages to the cell phones of all students and faculty members from the beginning of the pandemic, and also issued a comprehensive notice on the campus network and official WeChat account to inform everyone about the school's pandemic prevention plans. As of 27 November 2022, SISU had issued 140 notices, including 57 from 12 March 2022 to 27 November 2022, an average of 1–2 notices per week. On SISU's official WeChat account, 22 Q&As were posted to explain the latest arrangements and dispel our doubts.

Also, SISU's Office of Public Relations and College Communications, in cooperation with off-campus media organisations, repeatedly reported cases where faculty and students worked selflessly to spread positive energy for all.

The Second Line of Defence

Members of the Building Emergency Response Team were also referred to as TBMs. During the lockdown, three meals were prepared by support staff in disposable plastic boxes and sent to each building. TBMs counted the number of boxes for each floor and distributed them to each room with the help of student volunteers. Due to different job requirements, the league officers generally didn't have previous experience working with students. However, there was a severe shortage of TBMs. Hence, each TBM team had at least one member from the general office, faculty and student party, or student advisor staff. Student advisors have the most direct experience with students. They have already established good relationships with students and also have the greatest understanding of students, which can help TBMs work more efficiently and effectively because a familiar person acts as a stabiliser when everyone is under pressure, such as during a sudden lock-in.

In addition, the TBMs went to each room every night to take the students' temperature and conduct a roll call. In this way, the TBMs got to know the students as quickly as possible. As soon as the results of the nucleic acid tests or antigen detection were abnormal, the person(s) concerned and their close contacts would be moved to the quarantine zone for further examination and treatment. In the meantime, college psychological services took various steps to help students get through this period smoothly by giving online lectures on adjusting to new situations and offering online counselling services. SISU's Counseling Center established an online counselling service to help alleviate students' anxiety.

The Third Line of Defence

According to Collie and Martin (2017), adaptability refers to an individual's capacity to employ strategies in order to regulate their response to novelty, change, or uncertainty. In most cases, college students are the new adults. They were born around the turn of the millennium and grew up with the development of the Internet in China. They are referred to as Generation Z, who have already created their own worldviews and values, and whose cooperation and support is difficult to gain through rules and regulations. They need to be involved in things that affect them. Therefore, student volunteers were called upon to form the third line of defence. Their duties included delivering meals and packages to other students in the same dorm, helping TBMs take students' temperatures, and organising group activities, such as when the staggered shower time policy was implemented and different buildings had different shower times to avoid cross-infections. Unlike staff, students know their classmates and have a relationship with each other. New volunteers were recruited every other week so that most students could participate and help others. If some students wanted to drop out, they could tell the TBMs and other volunteers could replace them.

Recruiting volunteers from the student body and involving them in control management not only distracted them from the unfamiliar and comparatively tense atmosphere created by the COVID-19 control, but also made them feel like they were contributing and belonged.

Conclusions

The COVID-19 outbreak caught Shanghai universities off guard. Having never experienced anything like it, they quickly formed the 'Three Lines of Defence' and mobilised everyone from college administrators to students. Students enjoyed an unexpected but organised life on campus, staying with roommates, taking online courses, and having food delivered to their dorms. There were few reports of major outbreaks.

With China releasing a new 10-point plan to optimise COVID-19 response on 7 December 2022, it is safe to assume that 'collective online learning' will soon be a thing of the past for students in China. But in a rapidly changing world, a new crisis is bound to happen. Universities around the world, with students from different parts of the country and/or from different countries, may face the same dilemma: How to manage a crisis when large numbers of students are stuck on campus? The *Three Lines of Defence* policy at Shanghai universities may be a good example for others to learn from in the future.

References

Collie, R. J., & Martin, A. J. (2017). Students' adaptability in mathematics: Examining self-reports and teachers' reports and links with engagement and achievement outcomes. *Contemporary Educational Psychology*, *49*, 355–366.

Li, T. (2020). The current situation, dilemma and path exploration of "Live + Education" in domestic universities. *Media*, *17*, 82–84.

Da Shu Cheng Zhang Ying. (2022). Over 60 Shanghai Universities in Full Lockdown, with 750,000 Students, 75% from across the Country. *Sohu*, March 16. https://learning.sohu.com/a/530306401_120175571.

Restubog, S. L. D., Ocampo, A. C. G., & Wang, L. (2020). Taking control amidst the chaos: Emotion regulation during the COVID-19 pandemic. *Journal of Vocational Behavior*, *119*. Article 103440. https://doi.org/10.1016%2Fj.jvb.2020.103440

Rutkowska, A., Cieślik, B., Tomaszczyk, A., & Szczepańska-Gieracha, J. (2022). Mental health conditions among E-learning students during the COVID-19 pandemic. *Frontiers in Public Health*, *10*. Article 871934. https://doi.org/10.3389/fpubh.2022.871934

Wang, J. (2022). A comparative analysis of online and offline undergraduate teaching quality – Based on teaching evaluation data from Tsinghua University. *China Educational Technology*, *3*, 90–95+102.

Zheng, Q. (2020). Status, problems and suggestions for countermeasures of online teaching during COVID-19 pandemic. *China Educational Technology*, *5*, 34–43.

General Conclusion: Global Multidimensional Crisis and Hope

Fernando Calderón Gutiérrez[1]

Universidad Nacional de San Martín, Argentina

We are living in times of a multidimensional global crisis. It is difficult to pinpoint when it started. Today I have the impression that I am among the 'privileged' who can, as they say, see the fire from the top of the hill. And yet I feel compelled, generationally and existentially compelled, to hope. To insist. To look for glimmers, 'little lights', of hope. That is why I have been enthusiastic about this work of a Tocquevillian nature, given its determination to recover local experiences, anchored territorially, such as the experience of the orçamento participativo in Porto Alegre, Brazil, and several other cases of decentralisation and mobilisation that I had the opportunity to analyse, together with various colleagues, in the 2003 Human Development Report.[2]

Alongside a well-selected gallery of hopeful glimpses, this book raises issues and opens up questions.

Global South is neither a simple nor a transparent category. As is well known, there is neither a single North nor a single South, and, moreover, there are Souths in the North and Norths in the South. Rather than dependence, it seems necessary to speak of asymmetrical interdependence. In the South of Chicago, in the North of New York and in the North of Paris there is poverty, hunger, violence,

[1]He is one of the most prestigious sociologists in Latin America. Of Bolivian origin, he currently lives in Buenos Aires. He was Executive Secretary of CLACSO in the 1980s and later Advisor to ECLAC and UNDP. He has held the Simón Bolívar Chair in Latin American Studies at the University of Cambridge. In 2017, the UNSAM awarded him an Honorary Doctorate.

[2]UNDP, Human Development Report 2003. The Millennium Development Goals: A compact among nations to end poverty, esp. chap 7: 'Mobilising popular support'. That report was led by Sakiko Fukuda-Parr and included the participation of Jeffrey Sachs, among other experts. According to Amartya Sen, public discussion and social participation should be central to the elaboration of public policies in a democratic framework, including, of course, the evaluation of such policies.

Exploring Hope: Case Studies of Innovation, Change and Development in the Global South, 249–252

Published under exclusive licence by Emerald Publishing Limited
doi:10.1108/978-1-83549-736-420241043

insecurity and fear. Fortunately, people also drink and dance. But drug trafficking networks are at work there. The fentanyl crisis is just one example among many, but it is eloquent: to what extent can the elites of the North speak of ethics when they launder 20 billion dollars a year in cocaine alone? There is a universal culture that is made in the big cities: Afghans in Paris, Indians in New York. And what about the elites of the global South…? In the territories of the South there is poverty, hunger, violence, insecurity and fear, of course, but also, above all, there is inequality: the contrasts are shocking, you can see them in the big cities of Brazil, Nigeria and India.

And then there are the migrants. The huge global diaspora. To a significant extent, the people who painfully migrate to the North sustain the South with their remittances. Visualising and claiming them is crucial. There is, in fact, a process of universalisation of the South. However, it is necessary to strike harder: they will have to realise how many Latin Americans there are in the United States, how many Africans and Asians there are in Europe…

'Informational capitalism' (Manuel Castells) would tend to dispense with the labour force. This is an important but insufficient idea: it should not be reified, nor should simple linear trends be extrapolated from it, since reality is more complex. Times are intermingled, and the experience of temporality is neither univocal nor transparent. The urban marginalised, for example, have been and can currently be a renewing force in the struggle against exclusion. Castells himself has highlighted their centrality in the French Revolution of 1871 (Paris Commune).[3]

Throughout my career as a UNDP staff member, I have seen, and sometimes been part of, experiences that have been marvellous from the local level and that could well be 'exported'. Several of those recounted in this book reminded me of enthusiasms I was part of some years ago. For example, the project called Beautiful Sofia was carried out in the Bulgarian capital around 2000. The idea was to enhance places that had fallen into disrepair with the participation of the community. An experience not so different from that which took place in the historic centres of Salvador de Bahia, Quito and several other cities. Another example is the work carried out by Verónica Cereceda and the Asur Foundation (Sucre) on the recovery of ancestral weavings, in extraordinary combinations of shapes and colours. The local experiences associated with art are very numerous and significant. Another example is linked to the memory of something Mahbub Ul Haq once said: 'The future of Bolivia lies in El Alto, in the tremendous work skills of its inhabitants, in their honesty, in their pride in fighting'. At another time, Joseph Stiglitz commented, in the same vein, that Bolivia should build on this factor, and not fail to look at the experiences of Norway (a major oil and gas exporter) and Southeast Asia (with its multicultural reality). The peripheral, the marginal, can often become central and inspiring. The problem is that it is often confined to a small scale and the rest of society simply does not look at it. However, there is an indisputable strength in all this.

[3]Castells, M. (1983). *The city and the grassroots.* University of California Press.

The key to tackling the multidimensional global crisis is none other than the recovery of people's ability to lead their own lives and to be dignified. The logic of financial and technological capital is, in principle, going the other way. Change has to be thought from an ethical point of view. Thinking exclusively from the economic point of view is not enough. We need a pedagogy of ethics, to show ways of being and doing. Amartya Sen's contributions remain fundamental references in this regard. He wrote:

> In the contemporary world there is a compelling need to ask questions not only about the economics and politics of globalisation, but also about the values, ethics and sense of belonging that shape our conception of the global world.[4]

The experiences recovered in this work are not so much about scholarly intellectual production. It is about drawing attention to productive, territorial and cultural experiences. In them, through them, thanks to them, people rebuild solidarity and weave ties that allow them to forge their own lives. If they are still, or seem to be, insufficient, it is because they are not adequately connected.

My thesis is that we need bridges between the different spaces that make up the South and between them and the North. For instance, given its constitutive multiculturalism, Latin America can play an important role in this. However, I also believe that in the other southern territories they listen to us and see us more than we Latin Americans see them. There is little dialogue and discussion, but the possibility is open, as the existence of this book proves. There is the political level, as illustrated by a figure like President Lula, but there is also the promise of cultural exchange based on respect for otherness. It is important to recover what we are: rich cultures and civilisations, sometimes not sufficiently recognised (by ourselves, to begin with). For example, it is important to value the meaning of Quechua words such as waqcha and its antonym qhapaq, which mean poverty and wealth, but with a strong allusion to the social bond, to solidarity. Amartya Sen was very much struck by these nuances. However, the surveys I am currently receiving are disheartening: for example, more than half of Bolivia's young people do not know the main historical facts, many of which have to do with experiences of struggle.

It is key to learn from other parts of the world and to provide ourselves with other mirrors, especially because the mirrors in which we have looked at ourselves for many decades now return problematic images. An experience such as that of Southeast Asia is worthy of attention. It was in Fernando Fajnzylber's mind when he shaped, in the framework of ECLAC, his powerful proposal on 'productive transformation with equity'. I reflected on this set of issues in depth during a visit to Kerala that I had the privilege of making recently. Also, contemplating the magnificent work of the artist Tomás Saraceno, who thinks from and with new

[4]Sen, A. (2007). *Identidad y violencia. La ilusión del destino* (p. 244). Katz.

technologies, from and with an ecological sensibility. Saraceno is an artist who builds with communities and focuses on the issue of peace, which is fundamental.

Art has a specific, very special strength. Above all, music. The cumbias, all of them. Salsa. You hear Brazilian music in Africa. There are successful popular expressions in the framework of asymmetrical interdependence. It also happens in painting. The women's movement, with all its modulations, is also crucial. I am thinking of Chilean women, in a space like the Colectivo Las Tesis, their interventions and performances, with a high power of interpellation.

Can we be optimistic about the new technologies? It is a delicate issue, but what is certain is that the Mexican neo-Zapatistas would have lasted very little if it had not been for the external support they received, without the communication platforms. Many indigenous communities rely on support from Europeans and Americans when it comes to raising and disseminating their demands. But neither can it be denied that new technologies do not always contribute to improving the quality of democracies. Technosociability is a central, unavoidable dimension for thinking about possible futures. Is there a technosociability of the global South? It does not seem so, at least not yet. Questions arise about how to appropriate, how to renew, and how to move towards the conformation, deployment and projection of transnational networks that we can feel as 'ours'. These are shuddering questions, which go to the heart of the challenges facing democracies. They allude to a problem of the South, but not only of the South.

Challenges are enormous. It is necessary to move slowly and keep a global perspective, of the South, yes, but not limited exclusively to the South. And without forgetting that it is difficult for anything new to emerge if the old has not been critically reviewed first.

How much of this makes sense in the face of the logic of a brutally concentrated and extremely dynamic informational capitalism, which can even have authoritarian overtones? What will happen in China with all this? There is also 'commodity fetishism' there. The dark side is appalling. It is legitimate to try to focus on the bright side and to seek to think about it, as is done in this book. We intellectuals have to make a critical historical review and construct options from ethics, putting the question of dignity at the centre of the debate. Dignity: I do not see that we have any other notion with equivalent heuristic power.

Index

Printed and bound by CPI Group (UK) Ltd, Croydon, CR0 4YY

09/09/2024

14553446-0003